W9-BNW-849

# STRATEGIES FOR
# SCHOOL IMPROVEMENT

# STRATEGIES FOR
# SCHOOL IMPROVEMENT

Cooperative Planning

and Organization Development

119240

DANIEL C. NEALE          WILLIAM J. BAILEY
*University of Delaware*          *University of Delaware*

BILLY E. ROSS
*University of Delaware*

LIBRARY

## Allyn and Bacon, Inc.

BOSTON   LONDON   SYDNEY   TORONTO

Copyright © 1981 by Allyn and Bacon, Inc.,
470 Atlantic Avenue, Boston, Massachusetts 02210.
All rights reserved. No part of the material
protected by this copyright notice may be reproduced
or utilized in any form or by any means, electronic
or mechanical, including photocopying, recording,
or by any information storage and retrieval system,
without written permission from the copyright owner.

**Library of Congress Cataloging in Publication Data**

Neale, Daniel C        1931–
    Strategies for school improvement.

    Bibliography: p.
    Includes index.
    1.   School management and organization.
2.   Educational sociology.   3.   Educational
equalization.   I.   Bailey, William Jay, 1929–
joint author.      II.      Ross, Billy E., joint author.
III.   Title.
LB2805.N465        379.1'54          80-10740
ISBN 0-205-06950-9

Printed in the United States of America

LB
2805
.N465

Alwar 16.95

4-15-81 Alaraw

# CONTENTS

# FOREWORD

Planned change in schools is slow for many reasons. One reason is that Americans disagree about the goals of education. Because goals are ambiguous, clear and definite programs of change are difficult to identify and implement. Another reason that change is slow is that new educational practices are rarely supported by solid research nor communicated to practitioners in effective dissemination programs. Still another reason is the bureaucratic nature of public schools, in which few incentives exist for institutional change. Thus, the time lag for diffusing innovations that was lamented by Paul Mort so long ago still exists.

Unfortunately, the need for change in schools is great. Not only do basic skill programs need to be strengthened, as is the current focus, but also creative solutions to other long-standing problems of curriculum, organization, and technology need to be found.

The fact is that we know *how* to educate far better than we are *doing* it in practice. Consequently, although schools do some things extremely well, many students are served very poorly. For many students schools are largely irrelevant—an "aging vat" as some have said.

The authors of *Strategies for School Improvement* have maintained a broad perspective on the problems of planned change in education. Provision is made for how to improve basic skills, but provision is also made for how to attack other important problems of education. The emphasis is upon how to make planned change efforts succeed in schools, whatever the need for change might be.

The authors have carefully screened the extensive literature on planned change and organizational development. They have selected four successful models of change to develop in some detail. Each of these models—Ronald G. Havelock's Linkage Model, Richard A. Schmuck's Organization Development in Schools, John I. Goodlad's Responsive Model of Educational Improvement, and the Rand Change Agent Study Model— represents a significant body of research and experience in educational change. Each model contains a common ingredient that is likely to produce successful educational change. That ingredient is *collaboration* among all members of the educational community, including students, parents, teachers, administrators, college educators, and state education officials.

My experience in the management of public education supports the authors' views on collaboration, including the recommendation that local partnerships for school improvement be formed. Members of such partnerships would include the school administration, teachers' organizations, local colleges, and a state department of education. Because interactions in our society are becoming increasingly complex, schools must become better connected to the educational environment in order for school reform to succeed.

The obvious message is that school administrators need to understand better the complexities of change and how processes of local school improvement may be stimulated. Dan Neale, Bill Bailey, and Billy Ross do not just present abstractions from change theory; they also develop practical examples to demonstrate how principles could apply in specific circumstances.

If the time lag in education is to be reduced, educators should become more familiar with the concepts and practices reported in this book. This is an important book for teachers, administrators, and professors of education, everywhere.

Gordon Cawelti

# PREFACE

This is a book about how to improve elementary and secondary schools in a time when enrollments are declining, resources are scarce, and the public is pessimistic about school reform. The book is written especially for educators who are seeking a careful summary of current knowledge about planned change in education.

Although the authors have drawn extensively upon research and theory, this is not primarily a work for educational theorists. Instead, the book concentrates on what can be recommended to practitioners on the basis of recent research.

This book is not intended for the "seat-of-the-pants" educator who is skeptical about all educational theory. The authors believe that the recent past in American education was a unique period of educational thought and invention. Never before on such a scale were human resources devoted to the task of educational innovation. The lessons from these efforts, while they did not yield precise recipes for school reform, are an excellent resource for practitioners thinking about how to improve schools.

The central ideas in this book originated in the practical experiences of the authors as each of them was involved in trying to improve American schools. As the 1970s unfolded, dramatic changes in the educational scene brought about "a new reality" for schools. As the authors attempted to understand this new reality, the following convictions emerged:

1. The new context for school improvement was an "Age of Slowdown" in which enrollments and resources would decline; a new emphasis on reallocation and efficient use of existing resources was therefore needed. In public elementary and secondary education, this new emphasis would require higher levels of cooperation among elements of the educational system, that is, local school officials, state and federal education agencies, colleges and universities, and teachers' organizations.

2. Despite disappointments with attempts at school reform, much knowledge had accumulated about how to succeed with planned change in schools. Particularly promising were organization development strategies that included: (a) a focus on the local school-building organization, (b) clear identification of the need for change, (c) strong commitment to change at the school and district levels, (d) sustained involvement and support of staff to adapt new ideas to the local setting, (e) cooperation among all members of the local school community, and (f) strong links to outside resources to support local change efforts.

3. In the new reality, radical changes in attitudes toward school improvement were required. The illusion that progress was inevitably tied to growth had to be discarded. The view that schools could quickly solve deep-seated social problems had to be abandoned. An overreliance on hardware and the design of new educational practices needed to give way to an emphasis on

human resource development and on the process of implementing new practices within individual school organizations.

These convictions led to a systematic review of the literature on educational change. From that literature the authors selected works that were particularly relevant to "the new reality." Using feedback from practitioners in graduate seminars, the authors developed The Partnership Model of School Improvement. This model, which is the subject of this book, is used to synthesize and communicate our findings. The emphasis is on translating the results of practical experience, research, and theory into useful recommendations for educational personnel. We hope that the Partnership Model will not be misunderstood as a rigid prescription for educational change, nor as a simple formula for solving all educational problems. We hope, instead, that the Model puts thoughtful practitioners conveniently in touch with the best of current ideas about how schools can be improved. It is such practitioners who will be working out strategies for school improvement in the 1980s.

Because collaboration is a central theme in this book, it seems particularly appropriate to acknowledge the contributions of those who collaborated in the development and writing of the book itself.

The central ideas in the book were jointly developed by Drs. Neale, Bailey, Ross, and Patricia Campbell-Stetson, with considerable help from students in successive sections of a graduate course in planned change at the University of Delaware. Drs. Bailey and Neale were principal authors in the writing stage, making equal, and sometimes indivisible, contributions. Dr. Ross contributed substantially to the writing and participated in major decisions about the manuscript.

Patricia Campbell-Stetson was an important partner until other commitments forced her to withdraw from the project. We are especially indebted for her early drafts of material on partnerships, consortia, and collaboration. Naturally, she should not be held accountable for the final result, which is the responsibility of the three principal authors.

Special thanks are due to Ms. Edna Johnson, our typist, and Ms. Kathleen Liebhart, who assisted us with editorial advice.

Each of the authors also acknowledges the many teachers, colleagues, and students who, through the years, contributed to the ideas of each author about educational change.

*Newark, Delaware*                                                D. C. N.
                                                                 W. J. B.
                                                                 B. E. R.

# PART I

# A NEW REALITY FOR SCHOOLS

## INTRODUCTION TO PART I

A new reality exists for American schools. A period of dramatic growth, when enrollments and resources expanded year after year, is gone. Here instead is an "Age of Slowdown," with declining numbers and resources. Gone, too, is a period of strong faith in the power of American schools to strengthen America's world leadership, to reduce poverty and discrimination, and to maintain economic prosperity. Instead we have doubts about our schools and pessimism about the possibilities of social progress.

This new reality is forcing schools to change. Declining enrollments and escalating costs, for example, are forcing many school districts to reduce staff, close buildings, and reexamine educational priorities. Many of these changes—terminating experienced staff, closing neighborhood schools, and ending valued educational programs—have been traumatic.

A special problem is the widespread opinion that schools have somehow failed. Despite large investments in education and despite much fanfare about educational reform, schools do not appear to have changed much for the better. Although the need for school improvement remains strong, skepticism about school reform is common and special resources for educational improvement are absent.

The purpose of this book is to examine the problem of how to improve schools in this "new reality." Can schools become smaller but better? Can they be less costly and more effective? Where are the resources to be found for improving schools? What strategies for improving schools will work in an "Age of Slowdown"?

To answer these questions, we shall first examine the changes that define the new reality for school improvement. The period from 1950 to 1970, which we have called, "A New Progressivism," is described in terms of (1) an unprecedented expansion of population, resources, and educational opportunities, (2) high expectations for school improvement and social progress, and (3) a profusion of educational innovations. The optimism about school reform as a means for social progress is strikingly similar to the earlier "Progressive Era" of social reform.

By contrast, the period since 1970 is described as an "Age of Slowdown" with (1) declining school enrollments and resources, (2) pessimism about the role of schools in social progress, and (3) uncertainty about whether and how schools can be improved. This contrast with the former period leads directly to a consideration of strategies appropriate to the new reality for school improvement. Briefly, the changes require: (1) a conscious deemphasis of "bigger is better," (2) a concentration on economy and efficiency, and (3) a focus on improving the use of existing human resources.

Lessons from recent attempts to improve American schools must also be incorporated into new strategies for school improvement. In particular, two lessons are apparent: (1) a focus on the organization of the individual school is helpful in bringing about desired change, and (2) local school organizations need outside resources to create the conditions required for change. These lessons are presented in the form of practical recommendations in a Partnership Model for School Improvement. Part I concludes with an overview of the Model, which is explained in detail in later sections of the book.

# Chapter 1

# A New Progressivism, 1950–1970

During the 1950s and 1960's, American educators enjoyed a period of growth and abundance in which hopes were high for social progress through investments in education and technology.

## GROWTH AND ABUNDANCE

For several generations, Americans became accustomed to growth in almost every aspect of life: population, gross national product, productivity, and per-capita income. American schools, especially in the years from 1950 to 1970, experienced striking growth in enrollment and resources. This growth is shown graphically in Figure 1–1 by the increasing numbers of instructional staff members employed in elementary and secondary education since 1870. The years, 1950–1970, stand out dramatically as a period of unprecedented growth.

During this time, American educators performed a quantitative miracle. Somehow, enough schools were built, enough staff provided, and enough materials purchased to handle the growth. Naturally, school officials were preoccupied with this growth and came to accept it as a normal circumstance. Each year enrollments grew, and new resources, justified primarily on the basis of growth, were added. Each year this new pool of resources was available for allocation to the development of new programs and the expansion of old. Plans for new buildings provided opportunities to devise new patterns of staffing and new educational programs.

Resources to accommodate burgeoning enrollments came from local, state, and federal governments. Funds were also furnished by private foundations for new media, new organizational patterns, and new teaching strategies. Thus, "the bigger the better" became a watchword for progress in educational enterprises.

## FAITH IN SOCIAL PROGRESS

Along with growth and abundance came high aspirations for social progress. In retrospect, American educators became principal actors in a broad social drama of progress and reform. Severe criticisms of an earlier progressive education, which had become a scapegoat for school problems, were transformed into a

5

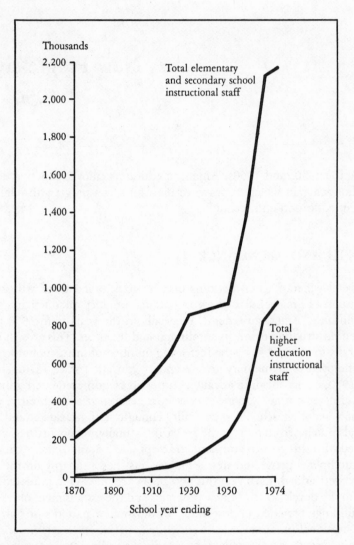

**FIGURE 1-1.**  Faculty in Educational Institutions

*new progressivism,* in which American faith in education as a means of achieving social progress became a national policy.

Change became a general value in the schools. Substantial investments were made in schools to: (1) strengthen the United States' role as a world leader; (2) equalize social and economic opportunities for disadvantaged groups; and (3) perpetuate growth and abundance.

**Strengthening World Leadership.**    Sputnik became a central symbol to American educators in the late 1950s and the early 1960s. Although efforts to revitalize and update school curricula had already begun, school reform acquired a sharp new focus resulting from charges that Russian missile and space technology would soon be superior to ours. The view that schools had a central role in the cold war was sanctioned by the federal government through The National Science Foundation's efforts to improve science and mathematics education and the National Defense Education Act of 1958. This view was widely publicized by Dr. James Bryant Conant, who became particularly sensitive to the "global struggle" while serving as High Commissioner and later Ambassador to the Federal German Republic. Improvement of mathematics and science education was given high priority, but the rationale also served to support other efforts to improve the organization, financing, content, and methods of American education.

**Reducing Poverty and Discrimination.** Among educational criticisms in the 1950s was the charge that schools had failed to provide equality of opportunity for certain disadvantaged groups, especially minorities in urban centers. With the growth of the civil rights movement in the early 1960s, more and more emphasis was given to improving education for the "culturally deprived" (later "culturally disadvantaged"; later still, "culturally different"). Subsequently, the drive for equal opportunity expanded to include Chicanos, Indians, women, and others. Again, schools were primary agents of social reform through programs of compensatory education, school desegregation, and affirmative action.

Because the drive for social equality was inseparable from economic issues, compensatory education programs were also efforts to solve the pressing economic problems of the urban poor, most of whom were ill-equipped to prosper in the urban environment. Especially with the Elementary and Secondary Education Act of 1965, schools were enlisted as primary agents to ameliorate the problems of the poor.

**Maintaining Prosperity.** From 1950 to 1970, faith remained in economic progress to provide resources for both world leadership *and* social progress. Investments in education were expected to bear rich economic returns for society and lead to leisure and abundance for all in the evolving "post-industrial" society. At the end of the period, however, doubts about the inevitability of economic progress led to an emphasis on career education to satisfy labor force demands and counter the seeming disaffection of youth with the economic roles necessary to sustain continuing growth and abundance.

## OPTIMISM ABOUT INSTITUTIONS AND TECHNOLOGY

Throughout the period of 1950–1970, most Americans remained optimistic about their institutions and the promise of technology (broadly defined) to solve social problems. Only after failures in Vietnam, the disillusionments accompanying the Watergate scandals, and dramatic world shortages of food and oil did Americans fully face the limits of American institutions and technology in dealing with world problems. While it lasted, however, the new progressivism brought a profusion of new educational hardware and software, including a technology of systematic, large-scale educational reform.

**Educational Hardware and Software.**   Technology was enlisted to solve a variety of problems and to improve schools. An obvious example is what came to be called the "newer media" (for example, television, film, audio tapes, filmstrips, overhead projectors). Not only could these devices help accommodate swelling enrollments, but they could also enrich instructional methods at all levels and in all subjects. Another popular innovation, programmed instruction, was proposed as a technology of teaching. In a popular version by B. F. Skinner, programmed instruction was the application of principles from the science of psychology to the design of instruction. Similar principles were applied to a variety of learning and behavior problems under the label of "behavior modification."

The systematic development of school curricula was another example of educational technology. Scholars, educators, media specialists, and editors combined to revise and update school curricula in many areas, especially academic subjects.

Still another family of innovations was proposed for school and classroom organization. Differentiated staffing, team teaching, multi-age grouping, individually-prescribed instruction, and flexible scheduling are examples.

Computer applications in education came to be widely advocated, whether as computer-managed instruction, computer-assisted instruction, computerized scheduling, or as an aid to budget management and cost analysis.

Looking back, the number and variety of technological innovations is impressive, especially in light of the disappointment with the results of educational technology in the early seventies.

**Systematic, Large-Scale Educational Reform.**   The process of school improvement was also a subject for study in its own right. Theories of organizational change from sociology were adapted by scholars in educational administration to study innovations in the schools. Techniques for encouraging change that had been used in business and other fields, especially those developed by the National Training Laboratory, came to be widely employed in schools. Principles of educational change were formulated and models of the educational change process were invented. The concept of "educational change agent" became popular, and manuals for use by change agents were developed. Much of this work was sponsored by federal education agencies.

This book, itself a continuation of these efforts, is written in the belief that this search for methods of successful, planned change in education has produced valuable knowledge that can be adapted to the new reality in which growth has ended and a less optimistic view of the future prevails.

# Chapter 2

# The Age of Slowdown, 1970–?

The period of 1950–1970 was characterized by a new progressivism in American education. Growth was tied to improvement, schools were a primary instrument for achieving social progress, and technology was viewed as a major contributor to school reform.

By contrast, American educators are now in a period of declining enrollments, of doubt about the role of schools in social progress, and of pessimism about the power of educational technology to bring about school reform. This new reality must be well understood by educators seeking to be successful in school improvement.

## DECLINING GROWTH RATES AND SCARCE RESOURCES

As Kenneth Boulding has pointed out,[1] declining enrollments are the great problem facing our education system during the present decade. His phrase, "The Age of Slowdown," suggests the probability of declining rates of economic growth, productivity, and per-capita income. Thus, Boulding has suggested that the preparation of academic administrators who are skilled in the "management of decline" be given top educational priority.

Declining school enrollments should not mean the end of educational reform efforts. However, we have become so accustomed to the belief that schools that are bigger *are* better that we have difficulty imagining how to make schools smaller and better. Likewise, in the early 1970s Americans faced the traumatic new realities of a world-wide shortage of natural resources. In a widely-publicized report entitled, "The Limits to Growth,"[2] projected trends of world population, pollution, food, and natural resources showed a disaster for humanity in the twenty-first century. Despite objections to the specific conclusions of the report, there is, nevertheless, widespread agreement that we have entered a period of resource shortage that calls for a drastic revision of American expectations for continuing growth and abundance.

Highlighted by the escalation in oil prices, a world-wide inflation underlines the need for a radical reorientation of American views of the future. Indeed, this is a "new reality," which educators must face along with all other world citizens.[3]

Although the details of this new view of reality are uncertain, the following are sure to be among its general axioms.

9

1. All life on the planet exists in a profound state of interdependence, as a part of a single system, which has definite tolerance limits for disequilibrium.
2. Everything in the system has a trade-off, such that misuse of the environment produces inevitable costs. Humans have been systematically borrowing from their future in terms of natural resources and environmental renewal.
3. To guarantee a future for humanity, we must change our views of progress and growth, so that there is less cost to the natural environment. Industrial nations may need to reduce consumption of material goods and restrict growth of many kinds.
4. The solutions to current problems must be world-wide solutions. This requires a new level of human cooperation, which is among the most urgent needs of the present age.

This new view of reality must be examined closely to see its implications for American schools. One purpose of this book is to do so, proposing methods of school improvement that are consistent with this reality. Our stress is on "smaller but better," on realistic goals, and on collaboration so that schools can make better use of human resources to move positively toward a new future.

## DOUBT ABOUT SOCIAL PROGRESS

One of the continuing realities of American education is public criticism of schools. In the late 1960s, as part of a broad wave of social discontent, school critics were particularly vehement in challenging the belief that schools are a primary instrument of social progress.

First, American disaffection with the Vietnam War grew strong in the late 1960s. Among the young, the war became a base for widespread disapproval of American values and institutions.

The limits of American power in the world, brought home by the failure in Vietnam, were then accentuated by the crisis in energy supplies. Emphasis now must be given to the interdependence of nations and the need for international cooperation to preserve a future for humankind. Although many would argue that we need schooling for America's new role in the world, the task of the schools in this regard has been radically altered since the 1950s.

Second, as the decade of the 1960s progressed, faith in the ability of social institutions, including schools, to bring about social equality and to solve urban problems waned. Silberman's *Crisis in the Classroom*,[4] published in 1970, was a popular expression of the distance perceived between aspirations and the reality of existing schools. Student protests emphasized this distance as "hypocrisy" and called attention to institutional barriers to social change. Evaluations of compensatory education programs were disappointing and innovative practices established in schools appeared to be transitory.

Educational historians attempted to debunk what Colin Greer has called "The Great School Legend": "Once upon a time there was a great nation which became great because of its public schools."[5] As the 1970s began, the revisionists pointed out that schools had failed in the solution of social problems and, in fact, had helped to polarize American society into a self-satisfied, suburban middle class and a poor, despondent, predominantly ethnic, urban class. They pictured the primary purpose of the school system as social control for a corporate state, whose goal was efficient production and disciplined consumption of growing amounts of goods and services.

Finally, growing economic problems raised questions about the general health of the American economy, and during the Nixon years federal educational priorities were shifted to career education. The educational accountability movement was a way to question the return on investments in education and marked a change in the public faith that schools should be a primary instrument of social reform. This trend continued as a "back to the basics" movement of the mid-1970s.

## PESSIMISM ABOUT INSTITUTIONS AND TECHNOLOGY

Disillusionment with technological solutions to human problems is a general theme in American society. Examples of this theme include the growing awareness of the costs to the world environment of technological progress and the failures of systems analysts to manage either war, peace, prosperity, or equality of opportunity. The unending blunders of the Vietnam War and "Watergate" symbolize the disillusionment with our social institutions.

Public schools have experienced similar, if less traumatic, events. In the first place, new instructional media, including television and computers, failed to bring about promised revolutions in schools, although each has found an important place in education. Machines have not, in fact, replaced teachers, and the escalating costs of education are still primarily those of personnel. While systematic efforts to develop new curricula were successful, the experiences of school children were not altered in any fundamental way. The successful implementation of curriculum changes remains a poorly developed science. Proposals for new patterns of school organizations, such as differentiated staffing, team teaching, multi-age grouping, and individually-prescribed instruction, have enjoyed only local or temporary successes. The problems that these technological innovations were designed to solve remain.

Not only were the results of school improvement programs disappointing, but also evidence from a landmark national study, the *Coleman Report*,[6] showed that social and economic background variables could explain most of what students learn and that variations in school inputs appeared to make little difference.

Although it can be argued that these efforts to improve schools were deficient and that our methods of research are faulty, nevertheless, it is clear that the results of school reform efforts have fallen far short of expectations. We must at least recognize that the improvement of schools through the application of educational technologies is much more difficult and costly than we had hoped.

Attempts to develop theories of systematic, planned change in education, while promising, are still in a primitive stage.[7] We seem to have learned more about obstacles to change than about strategies to produce improvements. Thus, while this book attempts to systematize current knowledge about successful school improvement, it will necessarily fall short of a comprehensive and scientifically verified technology of educational change.

## NEW STRATEGIES FOR SCHOOL IMPROVEMENT

Our analysis of the new reality for schools is summarized in Figure 2–1. The current Age of Slowdown is contrasted with the 1950–1970 period (The New Progressivism) in terms of three factors: (1) population and resource trends, (2) social goals and expectations, and (3) means and methods for reaching social goals. As indicated, general social and economic conditions have had strong effects on schools. From 1950 to 1970 economic and population trends led Americans to connect school improvement to growth; a faith in social progress was accompanied by faith in the power of school reform; and optimism about technology was reflected in an array of new educational hardware and software.

Also indicated in Figure 2–1 are the contrasting social and economic conditions following 1970. Declining rates of population growth and economic problems produced declines in school enrollments and resources. Doubt about the possibilities of social reform were reflected in criticisms of schools, such as the "back to the basics" movement. A new pessimism arose about the value of social innovations and the technology of educational reform.

The new reality for American schools, an Age of Slowdown, requires a reexaminaton of beliefs about how schools can be changed for the better. Certainly, American educators must be more modest than in the recent past in their aspirations and expectations for change. Also, American educators should admit uncertainty in knowledge about how to improve schools. Finally, because educators must now make do with less, the stress must be on new combinations of existing resources and especially on improving the utilization of existing human resources.

Thus, we propose to elaborate in subsequent chapters three convictions about school improvement in an Age of Slowdown:

1. In a period of stable or declining educational resources, new emphasis must be given to the reallocation and efficient use of existing resources. In public elementary and secondary education, this new emphasis invites and requires higher levels of cooperation and collaboration among elements of the educational establishment, including local school officials, state and federal education agencies, institutions of higher education, and teachers' organizations.

| | A New Progressivism, 1950–1970 | | The Age of Slowdown, 1970–?? | |
|---|---|---|---|---|
| | Social and Economic Conditions | Effects in Schools | Social and Economic Conditions | Effects in Schools |
| Population and resource allocation | Continuing growth and abundance | School improvement tied to growth —new people —new facilities —new ideas "Bigger is better" | Declining growth rates / Scarce resources | Enrollment declines / Resource reductions "Can Smaller Be Better?" |
| Goals and expectations | Faith in social progress | Social progress through school reform / Innovations to strengthen world leadership, reduce poverty and discrimination, maintain prosperity | Doubt about social progress | Emphasis on essentials / Innovations to improve efficiency and effectiveness |
| Means and methods | Optimism about institutions and technology | New educational hardware and software / Systematic, large-scale educational reform | Pessimism about institutions and technology | Need for partnerships to improve utilization of human resources in local schools |

FIGURE 2-1. The New Reality of School Improvement

2. Despite recent disappointments with attempts at school reform, much is known about processes of school improvement, especially that local efforts, properly managed, can lead to desired changes. Successful strategies include: focus on the individual school organization; clear identification of the need for change; strong commitment to change at school and district levels; sustained involvement and support of staff who must adapt new ideas to the local setting; flexible, on-going training to provide staff with needed skills, and close communication among all members of the local school community. School improvement requires changes in individuals and in organizations; these changes take the involvement and interaction of many people.

3. A humanistic attitude should be taken toward school improvement. Restraint, recognition of human limits, and a commitment to a reasonable future for humankind must pervade our efforts to improve schools. We must dispel the illusion that progress is inextricably bound to growth and understand that people are part of a larger biosystem, inevitably limited by it. Technology has its place, but a limited place, in the solution of human problems.

## ENDNOTES

1. Kenneth E. Boulding, "The Management of Decline," *Change* (June 1975): 8–9, 64.
2. Donella H. Meadows et al., *The Limits of Growth* (New York: Signet, 1972).
3. Edwin O. Reischauer, *Toward the 21st Century: Education for a Changing World* (New York: Vintage, 1974).
4. Charles E. Silberman, *Crisis in the Classroom* (New York: Random House, 1970).
5. Colin Greer, *The Great School Legend* (New York: Viking, 1973), p. 3.
6. James S. Coleman et al., *Equality of Educational Opportunity* (Washington, D.C.: U.S. Office of Education, 1966).
7. Victor Baldridge and Terrence E. Deal, *Managing Change in Educational Organizations* (Berkeley, Calif.: McCutchan Publishing Corp., 1975).

# Chapter 3

# Coping with Reality:
# New Policies for School
# Improvement

Because educators are facing a new reality for public elementary and secondary schools, new and different means for improving schools are needed. This chapter will highlight the kinds of policy changes that are required to improve schools in the new reality. The analysis, which is based on Figure 1-1, emphasizes the need for dramatic changes in resource allocation policy as well as new policy goals and expectations. Means and methods for school improvement will be introduced in Chapter 4. The analysis leads to the authors' recommendation that policies for educational change should include *partnerships for local school improvement*. The purpose of these partnerships, involving school districts, state education agencies, higher education institutions, teachers' organizations, parents, and community is to supply the leverage and coordination needed to mobilize available resources for school improvement.

First of all, the new reality for schools requires that major changes be made in the procedures by which resources are allocated for school improvement. In the fifties and sixties educators depended on conditions of growth to supply resources for improvement; being better depended upon being bigger. Now policies must be developed for schools to be smaller *and* better.

## BUDGETING FOR IMPROVEMENT

In a period of growth, educational budgets tend to rise each year. New money, justified on the basis of growing enrollments, is available for allocation. Budget-making strategies in such a situation emphasize competition among various new proposals. The difficult job of program cuts and reallocation may be avoided while new program initiatives are made.

During the recent era of expansion, for example, new staff were continually required. American educators depended on this fact in changing schools. To install new educational programs, new staff members with appropriate training could be hired. The presence of fresh college graduates was a "natural" force to keep new life in a teaching staff.

The need for new school buildings also provided opportunities to improve schools. New ideas for school organization, such as team teaching and flexible scheduling, could be implemented in connection with plans for a new building, which also brought funds for the purchase of new equipment and materials.

Now, of course, American educators have had to change their ways because the conditions of expansion no longer exist. New staff members are increasingly rare, money for new facilities is gone, and budget cuts have replaced budget additions.

Clearly, new initiatives must come primarily from the reallocation of existing resources. This means developing new and better policies for establishing goals and priorities, for cutting back programs and people, and for reallocating current resources to new initiatives. In particular, we must depend increasingly upon existing human resources as the primary vehicle for improvement. Change must come more and more from the reassignment of existing staff and in changes made by staff members themselves. The focus must be on changes in the duties, skills, and relationships of existing staff members.

**Control through Budgeting.**  Because enrollments are declining, but even more because educational costs are escalating, school managers are called on to find new efficiencies. Many are discovering that the key to efficiency lies in increased attention to the concept of "control" as it is used in administrative theory. Control procedures function to ensure that a management plan is achieved, placing limits or boundaries on acceptable activities of an organization or people. As interpreted in budgetary decisions, increased emphasis on control means allocating resources according to specific plans that have clear relationships to institutional goals.

Thus, new emphasis is being given to the analysis of educational expenditures at the school, district, and state levels to develop a better data base for budgetary decisions. To be useful, such expenditure analysis must include financial breakdowns according to each function and activity within the organization. If comparisons are to be made between schools or districts, care must also be taken that procedures used in the analysis are precise and uniform. For maximum benefit the analysis of expenditures should be made periodically to permit analysis of trends. Without a good system of expenditure analysis, management controls necessary to improve efficiency are difficult or impossible to establish.

Another way to improve efficiency through budgetary control is to strengthen systems for setting priorities. Often, clarity about goals or educational needs, especially when these are placed in priority order, can give essential guidance in making difficult budget choices. Too often, budget crises arrive suddenly, without time to permit a careful study of alternatives. Decision makers must have a finely-tuned set of priorities constantly ready.

A third ingredient in budgetary control is an improved system of feedback on the effectiveness of budgeted activities. Much has been made of "accountability" in this regard, and the basic principle holds: judgments about *costs in relation to effectiveness* are central to bringing about increases in efficiency and productivity. Although effectiveness is extremely difficult to appraise in educational activities, this appraisal must be made and must be a basis for deciding what pattern of budgeted activities yields the most education for the limited number of educational dollars available. Later in this book, we propose specific means for improving such appraisals and thus for improving efficiency through budgetary controls.[1]

**Decentralized Control for School Improvement.**    The word *control* often implies rigid policies and rules that are devised and enforced from the top down. Such a tendency in management style has been an all too frequent response to economic problems in education. Although it is tempting to equate efficiency and cost-cutting with an autocratic, centralized administrative plan, in fact, improved efficiency, as opposed simply to reducing expenditures, requires the participation of those throughout the organization.[2] Thus, a decentralized approach to financial controls is recommended. Responsibility for efficiency is delegated—school building administrators, supervisors, and teachers are asked to become more accountable for budgetary control (in the sense of justifying the allocation of budgeted resources according to specific plans that relate to school or district priorities).[3]

In keeping with this emphasis on decentralized control, we recommend particularly that control over school improvement projects and staff development be decentralized. If schools are to become more efficient or more productive, resources must be allocated for the improvement process. Primarily, this means resources for developing staff. To make the most of these resources, moreover, we strongly recommend a decentralized approach to staff development and innovation.[4]

Through decentralization, local school building teachers and principals experience a greater sense of ownership over the programs and activities of the school and will be much more willing to accept responsibility for the same.

## ATTITUDES TOWARD RESOURCES

The new procedures for resources management required in an Age of Slowdown must also be accompanied by new attitudes toward resources. We must consciously work to dispel the illusion that progress depends upon growth. To be smaller and better must be adopted as a deliberate policy of educational organizations.

Likewise, we must deliberately adopt a policy of conservation of scarce resources. Although most Americans are by now aware that energy and other natural resources are dangerously scarce, we have not changed wasteful policies and procedures throughout our social institutions. Schools should be, *must be,* places where new economies and efficiencies are found. To be less wasteful, to be more economical—these are, by themselves, improvements.

Perhaps educators would be wise to learn some of the lessons from business and industry where the economic factors relating to efficiency and effectiveness have always been instrumental in management decisions regarding utilization of resources. In a sense, educators have been spoiled by an absence of economic accountability. Prudence in the use of educational resources is now clearly an educational management function and responsibility.

Obviously, the largest resource in any educational organization is the teaching staff. Therefore, the resource-oriented school manager will be looking for ways and means to optimize the quality of the teachers' work life. The improvement of the quality of work life is primarily accomplished through management behavior that emphasizes morale, which, in the case of professional employees, means an emphasis on participation and involvement. These themes will be a focus of this book, and later we plan to show how involving teachers and parents in decision making is a key step toward maximizing human resources. Part of the process involves a change of attitude about human resources.

As a beginning, we believe that school managers should closely reexamine their own attitudes toward human resource development in the schools. What priorities are given, in fact, to the development of school staffs? How many features of present-day schools, now accepted as "given," might be less important than attention to the improvement of human resources? As examples, consider the following list of concepts that might be changed if greater value were placed on the development of the human resources in schools.

- The concept that 180 (or however many regulations dictate) school days are necessary for children to learn. Might fewer days in school for children and more days in training for teachers improve the effectiveness of the learning and teaching?
- The concept that six or seven pupil contact hours in a school day are the most productive number of hours for teachers. Perhaps the number of hours per day of active teaching should be reduced to be replaced with increases in teacher and administrator training. The school day for students can be shortened.
- The concept that all teachers (with equal education and years experience) should receive the same amount of pay. Could not differentiated pay scales reward certain teachers with development skills?
- The concept that all learning has to take place in modern expensive buildings with comprehensive facilities. Why not save money with alternative schools, street academies, and field experiences?
- The concept that every time a teacher is absent, a substitute teacher should be hired at a tremendous expense to school districts. Team teaching, individualized programs, volunteers, or student vacation days may have to be substituted for the substitute pay which is draining our coffers.
- The concept that instructional devices such as audiovisual equipment, visual aides, supplementary textbooks, hardback books, learning kits, etc., are necessary to valid teaching/learning situations. Might not human resource development be more important? And what's wrong with teacher-made materials?

Educators must make some hard decisions about the utilization of resources. Particularly in the face of reduced resources, we advocate the highest
priority on staff development projects, change/improvement activities, and
organization development. Smaller can be better. Improvement can occur during hard financial times, but it will require fundamental changes in attitudes
that have been long-accepted.

## POLICIES TO DEVELOP HUMAN RESOURCES

Along with new attitudes toward resources must come new policies and procedures. After a period when personnel policies emphasized the recruitment of
new staff, we must make special efforts to change our concepts of personnel
management in schools—compensation patterns, promotion opportunities,
and staff training programs to foster development of existing staff. These adjustments in educational policies will require involvement of those beyond the
local school and district. At state and federal levels and in institutions of higher
education, major readjustments are needed so that existing human resources in
the public schools can change and adjust to new conditions.

Again, lessons can be learned from business and industry. An analysis of
the components of morale and motivation in business, for example, suggests
four factors: *pay, direction and control, job design,* and *benevolence.*[5]

*Pay* has long been the subject of controversy for teachers and school districts. Because of changes in the employment picture with an excess of teachers,
salary schedule policies need to be reexamined. Policies designed to attract new
personnel in a time when teachers were scarce should be changed. Consideration should be given to additional pay incentives for professional growth and
for leadership in school improvements.

*Direction* means telling someone what to do; *control* means making sure
they do it. The "workers" of the education world, the teachers, must be
allowed increased self-direction and greater peer control in the future.

A major shift in *job design* in education for the Age of Slowdown must be
in the direction of shared leadership among the various roles in the education
community. Much of this shared leadership should be directed at school
improvement. At least some teachers, parents, administrators, and college professors must begin to have school improvement as a major assignment. We can
no longer afford to retool while in operation (something industry very seldom
attempts). Instead, personnel must be assigned in a manner that directs talent
to the organizational development and change process.

The *benevolence* factor is simple. Management scholars have long known
that satisfied workers are more productive than unhappy workers. What is the
quality of the work life for educators, and what factors will create satisfied
teachers in the Age of Slowdown?

In specific terms, the concern for these policy areas may reinforce the case
for expanded roles of teachers. This could be manifested in differentiated staff-

ing patterns, increased responsibility for new teacher certification, licensing and other training, peer evaluations, and unique job descriptions. Other professions take responsibility for conditions other than welfare concerns and this direction holds promise for maximizing human resources in the teaching community.

## POLICY GOALS AND EXPECTATIONS

Readjustments are necessary not only in resource policies but also in the goals and expectations we hold for school improvement. In particular, we must reduce the unrealistic expectations held by many persons during the New Progressivism without losing a justified recognition of past progress and a realistic role for education in solving new problems.

**Realism about Education and Social Progress.**    Opinions about American schools shift periodically. Like a pendulum, the impulse for school reform seems to swing between a limited focus on basic skills subjects and an emphasis upon broader goals for schools. The period 1950–1970, the New Progressivism, was characterized by a strong faith that school reform could solve social problems. As embodied in the legislative record, the rhetoric of school reform promised a "head start" to those who were educationally disadvantaged, "equal opportunity" for poor minorities in American society, and "career education" to guarantee job placement and satisfaction. Through education, human relations between antagonistic groups would be improved, school and social failure would be reduced, individual needs would be met, and the quality of life for everyone would be better.

High aspirations were often followed by disillusionment. Evaluations of programs for the disadvantaged failed to uncover lasting gains in academic achievement. Problems of poverty and unemployment persisted. Schools and other social institutions proved remarkably resistant to change. America's failure to end the Vietnam War decisively changed Americans' hopes for the United States as the irresistible leader of the world community.

The Ford Foundation Fund for the Advancement of Education, for example, invested substantial sums of money in efforts to produce widespread educational changes. Yet, in retrospect, the Foundation was disappointed to find that changes were random and transitory.[6]

The Coleman Report, *Equality of Educational Opportunity*, underlined the resistance of American educational systems to school integration goals. As noted earlier, Coleman interpreted his evidence to indicate that social and economic background variables were the primary determinants of educational outcomes, not characteristics of schools.[7]

Evaluations of federal programs designed to stimulate educational change were disappointing. Despite the many millions of dollars invested, little concrete evidence appeared to show that students learned more from special programs for the disadvantaged, or new media, curricula, or instructional methodologies. After an extensive survey of school classrooms, John Goodlad reported almost no evidence of the many educational innovations which had, supposedly, been introduced in schools.[8]

Although disappointing, these reports, and others like them, represent a rich resource to Americans interested in changing schools. Two lessons from them deserve attention at this point. First, bringing about widespread change in American schools is much more difficult and expensive than was imagined during the New Progressivism. Second, the schools are as much a *product* of political, economic, and social forces as they are a force for social change.

Thus, compared with the 1950s and 1960s, we are now conservative about the role of schools in social progress. Although some may yearn for a return of optimism, others believe that, because expectations for schools are now more realistic, success in reaching goals is more likely.

**Improving Schools.**   Although many people now doubt that school reform can be a primary means for social progress, nevertheless, substantial evidence and belief remain that schools can be improved and that education is a vital resource in the solution of human problems.

We realize, for example, that racial minorities have made substantial political and social gains, although progress has not been as fast as many had hoped. And substantial changes have occurred, especially in the South, in race relations in the schools. Strong, positive examples exist of successful, integrated schools.

A startling example of successful change was reported by Robbins and Teeter. Twenty years after forced integration in Little Rock, Arkansas, Central High School is regarded as one of the best in the nation.[9] Other examples are found in *Affirmative School Integration.*[10]

Likewise, although many large-scale educational change projects appeared to be unsuccessful, many examples of successful change in local areas have been documented. Furthermore, we recognize the limitations of our methods of evaluating change. Many disappointments are failures in research and evaluation, not in the possibility of school improvement.[11]

We believe that efforts to improve schools during the 1950s and 1960s have left a substantial record of positive achievement, which shows that valuable improvements can be made in schools. Furthermore, when reasonable goals and expectations are established, one can be quite optimistic about the probabilities of success. Specifically, we believe the record shows:

1. Dramatic changes in local schools are possible through systematic and deliberate efforts at improvement.
2. Large amounts of money to initiate and sustain educational innovations are not essential.

3. Hard evidence exists showing that such local change efforts produce desired changes in pupils.
4. Much is known about factors associated with successful local change, such that school improvement can be planned and managed.

We will draw extensively upon this record of success and failure in school reform to make our own recommendations about methods of school improvement in the Age of Slowdown.

## ENDNOTES

1. See also, R. A. Rossmiller and T. G. Geske, "Toward More Effective Use of School Resources," *Journal of Education Finance* 1 (1976): 484–502.
2. See, for example, L. Craig Wilson, *School Leadership Today: Strategies for the Educator* (Boston: Allyn & Bacon, 1978).
3. T. H. Jones, "The Case for Local Control," *Journal of Education Finance* 2 (1976): 110–122.
4. Milbrey McLaughlin and Paul Berman, "Retooling Staff Development in a Period of Retrenchment," *Educational Leadership* (December 1977): 191–194.
5. Saul W. Gellerman, *The Management of Human Resources* (Hinsdale, Ill.: The Dryden Press, 1976), p. 17.
6. Ford Foundation, *A Foundation Goes to School* (New York: The Foundation, 1972).
7. James S. Coleman et al., *Equality of Educational Opportunity* (Washington, D.C.: U.S. Office of Education, 1966).
8. John I. Goodlad and M. F. Klein, *Behind the Classroom Door* (Worthington, Ohio: C. A. Jones, 1970).
9. J. Robbins and T. Teeter, "The Phoenix of Little Rock: Central High 20 Years After Forced Integration," *Phi Delta Kappan* 59 (October 1977): 111–112.
10. Roscoe Hill and Malcolm Feely, *Affirmative School Integration* (Beverly Hills: Sage Publications, 1968).
11. Milbrey W. McLaughlin, *Evaluation and Reform* (Cambridge, Mass: Ballinger Publishing Co., 1975).

# Chapter 4

# Methods for School Improvement

In addition to new policies for resource allocation and new realism in policy goals and expectations, it appears that the new reality for public schools also requires new means and methods to bring about desired changes. Furthermore, lessons learned from recent school reform efforts, both successes and failures, provide an important new basis for choosing methods likely to succeed. Two important lessons from the recent past are central to the selection of such methods.

1. The local school, as a social organization, is the optimal focus for change; successful change can best be brought about by continuous efforts to improve the local school building organization as a total unit.
2. The local school building organization, as a part of a larger educational system, must be linked to other organizations for maximum success in school improvement.

## LOCAL SCHOOL ORGANIZATION AS FOCUS FOR CHANGE

After more than two decades of federal, state, and local efforts to stimulate change in schools, it is clear that educational policy and decision making are still centered at the local school district level. Furthermore, for a number of reasons, the local school building appears to provide the optimal unit for educational change.

**Goodlad's Change Strategy.** A major statement of this view has been presented by John I. Goodlad. Out of more than fifteen years of study and personal experience with educational change, Goodlad adopted as a primary principle that:

> . . . the optimal unit for educational change is the single school with its pupils, teachers, principal—those who live there every day—as primary participants. The interactions of these people, the language they use, the traditions they uphold, the beliefs to which they subscribe, and so forth, make up the culture of the school.[1]

It is the culture of the local school, in Goodlad's view, that should be the focus of change.

. . . the single school falls nicely between the depersonalized, complex, amorphous school system and the somewhat intimidated, impotent, individual teacher. The schoolhouse is a physical entity (even when schooling is treated as a concept rather than a place, which I favor, there can still be a place called school); it is occupied by real people—not just "they"—who can be seen and talked with, face to face; it has an identity characterized by roles and people who occupy them, activities, ways of behaving, perceptions, and even elements of a special language. It satisfies at least some of the components of a culture, shaped in part by those who occupy it and, to a degree, shaping them.[2]

According to Goodlad, the internal processes necessary for self-renewal are uncommon. With outside assistance, however, schools can develop the processes that lead to constructive change.

Goodlad's views were elaborated in a League of Cooperating Schools and subsequently adopted as the basis of the Change Program for Individually Guided Education of the Institute for the Development of Educational Activities (/I/D/E/A/).[3] We have drawn substantially on these strategies in making our own recommendations.

**Rand Change Agent Study.**    Additional support for choosing local schools as the focus for educational change is provided by the Rand Change Agent Study.[4] Combining survey techniques and case studies, this extensive investigation of federal projects in support of educational change concluded that successful change was not associated with the amount of money spent or with the particular type of change introduced, but with the use of a particular *local school implementation strategy*. The successful strategy included such features as:

1. local development of educational materials, which produced a sense of local ownership in a new practice;
2. on-line planning, with regular staff meetings to solve problems and adapt an innovation to local conditions;
3. on-going training, flexible enough to provide new skills as the need for them was perceived;
4. a critical mass of local staff members to provide mutual support and stimulation.

The investigators characterized this process of successful change as one of *mutual adaptation*, in which the innovative practice and the local school organization both were changed. Theirs is a developmental model of educational innovation, in which the local school *grows* better. Change is inherently a local process.

In a follow-up to the Change Agent Study, the Rand investigators chose five school districts for intensive study. Districts with successful records of innovation used a decentralized approach to improvement, with chief responsibility for improvement given to school principals and school building staffs. The implications of these studies for improving schools in the present climate of educational cutbacks are substantial, and we believe the strategies suggested are excellent guides for current efforts to improve schools. We shall return to them in later chapters.

**Ford Foundation Comprehensive School Improvement Program.**   That successful innovation in education is a local process was also a major lesson learned by the Ford Foundation in the 1960s. After more than $30,000,000 was granted to promote comprehensive changes in selected schools, Foundation officers were disappointed that the changes introduced successfully in some schools did not spread widely to others. Likewise, successful changes were often temporary, losing momentum with the end of Foundation support or with the departure of a key local leader. Nevertheless, successful changes *were* made in many "lighthouse" schools, where local support was strong and a vigorous local leader stayed with the project.[5]

**Project LONGSTEP.**   Another significant evaluation of school innovation was undertaken in 1969 by the American Institutes for Research (AIR) for the U.S. Office of Education. Project LONGSTEP (the Longitudinal Study of Educational Practices) was an intensive study of thirteen school districts located in nine different states. Districts were identified on the basis of a nation-wide survey as ones that had educational programs with intensive, innovative practices. Over 30,000 students, 80 schools and 1,500 teachers were involved in such innovations as team teaching, multimedia emphasis, variations in scheduling, and individualized instruction.

Despite comprehensive data collection and analysis, including a study of achievement over a three-year period, no evidence was found that *amount of innovation* or *degree of individualization* were related to achievement gains across all schools. On the other hand, definite evidence was found to show that *selected* schools had unusually large gains.[6] Evidently, successful change, as measured in pupil achievement, is a local product, not guaranteed necessarily by the adoption of any one set of innovative practices.

**Project Follow Through.**   Similar support for an emphasis on local schools as the focus for improvement comes from extensive efforts to evaluate different approaches to compensatory education in Project Follow Through. Eleven different models of compensatory education were evaluated in terms of their success in raising achievement in basic skills, cognitive abilities, and self-concepts of disadvantaged children. On the basis of results at over sixty different sites, the major conclusion was that differences among the sites overshadowed the differences among the models. According to evaluators,

No model has shown itself to be powerful enough to raise test scores everywhere it has been tried. The most successful models had unsuccessful sites. Some of the least successful models had sites in which positive effects predominated.[7]

**Exemplary Schools and Programs That Work.**   That individual schools may be successful targets for change is most convincingly demonstrated in the research on exemplary schools.[8] A variety of investigations has uncovered a set of schools whose students are achieving well beyond expectations, that is, above achievement levels predicted by measures of the students' family and community background. Such exemplary schools reveal no single recipe for educational success; rather, each seems to have discovered a unique combination of ingredients from a longer list of promising educational practices.

Other local success stories have been documented by the U.S. Office of Education as *Educational Programs That Work.*[9] Each successful program is examined by the Joint Dissemination Review Panel, which applies rigorous evaluation standards to validate the results. Validated projects become part of the National Diffusion Network, as described in the final chapter. These validated programs are a frequently overlooked record of success in local school improvement efforts. They show that school improvement efforts can and do succeed!

**Studies of Educational Governance.**   Backing for what has been called "school site management" as the focus for educational change comes also from students of educational politics. During the last two decades scholars have drawn a complex, but fascinating picture of how educational decisions are made in America.[10] Briefly, scholars confirm the fundamental reality of local control of education, despite the influence of a variety of forces operating at the state and national levels.

Legally and historically, of course, educational powers and responsibilities have been divided among governmental jurisdictions. The federal government, under its powers to advance the general welfare, taxes and spends for educational purposes. Education, however, is primarily a state function, and states may enact any laws regarding education except those which specifically contradict the Constitution.

States, in turn, have delegated administrative control over education to local school districts, which thereby become instruments of the state with "quasi-corporate powers." The local school board, as the legally controlling, policy-making body at the local level, implements state mandates, but otherwise exercises whatever powers are necessary to its functions in the interest of local citizens. Thus, the strongest power in educational governance is local power, which flows, not through other local government, but directly to local school districts from the state. Education, it is usually said, is a state function, locally administered. As Laurence Iannacone puts it,

> . . . the structure of educational governance on the North American continent rests on the dynamic tension between local and state educational governance. That is the constitutional reality, if there is one. This dynamic tension is akin to a marriage without the possibility of divorce; it produces family conflicts, which are also often fruitful and productive.[11]

This primary fact of "dual sovereignty" in school governance means that local district and state school officials are charged by law with responsibility for schools. As we shall discuss later, their leadership is indispensable to creating a climate for local school improvement and to supporting local school building staffs in making needed changes.

Local educational politics, according to the generally accepted view, is one of a lay board, who selects a school superintendent. The operation of schools is then left to the superintendent and his or her staff. Shifts in the community or the development of educational problems may lead to defeats of incumbent board members followed by ideological and value differences between new board members and the superintendent. Open conflict often leads to a new superintendency. This general picture appears to hold even in large urban centers, although the particular coalitions and issues may be different from those in suburbs or rural communities.

While recognizing a complex background of political activity at all levels of government, it is thus clear that educational policy and decision making are centered at the local school district level. Furthermore, except in times of crisis or change, local boards defer to the school superintendent and staff in most matters.

This results in considerable autonomy in school management at the school building level. In a summary of research on educational governance, Michael Kirst concluded:

> Educational change . . . cannot be imposed from the top down or through parent pressure on uncommitted and reluctant teachers. The cutting edge of education is at the school and classroom level. This is where the child comes in contact with the educational process. Consequently, we need to give teachers more ability to plan and evaluate school reforms at the individual school level. Principal, parents and teachers at the school level can best insure implementation of educational ideas.[12]

Possibly the most important lesson to be learned from attempts to change American schools in the 1950s and 1960s is that generalized efforts to install new educational practices have failed to pass through *most* school house doors. On the other hand, we have repeatedly seen that selected local schools have been able to make dramatic improvements in their operations. Unless conditions for change exist at the school building level, no change will occur.

## NEED FOR PARTNERS IN LOCAL SCHOOL IMPROVEMENT

If school improvement is inherently a local process, what need is there for those outside the local school to be involved in change? Our view is that the *target* for educational change should be the local school. Without support from other agencies and people, however, the local school is unlikely to change.

Throughout its history, and today, the local American school has remained a conservative organization. This conservatism appears to be rooted in the type of person who becomes, and remains, a teacher and is reinforced by working conditions. For example, many teachers are also housewives or hold second jobs; they have little energy or incentive to be engaged in making dramatic changes. Likewise, the "cellular" organization of schools, where each teacher is isolated and autonomous with a group of students, tends to reduce the professional interaction with supervisors or colleagues that can lead to change. Furthermore, the status of teachers remains modest compared to other professions, without the power or prestige to support autonomous change. Teachers are clearly subordinates in a "flat," bureaucratic hierarchy.[13]

To take another perspective, the local school as an organization has few incentives for fundamental change. Unlike competitive business firms that must innovate to remain profitable, the local school acts like a public utility whose monopoly is secure. Superficial change is welcomed to satisfy clients' desires for "improvement," but fundamental changes that would rearrange the bureaucratic structure are resisted. Although the business analogy can be overdrawn, nevertheless, local school organizations have, in fact, been extremely resistant to structural change.[14]

Thus, the search for methods of school improvement must not only recognize the local school as a necessary focus for change, but also that the local school organization is normally a conservative organization. Therefore, our search has led us to the concept of "partnership," in which the local school is linked to a variety of resources to create conditions within the school that facilitate change.

One example of such a linking process is Goodlad's League of Cooperating Schools, in which local schools organize around an intermediate agency—a college of education or a state department of education—to gain leadership and mutual support for changing themselves.[15] Other examples are common in the teacher center movement and in the Teacher Corps.

In a similar vein, the Rand Change Agent Study emphasized the necessity of general school district support for local change projects with shared governance in decisions for change. The studies of educational politics have also emphasized that local schools exist and function with a very complex network of legal, financial, and political forces which both promote and limit local action.

Thus, we recommend that the resources devoted to school improvement can best be mobilized through partnerships whose purpose is to improve local schools, but whose membership transcends the school itself. We suggest that local teachers and administrators be supplemented by representatives of the state education agency and a college or university to provide needed linkages to the broader educational system and to contribute added resources to the local school improvement process. These partners—the teachers, the administrators, the state agency personnel, and higher educators—represent the primary resources for school improvement.

Unfortunately, these groups have not been working harmoniously to improve schools. Instead they have been engaged in competitions for power over educational governance, so that their collective force for educational improvement has been dissipated. Improved collaboration and cooperation among elements in the educational establishment is, in our view, a major requirement for new leverage in school reform. We now turn to a closer examination of these potential partners and the unique contributions we think each can make to local school improvement.

## THE ROLE OF LOCAL SCHOOL PERSONNEL

One lesson from the past is clear: teachers and administrators must be directly and continuously involved in any process of school improvement. Without their participation and committed involvement, significant changes are unlikely to occur. In the first place, these key figures must change their own skills, habits, attitudes, and relationships if the school organization is to change. Second, they must provide needed linkages to their constituencies—students and parents, on the one hand, and school district officials and teachers' organizations on the other. Third, they must be willing to seek and accept help from others, whether peers, colleagues in other schools, or state department, district-level and college personnel. If our analysis is correct, all three activities are necessary for successful change.

**The Principal.**    There is persistent evidence to demonstrate a strong relationship between the building principal and the behavior of the school as an organization.[16] In other words, the principal does make a difference. Although recent trends such as increased teacher militancy, accountability movements, parental involvement, and tenure laws may decrease some *powers* of the principal, educational leadership remains a crucial factor in efforts to improve schools. As a matter of fact, the so-called "erosion of the principal's power" means that an even greater premium is now placed on the *influence* of the principal. No longer can principals rule by edict; they must involve the entire staff in setting and accomplishing the school's goals. In the long run this requires more from principals than before. The importance of their leadership has not changed, but the necessary leadership behavior is different. This is consistent with experience in recent efforts to reform schools, in which successful change appeared to require a strong leader in the local school, usually a principal, who acted as an educational sparkplug to energize others.

It is evident that strong leadership from the principal can create change. It is also evident that without the principal's support, change and renewal activities are unlikely to succeed. Unfortunately, many school principals are poorly equipped to play change agent roles. This is partly a result of poorly designed graduate training programs for school administrators. But programs do exist to prepare the willing principal for this role. For example, some university graduate programs now emphasize change agent behavior. Also, the National Academy for School Executives (NASE) holds executive seminars and conferences with a similar emphasis. Likewise, the National Association of Elementary School Principals (NAESP), and the National Association of Secondary School Principals (NASSP) conduct programs of this type. However, much more help is needed by the practicing school administrator to develop the required skills. A major purpose of this book is to suggest the type of skills and knowledge needed by local leaders to bring about school improvement.

Even with the proper knowledge and skills, however, our analysis suggests that the change agent role is particularly difficult to play because the local administrator represents, on-site, the authority and policy of the local district, the state, and the federal government, while at the same time, he or she must win the support of teachers, parents, and students who may disagree with such policy. This situation brings a great deal of conflicting pressure upon the principal. The success stories from the change literature all point to strong leaders who thrive on such pressure. The principal is truly in the middle and deals with voices from every direction. Of course, just because principals are in such central positions, they are in the best place to bring interested parties together for concerted and collaborative efforts for school improvement.

**Teachers and Teachers' Organizations.**    Teachers are central in all attempts to improve schools. Too often, however, they have merely been *exhorted* to change. Clearly, teachers must be more involved in decision making and must be supported for introducing changes. Consideration must increasingly be given to the teacher, not only as a member of the school organization but also as a member of a professional group.

First, we recommend that teachers be involved in every phase of the school improvement process, from needs assessment to evaluation. Not only can their participation make decisions better, but such participation will result in greater enthusiasm and support for change. Unfortunately, in many schools the necessary processes of consultation, planning, and decision making are absent. Often, teachers lack the necessary skills or the time for participation. These are critical ingredients in any successful effort to change schools.

Second, a major fact of educational life in schools is the strength of teachers' organizations. During the 1960s, teacher organizations gained unprecedented power. This fact of life has often been overlooked in discussions of school improvement.[17] Because we believe that teacher power is here to stay, we recommend direct liaison between local school improvement projects and teachers' organizations. In fact, we believe that teachers' organizations have a crucial role in initiating and supporting school improvement, and that they must assume greater responsibility in this process.

At the building level, teachers may often be at odds with local school management because they reflect strong positions of state and national teacher organizations. A common conflict, for example, involves reimbursement for extra hours that may be needed for planning and implementing new school practices. Questions about new practices may also raise general issues of power or prerogative. Many a promising innovation has failed because someone saw it as a threat to power. The partnership strategy is designed to bring together all the necessary forces for school improvement, so that they may develop mutually agreeable goals and plans for making improvements in local schools.

Especially in a time when school budgets and staff may be reduced, efforts at school improvement must take into account vital labor-management issues. Likewise, solutions to problems of personnel reduction must not be solved at the expense of school improvement.

**District-Level Staff.**    A surprising finding of the Rand investigation was that school districts with elaborate provisions for staff development at the district level were not, in that study, the districts with success in school improvement.[18] In fact, a district with an elaborate, centralized staff development program was often a district preserving the status quo. "Developmental" districts, on the other hand, were those with highly decentralized approaches to change, and informal, flexible mechanisms for staff training. Another vital factor was support for local change efforts from the district level. Encouragement, recognition of local efforts, and special funds for improvement projects were helpful. It was quite clear that districts differed markedly in the climate of encouragement they provided for local school improvement.

There are many ways to implement district support for local school building change efforts, and the district office staff clearly has that responsibility. An example of one of the varied ideas that can encourage innovation in the school building can be the use of internal district curriculum grants. Bailey[19] suggests a plan in which teachers can submit mini-proposals to the district office for small funds to implement classroom innovations. The district office staff must set aside a small percentage of the budget (off the top) for these kinds of projects. In this example, the money made available demonstrates to the local school building that "we support change efforts." Bailey also suggests that a committee of teachers be established to judge proposals.

Another way to provide district support is for the district office staff to encourage individual school buildings to submit proposals for state and federal projects as an individual building. This implies a decentralization of curriculum control. If these projects are funded, there may be differences in educational programs among buildings. Reinforcing school building autonomy is an important role of school district staff.

Or, as is done in some larger school districts, a centralized staff can assist local buildings on a service basis, consulting about needs or providing staff training.

## THE ROLE OF STATE AND FEDERAL AUTHORITIES

A major incentive for this book is the disappointment with twenty years of federal efforts to reform American education. As is clear from experience, federal efforts to develop and install specific educational programs and practices "from the top down" failed. As American education is currently organized, only a decentralized strategy that recognizes great diversity in local settings can be defended.

On the other hand, federal involvement in school improvement is still essential. First, the schools do serve, *must* serve, national goals. Americans still believe, as a people, that education is fundamental to the continuation of a democratic society. Second, federal tax sources are incomparable as a means of funding social programs; state and local revenue sources are badly overextended. Thus, we agree with strategies that allocate federal funds for national purposes yet emphasize discretion at the state and local levels. It is a mistake that too many federal dollars are presently constrained in narrow program categories or tied to overly detailed regulations and procedures. Clearly, our federal system delegates responsibility for education to the states; thus, state departments of education should play vital roles in improving schools. Although federal funds have been employed to strengthen state departments, further strengthening must occur, especially in capabilities to assist individual schools to carry out improvement projects. The experience of the Elementary and Secondary Education Act (ESEA) Title III and IV C programs, for example, demonstrates the potential of state agencies to foster local school improvement.

We strongly recommend that state department representatives be included in school improvement projects both as liaison to state authorities and as a link between the federal and local level. Recent efforts in the U.S. Office of Education to improve state agencies as information brokers for local schools is an example of what is needed.

The philosophy of school inspection and regulation that seems to prevail in many state agencies needs to be supplemented by one that emphasizes assistance to schools in local improvement efforts, linking local school personnel to resources for change.

## THE ROLE OF HIGHER EDUCATION

Historically, higher education has provided rhetoric for school reform and sought, through the training of individuals, to be a force in school improvement. Direct service to schools, especially support in local school improvement processes, has been limited. This was particularly true during the 1950s and 1960s when higher education institutions were overwhelmed by the need to train new personnel for expanding schools. For example, from 1960 to 1970 approximately one-third of all bachelor's degree candidates in American colleges and universities were in teacher education programs. A similarly large fraction of all graduate students were enrolled in Education. No wonder that close connections with local schools were difficult to maintain. Although major institutions of higher education were and are active in developing and disseminating new educational knowledge, their participation in local implementation efforts has been quite limited.

As the 1970s began, criticism of higher education's role in the training of school personnel was increasing. Teachers' organizations challenged the traditional dominance of higher education in setting standards for teacher education programs and licensure. At the national level, teacher's groups gained new power in the National Council for Accreditation of Teacher Education and, in several states, lobbied successfully for teacher-dominated boards of licensure.

Local, state, and federal education officials have also criticized higher education institutions for their failure to be responsive to the needs of local schools. The competency-based teacher education movement was, in part, an effort to bring needed relevance into training programs.

Colleges, schools, and departments of education have been a particular focus of criticism—taking heat from school personnel for impractical studies but also from university colleagues critical of scholarship in education and the poor academic credentials of education students. The fact that school salary schedules are tied to graduate credits and degrees, and that graduate schools are often dominated by research scholars, has increased the friction between higher education and the schools.

Despite the friction, a thesis of this book is that higher education will and must continue to be involved in the education of school personnel. Furthermore, the absense of demand for new school personnel means that resources, especially in colleges and departments of education, are now available for the continuing education of school staffs. Resources on a similar scale do not exist elsewhere.[20]

The lessons of recent school reform efforts emphasize staff training as an essential ingredient in implementing new educational practices. Closer coordination, however, is needed between training resources and training needs. In our opinion, higher education and state department personnel need to be included in local school improvement projects, and these agencies must develop flexible programs for in-service training directly related to school improvement goals.

## THE ROLE OF CITIZENS AND PARENTS

Although the primary focus of this book is upon the opportunities and responsibilities of professional educators to bring about school improvement, citizens, especially parents, play indispensable roles in the improvement process.

First, citizens participate in political processes that influence government actions at every level—federal, state, and local. Through elected representatives citizens create educational policy, and through memberships in a variety of interest groups they influence governmental action. If, as we have stated, school reform is a local process that needs support from higher levels of government and from institutions of higher education, then public policies and programs should reflect these conclusions. Citizens should insist, through elected representatives and interest groups, that appropriate policies be developed. Citizens should insist that elements in the educational system—especially teachers' organizations, colleges, and state departments of education—work together, not against one another, for school improvement at the local level.

Citizens, and especially parents, can also play a second, more direct, role in school improvement at the local level. Because American schools remain, to a large extent, a local enterprise, direct action to improve local schools is possible—not easy, but possible.[21]

Many people are familiar with the difficulties of citizen involvement in local school activities. The Parent-Teacher Association, Home School Council, and citizen advisory groups are often disappointing as vehicles for school improvement. In many cases school officials hold such groups at a distance to prevent them from having real influence in school operations. In our view, this represents a serious problem because community support for school policies and community participation in school programs appear to be central aspects of successful schools.[22] Citizen support is often necessary to make needed changes.

The Institute for Responsive Education (IRE), an organization dedicated to increasing citizen participation in American schools, has identified over 100,000 building-level advisory groups with an estimated 1,200,000 members. Unfortunately, IRE studies reveal that such groups have been granted little influence, even when the groups have been mandated by federal or state legislation.[23]

One possible means to strengthen the role of citizens' advisory groups is to specify more clearly in legislation the specific powers and authority of such groups. Another possibility is to strengthen citizen-initiated, voluntary organizations at the grass-roots level. These citizen-initiated groups are often more successful than mandated advisory boards. Summarizing the results of his studies, Don Davies, President of IRE, makes the case well.

> I see citizen participation as an essential part of empowering the powerless, revitalizing grass-roots democracy and creating a more equitable and just society. It is also a necessary part of improving the schools. It is simply too important to be treated in a trivial way by policy-makers and educators, or to be left to domination by local, state and federal government agencies.
>
> It is clear to me that individuals and organizations who advocate citizen participation have an opportunity now to capitalize on the spirit of the times and to push toward making the widely accepted rhetoric of citizen participation a reality.[24]

We especially believe that school personnel interested in improving schools must learn to work with and grant genuine influence to citizens' groups. These new groups are important forces for change in the local school community.

## THE ROLE OF STUDENTS

"Adults have been exceedingly slow to admit students into collaboration on equal terms."[25] With that simple statement, Charlotte Ryan makes a telling observation about education in the United States. Mostly, students are ignored when discussions of change and school improvement take place.

There are countless arguments to restrict decision-making power of young people, but there are also examples of significant student involvement and participation in a few schools across the country. These examples are enough to discredit educators and parents who exclude students because they are too young, or too inexperienced, or irresponsible. The examples of the schools that have had high student involvement prove that most students at any age can be given more responsibility than they are typically given in our public schools.

What are some of the fears of involving students? First of all, there is the concern that adults will "give away the store." This concern is unfounded because in any properly managed organization, delegation of responsibility is commonplace and does not necessarily involve giving away authority. Principals delegate certain responsibilities to adults in the building and, with proper controls and adequate guidelines, they can also delegate certain responsibilities to students. Many students so appreciate being involved that they are often more respectful of authority. A liberal position on the part of adults will often get student cooperation more quickly than the usual stance of tight controls.

The second concern is that the students will make wrong or improper decisions. How, if they are not given a chance, will we ever know the extent of their maturity? Experiences from many administrators demonstrate that students can make mature judgments. One example is worth repeating. In a large Delaware suburban high school, students were asked if any of them wanted to be involved in the selection of new teachers. The student body thought that this was a good idea, but only twenty students actually showed specific interest in the project, and eventually about a dozen served. The other students were not so interested, but they respected the overture. The gesture gave a boost to student morale, which prepared the climate for several new innovations in the school. In the teacher selection process the students exhibited poise, sincerity, and remarkable perception.[26] There are countless examples across the country, but unfortunately, these are only happening in a few schools. Students *can* show maturity in decision making, and many times have insight from their vantage point that adults in the same environment fail to see.

We suggest that schools investigate the many possibilities for student participation, such as:

- Student screening committees for hiring new teachers
- Student representatives on the school board
- Student representatives at faculty meetings
- Student representatives on all curriculum committees
- Student judiciary groups
- Student newspapers
- Student participation on school improvement task forces
- Peer counselors
- Peer tutors
- Student aides in offices
- Student representatives on PTA councils
- Student representatives on citizen advisory groups
- Student forums after school for those who would like to express concerns about the school—on a regular basis
- Student surveys of morale, teacher/student relationships, evaluation of program, evaluation of special services, etc.

Ryan has summarized the authors' philosophy about student partners in the educational process as follows:

The basic need for adults, whether teachers, administrators, parents or employees, is to relax into acceptance of young people as individuals and avoid the compulsive expectation of conformity.

Secondly, adults must learn to listen. Most listen with preconceived ideas of what they will hear, and therefore hear nothing. Even a little relaxation of the felt need to control, a little redressing of the balance of acceptance, would in most cases go a long way.

And finally, adults must deal honestly with children and young people. Mutual trust between teachers and students, as between parent and child, is the most important ingredient of education. As adults open doors on opportunities and accept young ideas, they must expect frequently to join with young people in working out those ideas as partners, and take seriously the product of their joint endeavors. Trust grows out of mutual confidence in being treated fairly; in either schools or families, growth builds on trust.[27]

As members of the local school community, students are, necessarily, participants in any change. We believe that they can be willing participants, and more important, constructive sources for change if they are invited to be responsible members of the school community. We also believe that the responsibility for making this invitation rests squarely on school personnel—with backing from parents. These conditions will naturally contribute to a school environment conducive to change and improvement.

## ENDNOTES

1. John I. Goodlad, *The Dynamics of Educational Change* (New York: McGraw-Hill Book Co., 1975), p. 175.
2. Ibid., p. 173.
3. John M. Bahner, "A Significant Contribution to Teacher Education: The /I/D/E/A/ Change Program," *Journal of Teacher Education* 27, No. 3 (1976): 207–210.
4. Paul Berman and Milbrey W. McLaughlin, *Federal Programs Supporting Educational Change, Vol. 4, The Findings in Review* (Santa Monica, Calif.: Rand Corporation, 1975).
5. Ford Foundation, *A Foundation Goes to School* (New York: The Foundation, 1972).
6. Gary J. Coles et al., *The Impact of Educational Innovation on Student Performance: Project Methods and Findings for Three Cohorts, Vol. 1, Project LONG-STEP Final Report* (Palo Alto, Calif.: American Institutes for Research, 1976).
7. Linda B. Stebbins et al., *Education as Experimentation: A Planned Variation Model, Vol. 4A, An Evaluation of Follow Through* (Cambridge, Mass.: Abt Associates, 1977), p. xxiv.
8. Gilbert R. Austin, "Exemplary Schools and the Search for Effectiveness," *Educational Leadership* (October 1979): 10–14.
9. U.S. Office of Education, *Educational Programs That Work*, Volume VI, 1979.
10. Jay D. Scribner, ed., *The Politics of Education. 76th Yearbook of National Society for the Study of Education, Part II* (Chicago: The Society, 1977).
11. Laurence Iannaccone and Peter Cistone, *The Politics of Education* (Eugene, Ore.: Eric Clearinghouse on Educational Management, 1974), p. 28.
12. Michael W. Kirst, *Governance of Elementary and Secondary Education* (Cambridge, Mass.: Aspen Institute for Humanistic Studies, 1976), p. 23.
13. Dan C. Lortie, *Schoolteacher: A Sociological Study* (Chicago: University of Chicago Press, 1975).

14. John Pincus, "Incentives for Innovation in the Public Schools," *Review of Educational Research* 44 (1974): 113–144.
15. Goodlad, *Dynamics of Educational Change*.
16. See, for example, C. G. Miskel, "Principals' Perceived Effectiveness, Innovation Effort, and the School Situation," *Educational Administration Quarterly* 13 (1977): 31–46.
17. An excellent summary of the growth of teachers' organizations is found in Marshall O. Donley, Jr., *Power to the Teacher* (Bloomington: Indiana University Press, 1976).
18. Milbrey McLaughlin and Paul Berman, "Retooling Staff Development in a Period of Retrenchment," *Educational Leadership* (December 1977): 191–194.
19. William J. Bailey, *Managing Self-Renewal in Secondary Education* (Englewood Cliffs, N.J.: Educational Technology Publications, 1975), p. 14.
20. David A. Clark, *The Real World of the Teacher Educator: A Look to the Near Future* (Washington, D.C.: American Association of Colleges for Teacher Education, 1977).
21. See, for example, Murray Kappelman and Paul Ackerman, *Between Parent and School* (New York: Dial Press, 1977).
22. National Association of Secondary School Principals, *Guidelines for Improving SAT Scores* (Reston, Va.: The Association, 1978).
23. Institute for Responsive Education, *Sharing the Power? A Report on the Status of School Councils in the 1970's.* (Boston: Institute for Responsive Education, 1977).
24. Don Davies, "Citizen Participation in Schools: A Network of Illusions," *Citizen Action in Education* 5 (January 1978): 14.
25. Charlotte Ryan, *The Open Partnership* (New York: McGraw-Hill Book Co., 1976), p. 90.
26. Bailey, *Managing Self-Renewal*.
27. Ryan, *The Open Partnership*, p. 119. Used with permission of McGraw-Hill Book Co.

# Chapter 5

# Partnerships for Local
# School Improvement

In the new reality for schools, despite reductions in school staffs and education budgets, resources are still available for school improvement. These resources include the people that comprise the educational system—the teachers, students, parents, local and state school administrators, and college educators. Opportunities to mobilize these resources for school improvement exists in the formation of local partnerships for school improvement, consisting of representatives of local school administration, the teaching staff, the state education department, and an institution of higher education. These ideas are summarized in the Partnership Model of School Improvement.

## THE PARTNERSHIP MODEL

As shown in Figure 5-1, the Partnership Model provides linkages to the resources necessary to improve schools. A building administrator such as the principal would play a leading role in a partnership group and be a link to district-level resources and authority. A teacher representative would be both an advocate for teaching personnel in the school building and a liaison to the teachers' organization. A college educator, representing a local college of education, could treat staff training needs and be a connection with knowledge resources in higher education. A state department staff person could represent state policies and provide important links to state and federal program resources.

Also represented in Figure 5-1 is the conviction that partnership groups should establish and use an advisory committee of parents, students, and other interested citizens. In this way the partners can incorporate the views of all interested parties as the group addresses its central task: how to encourage educational improvements through the local school organization.

The functions of such a partnership group would be to identify local school improvement goals, to plan strategies to reach these goals, and to coordinate the continuing activity needed for the mutual adaptation of the local school organization and the new practices.

Unfortunately, those we have identified as partners in local school improvement have not been good collaborators in the past. Is it unrealistic to think that such collaboration is the key to school reform? Perhaps, but the case must certainly be made that each of these partners represents an important element in our system of public education, established and funded to serve the

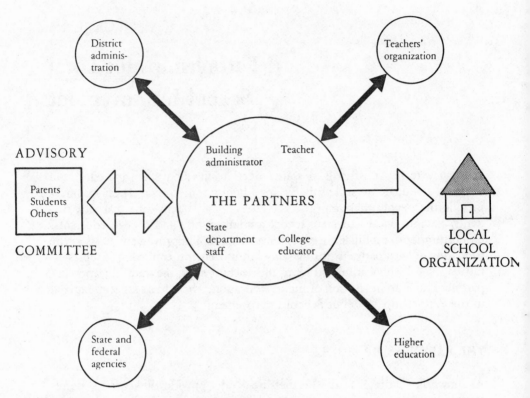

**FIGURE 5-1.**  **Partnerships for School Improvement**

public need. As participants in a public enterprise, collaboration among these elements of the education system is required in the public interest. We can, and we *must,* have such collaboration. The public can no longer afford to let internal competition among elements in the educational system divert resources from the goals of the system itself. Furthermore, each member of the partnership has much to gain through collaboration. In fact, collaboration is essential if each partner is to achieve both individual and collective goals for improving schools.

Because improved collaboration among elements of the educational system is crucial to school improvement in an Age of Slowdown, special attention must be given to the concept of collaboration and to barriers that must be overcome to make such partnerships succeed.

## COLLABORATION AMONG PARTNERS

A partnership is an agreement among parties to collaborate in some enterprise. Usually, partners take different roles in the enterprise, each contributing to mutually established goals and each receiving appropriate shares in the outcomes of collaboration. Collaboration, then, is the central process that makes partnerships succeed. Although each partner maintains an autonomous identity, for the purposes of the partnership each yields some autonomy in pursuit of partnership goals.

For example, Ladd has defined collaboration between two organizations as "ventures in which the people in organization A and people in organization B work together so that each group can achieve the things it wants, which by itself it could achieve either less satisfactorily or not at all."[1]

Hite and Drummond, in discussing the Teacher Corps, use the following definition:

> The term collaboration describes a voluntary association between two or more organizations, in which agents or representatives of each work together to achieve some separately held and some commonly held objectives. Collaboration involves some sharing of planning, decision making and resource utilization. Each organization in a collaborative venture maintains its own organizational independence and identity.[2]

For some, true collaboration must include a sharing of power, sharing in the planning, organization, operation and evaluation of programs, and sharing in the commitment of resources.

Figure 5–2 illustrates a partnership comprised of three partners representing three different organizations or institutions. The partners are collaborating on some activities of joint concern (represented by the areas of overlap), while at the same time pursuing unique goals. Individual partners collaborate selectively with one another (partners 1 and 2 are collaborating on B, while 2 and 3 share C, and 1 and 3 share D).

By collaborating, each organization achieves some common and some separately held goals. The common goals are improvements in the education of students in the local school. Some of the separately held goals might include:

1. For the local school administration: better education for students despite decreasing enrollments and inflation.

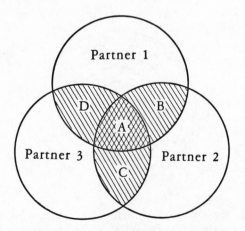

**FIGURE 5–2.  Areas of Collaboration in a Partnership**

2. For the teachers' organization: better working conditions and opportunities for the professional development of teachers.
3. For the state department: implementation of state-wide objectives for
   education.
4. For the local college: more effective in-service education programs for
   school personnel.

## DYNAMICS OF COLLABORATION

Kurt Lewin's concept of individual life space can be extrapolated to analyze
some of the dynamics of collaboration. For example, institutions are organized
in layers which can be represented by concentric circles. (See Figure 5-3.)

The circles on the outside represent areas that, while important, are not essential to the organization; as one moves closer to the inner circle, the organization's very existence is at stake.

If two organizations collaborate, the degree of involvement and commitment can vary. For example, in Figure 5-4, organizations A and B and B and C
are collaborating, but not to the same extent. The collaborative relationship between B and C is a much deeper one in which the partners have more control or
impact over the operation of the other.

As Ladd points out,

Most of the school system-university collaboration, in which we have been en-
gaging up to now, invades only the outer rings of the respective institutions. I
should like to suggest, though, that the kind we are going to be working on
in the next years will get us involved in each other's inner rings. We shall be
getting more and more involved with each other's policy-making, each
other's personnel selection, each other's basic style of operation and the like.
And these involvements will carry with them much greater threats and may
arouse much greater tensions and even antagonisms.[3]

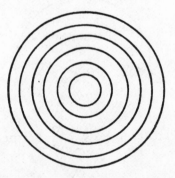

**FIGURE 5-3. Life Space of an Organization**    Adapted from E. T. Ladd, "Tensions in
School-University Collaboration," in *Partnership in Teacher Education*, ed. E. Brooks, et al.
(Washington, D. C.: American Association of Colleges for Teacher Education, 1967).

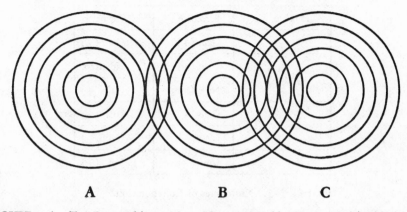

**FIGURE 5-4.    Two Partnerships**    Adapted from E. T. Ladd, "Tensions in School-University Collaboration," in *Partnership in Teacher Education,* ed. E. Brooks, et al. (Washington, D. C.: American Association of Colleges for Teacher Education, 1967).

Recent examples of such tensions are in teacher certification and licensing, formerly dominated by state departments and institutions of higher education. These have become areas of high concern to teachers' organizations. In several states, the establishment of teacher-controlled commissions on licensure has been a serious threat to the power of state department staffs and colleges of education. Also, teacher power has often threatened local school boards and administrations. Such increased threat, with accompanying tensions and antagonisms, does not necessarily mean that collaboration is absent. Rather, it can mean that the inner layers of one or more organizations are being affected—a healthy sign if conflicts are productively resolved.

While peace and tranquility may not be a measure of successful collaboration, mutual benefit to the several partners is such a measure. Therefore, peaceful or not, each member organization must gain from collaboration without too much expense to other partners.

Figure 5-5 shows simple alternatives that suggest how outcomes, either expected or real, may affect collaboration. Obviously, the first alternative, in which partners A and B both gain, is optimal; over the long run no partnership succeeds otherwise. In the second alternative one partner may gain without expense to another. This may be a frequent occurrence in the life of a partnership, as long as each partner gains from time to time. The third alternative, where partners may gain at one another's expense, is possible only when tradeoffs are possible or when partnerships are involuntary. In the fourth alternative, where both partners take a loss, the partnership is doomed.

One must be careful not to oversimplify the matter of gains and losses to individuals or organizations, whose goals are exceedingly complex and sometimes even contradictory. For example, a strong motive in many collaborations is the desire to be of service in a valuable cause; at the same time, a willing servant may be wary of being "used" for someone else's purpose.

| Alternative | Partner A | Partner B |
|:-----------:|:---------:|:---------:|
| 1 | Gain (+) | Gain (+) |
| 2 | Gain (+) | No effect |
|   | No effect | Gain (+) |
| 3 | Gain (+) | Loss (−) |
|   | Loss (−) | Gain (+) |
| 4 | Loss (−) | Loss (−) |

**FIGURE 5-5.**   Outcomes of Collaboration

Another complication is the problem of "coerced" collaboration, where relationships exist because they are mandated by an outside party. Federal programs, for example, may require collaboration before funding is granted. Such mandated partnerships have special problems, including tendencies toward low commitment and low morale of members. More desirable are "open," or voluntary, partnerships in which payoffs for collaboration are integral to the tasks undertaken.

## BARRIERS TO COLLABORATION

Three major barriers to collaboration deserve special consideration: (1) institutional territoriality, (2) the absence of partner parity, and (3) the lack of staff time required for collaboration.

**Institutional Territoriality.**   In order to collaborate efficiently, partners must relinquish some of their institutional autonomy, which often causes role conflict or "identity crisis" for representatives of each partner organization. Because vested institutional interests are often at stake in collaborative efforts, each member has to struggle with the question of whether his or her institutional loyalties are hindering collaborative progress.

It is important to remember that the amount of tension aroused among partner constituencies may depend upon the degree to which the joint activities of the partnership directly affect the policies and procedures of the involved institutions. In fact, according to Lancaster, as the degree of interdependency increases so does the conflict and competition. In other words, collaboration leads to conflict which should not be avoided since the outcomes are often beneficial.

> Sociologists of the Talcott Parsons School tend to see conflict in an organization as dysfunctional or negative in its organizational effect. Most administrators view it this way also. In the typical monocratic hierarchical structure, harmony is the goal and consensus is administered from the top. However, in an

interorganization—a consortium—conflict and competition may serve a positive function (e.g., defining boundaries, generating search behaviors, providing a sense of independence) and should be accepted and legitimatized.[4]

It is important for organizations who collaborate to provide procedures for resolving and managing conflict. In a later chapter, techniques for resolving such conflicts will be discussed.

**Absence of Partner Parity.**   Parity is defined as the state or condition of being the same in power, value, or rank. The phrase *partner parity* refers to two areas of concern. The first issue is the question, "Who will be represented?" In other words, what groups will be selected to become partners. There is widespread recognition that educational leadership is required that can effectively bring together the growing number of educational constituencies that are demanding involvement in educational decision making. Although we have recommended that membership in partnership groups be limited to education professionals, we have also emphasized the need for partnerships to seek advice from each of the constituencies that will be affected by the final decisions of a partnership.

The second area of concern focuses on the question, "Which partners will govern?" This question is of paramount importance since it implies what decision-making procedures will be utilized, who will conceptualize and initiate partnership activities, who has veto power, and who takes credit for meritorious achievement or blame for failures. We advocate the policy of parity for the members of an educational partnership. That is, each partner should have an equal voice in the decision-making process of a partnership group, where the responsibilities of the group are defined clearly in advance. This crucial question of parity among partners is discussed in later chapters on the tactics of school improvement.

**Staff Time for Collaboration.**   Even supposing that problems of institutional territoriality and partner parity can be solved, where do members of any educational organization find the time and energy required for successful collaboration? As mundane as the subject of staff time may sound, this barrier to successful collaboration may be the most difficult to remove. In each collaborating institution, staff members are fully occupied, even badly overworked. The daily pressures on school administrators are well known, as are the strenuous demands of teaching young people. Serving on additional committees is a serious burden, and extra duties without extra pay are rightfully resisted. State departments of education are often understaffed to carry out even regulatory functions; they have few staff members available to consult with individual school faculties. College educators are also busy with teaching and research. How can they afford the hours required to participate in local school improvement?

These are sticky problems. Certainly, the way roles of educational personnel are currently defined, little time is available for forming and operating partnership groups. Nor is it possible to see where additional monies might be found to provide new staff resources for such work. But isn't this just the point? In an Age of Slowdown, resources for improving education must be found by reallocating existing personnel or by changing staff duties. If school administrators, teachers, state department staff members, and college educators do not now allocate sufficient time to the task of local school improvement, they must decide to stop doing something else in order to find the time to collaborate.

On this matter there is no blinking. Either members of the educational system allocate time to school improvement or they don't. Unless we all believe that school improvement should come by happenstance, we must face the need to assign more time and energy of existing staff members to school improvement activities than is now the case. This is the most fundamental and urgent problem that exists in designing successful strategies for school improvement.

## PRACTICALITIES

Given the strong barriers to collaboration, is the Partnership Model practical? Even if one agrees that partnerships are theoretically desirable, is there any basis for believing that they can become a practical reality? Later in the book many specific examples of collaboration in school improvement are described. While most of these do not fit our Partnership Model exactly, each of them reveals some aspect of successful collaboration. Substantial bodies of practical experience exist to demonstrate the great power of collaborative models of school improvement. Educators are so accustomed to finding fault with one another or noting failures in cooperation that they do not see the many positive examples.

Another way to see the practicality of collaboration is to think again about how each member of the proposed partnership makes important contributions and gains practical benefits from collaboration.

School Administrators.    Aren't school administrators, especially school principals, responsible for school improvement? Why should others be brought in? The answer is, of course, that the school administrator cannot discharge these responsibilities alone. The cooperation and support of staff, students, parents, and others are needed. Also, if new practices are being introduced, staff members must have the necessary knowledge and skill to make the new practices function. The necessary planning and staff training resources are not available in most schools. School administrators need collaborators in order to exercise their responsibilities for improving schools.

Teachers.    Teachers are supervised by the principal in their work and represented by a teachers' organization at the collective bargaining table. Why should teachers spend time and energy on a local school improvement committee? First, teachers want and need more input into educational decisions. Increased input in decision making at the local school-building level will improve the effectiveness of school programs without unnecessary burdens being placed on teachers. Second, the organized profession needs more effective input at the local school-building level. Terms of collective bargaining contracts need careful implementation, and the voice of the organized profession needs to be heard by school-building administrators, not just district staff.

**College Educators.**   Can't school administrators and teachers do better without interference from higher education? Many school personnel believe that this is true. On closer inspection, it is apparent that local school districts and teachers' organizations do not have resources to undertake staff training on the scale required, nor do they have convenient connections to sources of formal knowledge. School budgets have little place for training staff, especially in tight financial times. Likewise, although teachers' organizations may wish to control training resources, their first priority is usually higher teacher salaries. Given choices at the bargaining table between staff development programs and higher paychecks, staff training usually comes second. Granted that resources in higher education are difficult to tap in making local school improvements, such resources do exist, if we have the will to apply them.

College educators, in turn, have much to gain from collaboration. Close connections with school practice are important to the operation of professional training programs and research. Furthermore, college educators obtain their students more and more from in-service, not pre-service, school personnel.

**State Departments of Education.**   Despite federal efforts to strengthen state departments of education, most are still primarily regulatory agencies and checkpoints for the distribution of federal funds. Many school personnel do not think of state departments as helpful. Yet, like it or not, state authority in education is substantial and links to federal agencies are real. If state department personnel could be designated to assist in local school improvement, they could supply needed expertise that would help, not hinder, local efforts. In some states strong programs have been developed to provide assistance to local school improvement efforts. As described in later chapters, the National Diffusion Network was an attempt by the federal government to strengthen the state education agency in this area of operation. Certainly state departments of education would discharge their mission better if they could make local school improvement succeed.


# A PHILOSOPHY OF COLLABORATION

The Partnership Model presented in this book is recommended primarily for its practicality. Based on recent lessons from school reform efforts, it appears that a concentration of a variety of resources on the task of improving education at a local school site is the best way to improve schools. Partnership groups are designed to bring together a group of people who can successfully initiate and coordinate this local process of school improvement.

Beyond immediate practicality, however, collaboration is a desperately needed process throughout human activity. Especially in the present Age of Slowdown, new levels of cooperation are needed to preserve the future of humankind. Our educational system is an example of the prevailing organizational forms found in industrialized nations—the technocratic bureaucracy. This form of organization is rooted deeply in competition and win-lose relationships. For the long-term success of all our institutions, we must move toward more collaborative, participative organizations.[5]

## ENDNOTES

1. Edward T. Ladd, "Tensions in School-University Collaboration," in *Partnership in Teacher Education,* ed. E. Brooks Smith et al. (Washington, D.C.: American Association of Colleges for Teacher Education, 1967), pp. 97–98.
2. F. H. Hite and W. H. Drummond, "The Teacher Corps and Collaboration," *Journal of Teacher Education* 26, No. 2 (1975): 133.
3. Ladd, "Tensions in School-University Collaboration," p. 97.
4. Richard B. Lancaster, *Conflict in Interinstitutional Cooperation* (Chicago: Loyola University, 1970), ED 039 839.
5. Eric Trist, "Collaboration in Work Settings: A Personal Perspective," *Journal of Applied Behavioral Science* 13 (1977): 261–78.

## SUMMARY OF PART I

The period from 1950 to 1970 was a time of unprecedented growth in American society and American schools. Faith in social progress was high, and schools were given a central role in social reform. With massive support from private foundations and the federal government, a variety of educational innovations were encouraged in schools. A systematic technology for planned change in education was created in the process. Because this optimism about the role of schools in improving society resembled the earlier Progressive Era in American history, we have labeled the period from 1950 to 1970 as "The New Progressivism."

By contrast, since 1970, very different conditions have emerged as a context for American education. World-wide resource shortages produced inflation and reduced economic growth. School enrollments nationally began to decline. Disillusionment about the role of schools in social progress was common, and schools were criticized for declining achievement test scores.

The "new reality" for public schools has meant that new and different means for improving schools were needed. Conservation of scarce resources became a major theme as budgets tightened. Attention to priorities was essential in a time of retrenchment and reallocation. More realistic attitudes developed about what schools could and could not accomplish, and new emphasis was needed on human resource development in schools.

Lessons from efforts to improve schools during the 1950s and 1960s suggest two basic principles: (1) the individual school as a social organization is the optimal focus for change, and (2) the local school organization must be linked to other organizations within the larger educational system to provide the conditions for improvement. With these principles in mind, we have recommended forming local partnerships for school improvement that link the individual school to the local district organization, the state education agency, the teachers' organization, and a local college or university. Members of the partnership collaborate to provide the conditions necessary for successful, planned change in the local school. A local partnership committee, with the help of an advisory group of parents and students, seeks to initiate and coordinate self-renewal projects in the local school.

Although significant barriers to such collaborations exist (such as institutional territoriality, absence of partner parity, and lack of staff time), a practical basis for partnerships can be found in the individual and mutual goals of the partners, especially under current educational conditions. Also, growing interdependence in the world-wide community underscores the need in all human institutions to foster values and techniques of collaboration.

## PART I DISCUSSION QUESTIONS

1. The period of New Progressivism in America (1950–1970) stressed the importance of education and technology in building a great society—one in which the rewards and benefits would be shared by all. What conditions, both national and global, led to the almost total rejection of our earlier belief in achieving social progress through education and technology during the Age of Slowdown?

2. During the period of New Progressivism (1950–1970), social, governmental, and educational leaders demanded that schools provide equal education to all children and youth, especially those thought to be culturally different. What means (grants, laws, etc.) were employed by federal and state governments to insure the full implementation of this egalitarian position?

3. School site management calls for decisions relative to the allocation of resources for educational purposes to be made by the local school principal and faculty. What are the implications for the traditional role and function of district school boards, superintendents, and staff personnel?

4. The Partnership Model for improving the instructional program of elementary and secondary school calls for the frequent interaction of representatives from the state department of public instruction, a college/university, teachers, and local school administrators. List specific suggestions for how each partner can find the time for this activity. What less important activity could each partner stop doing in order to make time for school improvement?

5. To be workable, the Partnership Model must contribute to the organizational goals of each participating agency. List advantages each partner (teacher organization, school administration, state department of education, and institution of higher education) gains from entering into a continuous, long-range school improvement process.

## SUGGESTED READINGS

Cremin, Lawrence A. *Traditions of American Education.* New York: Basic Books, Inc., 1976.

Donley, Marshall O., Jr. *Power to the Teacher: How America's Educators Became Militant.* Bloomington: Indiana University Press, 1976.

Fromm, Erich. *To Have or To Be?* New York: Harper & Row, Publishers, 1976.

Fuller, R. Buckminster. *Operating Manual for Spaceship Earth.* New York: Pocket Books, 1970.

Gardner, John W. *Self-Renewal: The Individual and the Innovative Society.* New York: Harper Colaphon Books, Harper and Row, 1963.

Lortie, Dan C. *Schoolteacher: A Sociological Study.* Chicago: The University of Chicago Press, 1975.

Reischauer, Edwin O. *Toward the 21st Century: Education for a Changing World.* New York: Vintage Books, Random House, 1974.

# PART II

# ORGANIZATION DEVELOPMENT THROUGH PARTNERSHIPS

## INTRODUCTION TO PART II

A focus on the individual school organization as the optimum unit for bringing about change can be understood from several perspectives. First, the great diversity among school communities makes each one unique. Second, the individual school functions as a distinct social unit with particular goals, norms, roles, and relationships. Third, the strong legal and social tradition of local governance in school matters continues in American life. Finally, a strong lesson from recent efforts to change schools is that adapting new practices to local circumstances is crucial to successful change.

Certain variables are critical when considering how to change the social organization of an individual school. Those emphasized in the Partnership Model are: (1) individual and organizational goals, (2) conditions related to organizational process and product, (3) formal and informal organizational structures, and (4) leadership.

Another concern is the process of change itself. A discrepancy model of change is presented as a useful way to approach the process of organizational change in a local school. Differences between *what is* and *what is desired,* defined at the local level, become the starting point in the school improvement process. This concept is fundamental to Organization Development (OD), which is proposed as a general framework from which to view the process of school improvement. The background of OD is summarized in relationship to the special problems of school organizations and to the concept of partnership presented in this book.

Part II concludes with specific recommendations for beginning the process of organization development through partnerships. Suggestions are made about how to form partnerships and how to conduct a preliminary organizational diagnosis. Finally, three stages of planned change are described: (1) initiation, (2) implementation, and (3) integration.

# Chapter 6

# The School As Target
# for Change

School improvement can begin from any number of starting points. For example, in recent years legislation at the state and national level has been a popular place to initiate educational reforms. Or, school districts may be the focus of changes introduced by the local board of education. Another common starting point is the individual teacher, whose training may be the vehicle for introducing new materials or methods in schools.

In the Partnership Model for School Improvement the starting point for change is the individual school as a unique organizational unit. Although reasons for choosing the school as the target for change have already been discussed, the topic needs closer examination as a background for selecting the most promising strategies for change. What does it mean to focus on the school as the unit of change? How shall we describe the school as an organizational unit? What characteristics of the school organization make it an optimal target for change?

## DIVERSITY AND COMPLEXITY

One way to understand the need to focus on the individual school is to consider the great diversity of American schools. In the fifty states there are still approximately 16,000 public and private school districts. These districts include approximately 75,000 elementary schools and 30,000 secondary schools.

American schools range in size from one-room elementary schools to large, comprehensive high schools. Furthermore, these schools are placed in a wide variety of community contexts—from isolated, rural settings to the inner city.

Students and their parents come from a variety of ethnic backgrounds and have differing educational histories. All of these factors, and many more, make each school unique. Even within the same school district individual schools develop their own distinct history, traditions, and ways of functioning. Each school is a human community with its own distinct culture.

The uniqueness of each individual school is a primary reason why "across the board" educational reforms are unsuccessful. It is a primary reason why a focus on the local school site is needed to bring about successful changes in school programs. Clearly, producing educational change is a complex process with many, many factors to be taken into consideration. These factors vary from school to school. Therefore, to be successful one must weigh these many factors in each local school and design a school improvement program especially for the local school site with its unique characteristics: its size, its community, its parents, its students, its teachers, its financial resources, its culture. This is not to say that the local school is unaffected by forces at the national, state, or local school district level. The local school culture is in the larger social context and is constantly influenced by it. Through the national media pervasive opinions about American education develop, for example, that children in American schools are weak in basic skills. Or, the Supreme Court may bring judgments, as in desegregation cases, that have profound influences on thousands of local schools. These general influences are strong, but it must be stressed that these influences operate differently in each local school setting because of the many other factors involved.

Likewise, it is not the case that school improvement efforts at the district, state, or federal levels are unimportant. But it is clear that such efforts must recognize the diversity of local schools and include provisions to change carefully identified elements in each unique, local school community. When reasons for educational change are identified, there should be an opportunity to consider the needs at the local school-building level. When alternative plans of action are considered, the uniqueness of the local school and its resources must be taken into account. When changes are implemented, local plans are needed and local adaptations are required. When structural or programmatic changes take place, the local school as a total social organization changes.

## THE INDIVIDUAL SCHOOL AS AN ORGANIZATION

One can appreciate the individual school as an organization by thinking back to schools one attended as a student. Or, if working in a school now, one has vivid impressions of that unique organization at work. Think of the people—students, teachers, administrators, support personnel, parents, citizens. Together, they comprise a unique community, working together as a social unit. These people have hopes and expectations, strengths and weaknesses, values and attitudes. Somehow, as a group, these individual characteristics are combined in one school community.

Think of the patterns of activity in the school. Each year brings its cycle of classes, exams, concerts, sporting events, PTA meetings, conferences, etc. Members of the school play their various roles, set their goals and standards, succeed or fail. Members of the school community experience pride or shame, gratitude or resentment toward the school. Many support and many criticize the school and what takes place within it.

Think also of the fact that individuals who are currently members of the school organization have taken the places of others who are now gone. Likewise, consider that they will soon be succeeded by other students, teachers, and administrators. Yet the school continues in its basic organizational form: its roles, its norms, its expectations, its traditions. This is what is meant by the school as an organization.

Behavioral scientists have provided useful ways to describe the local school as an organized, social system, that is, a set of social elements and subsystems that act together as an interrelated unit.

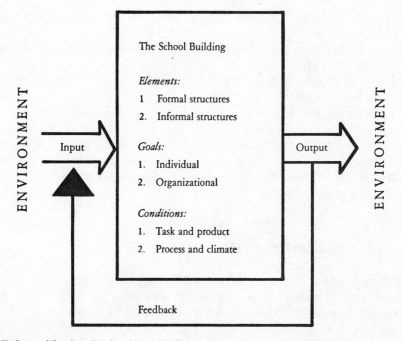

**FIGURE 6-1.    The Local School as a Social System**    Adapted from Wayne K. Hoy and Cecil G. Miskel, *Educational Administration: Theory, Research, and Practice* (New York: Random House, 1978), p. 38.

An example of a school described as a social system is given in Figure 6-1. The boundary of the system is the school site as the main focus of interaction. Components of the system include both the formal social structures (for example, formal positions, roles, responsibilities, etc.) and the informal social structures (for example, unwritten rules, influence, norms, etc.). These structures include the various individual roles within the social systems (administrators, teachers, students, etc.).

A second aspect of the school as a social system, also indicated in Figure 6-1, is the goals held by individuals and by the organization itself. A third important aspect of the social system is the product or process conditions. A product condition might refer to learning outcomes, such as reading achievement, while a process condition might refer to the morale of teachers and learners. The diagram also shows that the school as a social system exists in a larger environment from which inputs are received and into which outputs are made. The outputs of the system produce reactions which influence further inputs to the system.

Those who adopt a social systems view are making a number of general assumptions.[1]

1. Because social systems are comprised of interdependent elements, a change in one element affects other elements in the system of interrelationships.

2. The social system is goal-directed; that is, the system functions to achieve one or more goals.
3. A social system has a structure in which different elements carry out specific functions.
4. Social systems are normative in that the individual's behavior is guided by formal and informal prescriptions.
5. Behavior norms are supported by formal and informal sanctions.

Although this description may appear to be unnecessarily theoretical, it points to crucial aspects of the school as an organization that must be considered when seeking to bring about changes. These concepts will find further applications in later chapters.


## SCHOOL SITE MANAGEMENT

Making the local school organization the target for change is consistent with recent recommendations for "school site management." In a review of such recommendations, Pierce[2] gave two strong reasons for a new emphasis on the local school site as the basic unit of educational management. First, fiscal problems of schools have forced many school districts to search for cost-cutting steps. This search has led to decision-making procedures at the local school to choose between programs that are necessary and those that are not. Second, school site management reflects a desire to increase public participation in school governance. The pendulum of governance, which had swung to the state and federal levels and toward greater professional autonomy and executive control, is swinging back toward representativeness and local citizen control. According to Pierce,

> Between the 1920s and the 1970s the governance of public education became more and more centralized. Steps designed to increase the authority of education executives also increased the distance between education managers and the public; at the same time, they made it more difficult for teachers to influence education policy. As school systems have come increasingly under the dominance of professional managers, teachers have lost their ability to communicate freely with their superiors. Furthermore, teachers' discretion over classroom procedures has been eroded by management's efforts to introduce educational innovations. Public dissatisfaction with schools has been coupled with a growing alienation of school teachers, who find themselves being criticized for the failure of programs and policies over which they have had very little influence. Recent demands for citizen participation and community schools reflect a desire to nudge the pendulum back toward greater representativeness.[3]

Recommendations for school site management are often accompanied by suggestions that individual school advisory councils be established. Such councils are usually made up of citizens who meet with teachers and school administrators about local school matters. Some state and federal programs even mandate such citizen advisory groups.

In describing Ford Foundation support for community participation in local school governance, Harold Howe II, former U.S. Commissioner of Education, emphasized the extent to which school governance is dominated by three parties: (1) local and state boards of education, (2) professional school managers, and (3) the organized teaching profession. Granting that each party works to improve education for children, nevertheless, Howe observed that:

> . . . they exist and conduct their rivalries for power within a triangular preserve about which they make a common assumption—that no one else should be allowed within that preserve. As long as they are successful, there is little hope of accomplishing what I am recommending: the recognition of new voices in decision-making about the nature of education broadly defined at the local school level.[4]

Howe recommended the establishment of citizens' advisory groups to focus on the individual school, not the school district, going back to "that fundamental unit in order to bring the changes we need and enlist the parties needed to make those changes."[5]

The central ingredient in a move toward school site management is a shift of responsibility for decisions from the school district to the school site. This shift includes decisions about budget, personnel, curriculum and instruction, and community involvement. The school site manager is made accountable to higher levels of authority and also to a citizens' advisory group. Although many obstacles exist in decentralizing school management (think of collective bargaining, which is conducted at the district level, for example), there is considerable interest throughout the country in moving toward greater school decentralization.

## IMPLEMENTATION OF CHANGE

Another reason for focusing on the local school as a target for change is the importance now given to the process of implementation in change programs. During the 1950s and 1960s attention was directed primarily at the process of *adoption*. Studies were made of the factors related to deciding whether or not to adopt a particular educational practice. Since then, it has become clear that many educational innovations, although "adopted," were never implemented, that is, actually put into practice. Studies of implementation have shifted attention from such factors as the characteristics of the innovation, cost, and characteristics of the school, to whether or not an adequate implementation process, such as on-site planning, localized teacher training, participation in decision making, etc., were used. These are things that need management at the local school level because they involve important rearrangements of the formal and informal organization of the school. That many failures in educational reform efforts during the 1950s and 1960s were failures in local implementation has been documented in a review of research on curriculum and in-struction implementation by Fullan and Pomfret.

> . . . why do so many difficulties arise during attempts at implementing cur-ricular innovations? The source of the difficulty does not appear to reside in the actual development and production of curriculum materials, although this may be an important factor in some instances. Nor is it simply a matter of getting people to agree to try the innovation. It also involves more than con-vincing various individuals who have agreed to try the curriculum to actually use the materials in certain ways. The main problem appears to be that cur-riculum change usually necessitates certain organizational changes, particu-larly changes in the roles and role relationships of those organizational mem-bers most directly involved in putting the innovation into practice. That is, role occupants are required to alter their usual ways of thinking about them-selves and one another and their characteristic ways of behaving towards one another within the organization. Often the organizational (role relationship) change aspects of curriculum projects are left implicit in the plans. Less often, an effort is made to address them directly. In either case, problems inevitably arise during the attempt to put such changes into practice.[6]

Based on their review of implementation studies, Fullan and Pomfret em-phasize the following factors as important for successful implementation in the local school:

1. Any proposed change must be clearly understood by users in the local school. The reasons for making changes and the precise nature of the changes must both be understood. Innovations that are particularly com-plex may present special problems in this regard.
2. Successful implementation usually depends upon intensive in-service training that is specifically directed to the changes being introduced.
3. School personnel need adequate time, materials, and facilities during im-plementation. Making curriculum changes is an arduous, specialized ac-tivity above and beyond normal routines.
4. Continuous feedback on implementation efforts is also desirable. This feedback between managers or consultants and local school personnel is important; so is feedback among peers at the local level.
5. The extent to which an innovation meets local needs, as perceived by school personnel, is related to successful implementation. Participation in decisions about innovations by local personnel is widely accepted as a cru-cial factor, although the research evidence is still inconclusive.

In summary, Fullan and Pomfret state:

> If there is one finding that stands out in our review, it is that effective imple-mentation of social innovations requires time, personnel interaction and con-tacts, in-service training and other forms of people-based support. Research has shown time and again that there is no substitute for the primacy of per-sonal contact among implementers, and between implementers and plan-

ners/consultants, if a difficult process of unlearning old roles and learning new ones is to occur. Equally clear is the absence of such opportunities on a regular basis during the planning and implementation of most innovations. All of this means that new approaches to educational change should include longer time perspectives, more small-scale intensive projects, more resources, time and mechanisms for contact among would-be implementers at both initiation or adoption stages, and especially during implementation.[7]

Factors in successful implementation will be discussed again when strategies and tactics of school improvement are presented.

## TARGET SIZE AND INTENSITY OF EFFORT

A study of the successes and failures in efforts to change schools underscores the difficulty of the effort required to bring about change. The implications of these facts for those seeking to bring about change may be understood by considering Figure 6-2, which suggests relationships among effort, size of target, and success. Intensity of effort means the degree to which there is a total commitment within a school organization for change. Such commitment includes social-psychological factors such as relationships, structures, technology, involvement, and finance. Naturally, the greater the intensity of effort, the greater the expected success in making changes. Also suggested in the diagram is that, with a given amount of effort, change will be more or less successful depending on the size of the target for change. Thus, intense effort toward change in a small organizational unit will tend to be more successful than the same effort distributed over a wider organizational territory. Low effort directed toward changing a large organizational unit is likely to fail.

|  | Size of Target | |
| --- | --- | --- |
|  | Small unit | Large unit |
| High intensity | highly successful | somewhat successful |
| Low intensity | somewhat successful | unsuccessful |

Effort: The degree of commitment of social-psychological features of the organization, including relationships, structures, technology, involvement, finance, etc.

Target: The size of the school building or organizational unit which is undergoing attempts to change.

FIGURE 6-2.  Successful Change as a Function of Target Size and Intensity of Effort

Because the process of changing an organization requires intense effort, we have recommended the local school building as a target for change. The local school organization is a unit small enough so that efforts to produce changes are not spread too thin. Also, we have emphasized the need to add to local efforts resources from the local district, the state department, and institutions of higher education.

Recognizing that the local school building as the most appropriate organization for change efforts has definite implications for school board policy and district administrative practice. Both policy and practice should be established with a high degree of school building program autonomy, decentralized fiscal management, and a delegation of personnel authority. One cannot adopt a centralized management system on one hand and talk school-building change on the other hand. A decentralized concept calls for adept and well-trained principals who are accountable for their building, but who also are given a high level of professional freedom to be creative managers responsible for their own and their school's destiny.

## ENDNOTES

1. Wayne K. Hoy and Cecil G. Miskel, *Educational Administration: Theory, Research, and Practice.* (New York: Random House, 1978) pp. 38–40.
2. Lawrence C. Pierce, *School Site Management* (Cambridge, Mass.: Aspen Institute for Humanistic Studies, 1977).
3. Pierce, *School Site Management*, p. 2.
4. Harold Howe II, *Citizens, Schooling, and Education* (New York: Ford Foundation, 1977), p. 8.
5. Howe, *Citizens, Schooling, and Education*, p. 12.
6. Michael Fullan and Alan Pomfret, "Research on Curriculum and Instruction Implementation," *Review of Educational Research* 47 (1977): 337. Copyright 1977, American Educational Research Association, Washington, D.C.
7. Ibid., p. 391.

# Chapter 7

# Organizational Variables in School Improvement

Because the organization of the individual school is the optimal target for change and because intense efforts, including resources from outside the local school, are required to bring about change, certain variables are crucial to the process of school improvement. These variables are three dimensions of the school organization plus additional leadership supplied by the partners recommended in this book.

While there are many organization theories, three major categories of variables are proposed for special attention in the Partnership Model: *goals, conditions,* and *elements*. *Goals* may pertain either to individuals within an organization or to an organization itself. *Conditions* are divided into categories of organizational products and organizational processes. *Elements* are the formal and informal structures in organizations.

Another factor that is absolutely crucial to organizational effectiveness is *leadership*. Leadership must be supplied by the several partners that have been proposed as collaborators in the school improvement practice. These include the local school district (represented by the building administrator), the state education agency, a college of education, and a teachers' organization. Let us turn to a brief explanation of each of the variables to see how they relate to the process of changing an individual school organization.

## GOALS—INDIVIDUAL AND ORGANIZATIONAL

Attention to individual and organizational goals and their interrelationship has had long-standing usefulness in the analysis of organizational behavior. On the one hand, individuals within an organization have needs and goals. On the other hand, the organization itself has a mission and related goals. The fact that individual goals may not be reached even when the goals of the organization are maximized is a source of continuous tension within every organization. Likewise, the extent to which individual needs are satisfied within an organization has a crucial effect on the morale and productivity of individuals.

One prominent theoretical presentation of these forces in organizations is Getzels'[1] distinction between nomothetic and idiographic dimensions of a social system. The nomothetic dimension is the institutional, or organizational, dimension and emphasizes contributions to the goals or tasks of an organiza-

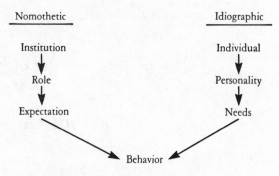

**FIGURE 7-1.    Dimensions of a Social System**

tion. The idiographic dimension emphasizes individuals with their unique personalities and needs. Organizational behavior in a social system is a product of nomothetic and idiographic forces.

As shown in Figure 7-1, the nomothetic dimension takes into account the institution, the social roles within the institution (for example, positions, offices, statuses), and role expectations. The idiographic dimension considers the individual, his or her personality, and need-disposition. According to the theory, organizations differ in the extent to which observed behavior is determined by nomothetic or idiographic forces. Thus, in one school, organizational goals might predominate, while in another, behavior is determined more by individual goals.

Regardless of the emphasis given within a certain organization to either nomothetic or idiographic dimensions, the tension between individual and organizational goals is a central problem for all organizations. As summarized by Likert in his "Principle of Supportive Relationships,"

> The leadership and other processes of the organization must be such as to ensure a maximum probability that in all interactions and all relationships within the organizations, each member will, in the light of his background, values, and expectations, view the experience as supportive and one which builds and maintains his personal sense of worth and importance.[2]

Within the local school, for example, bringing organizational and individual goals into harmony is a central strategy for increasing the productivity of the human resources. Furthermore, in making any changes in a local school organization, the needs of individuals involved in making the change, the idiographic goals, must be taken into account.

## CONDITIONS—PROCESS AND PRODUCT

Another useful distinction is between process and product dimensions of organizations. Product variables include an organization's formal outputs, tasks, and products, while process refers to the interaction pattern, the dynamics of

Goals

| | | Individual | Organizational |
|---|---|---|---|
| Conditions | Product | Ex:<br>Improved teacher<br>techniques | Ex:<br>Achievement<br>scores |
| | Process | Ex:<br>Improved student-<br>teacher relations | Ex:<br>School<br>climate |

FIGURE 7-2. Relationship Between Goals and Conditions in a School Organization

decision making, the means, the procedures, the motivation, and the organizational climate. Product deals with the outcomes of organization; process deals with the meaning of behavior in that organization. Product answers questions of "what" and "where"; process answers questions of "when" and "how." The primary products of schools are the knowledge, skills, and attitudes acquired by students. Major processes include teaching, learning, counseling, and administering.

At any one time in organizational life, these two conditions are always present. Those interested in organizational improvement must simultaneously deal with both product and process. Also, as indicated in Figure 7-2, each of these dimensions is related to the individual and organizational goals. Thus, in analyzing the local school organization, one must study the relationship of both product and process to organizational and individual goals.

For example, a school may be concerned about student achievement on standardized test scores. The organizational goal may be to raise mean scores as they compare to national norms. The "product" in this case could be interpreted as the combined scores on the tests given at the end of the school year. The organizational process might be measured in terms of the "climate" in the school before and after the push to "excellence." Climate might be defined in terms of staff morale and student attitudes about learning.

## ELEMENTS—FORMAL AND INFORMAL STRUCTURES

The third category of variables to be considered is the organizational elements of structure—formal and informal. Structure usually involves concepts of organization such as authority, division of labor or roles, control mechanisms, grouping patterns, and communications; all of these may be represented on an organizational chart. The seasoned administrator, however, knows that the chart may be misleading. If something needs doing, informal means may be best. Administrator style varies in terms of reliance on formal and informal structure as shown in Figure 7-3.

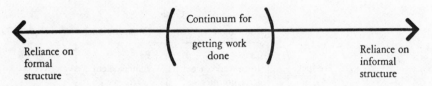

**FIGURE 7-3.** Administrative Style Varies in Reliance on Formal and Informal Structures

Newell[3] has described the distinction between formal and informal organization structures well. It has been recognized for several decades that in any organization there are both formal and informal structural relationships; that is, relationships which are designated formally and explicitly in the organizational structure, and relationships which are informal in the sense that they are not officially recognized. Without any designation in the formal organization, small groups of compatible persons form to discuss work-related and nonwork-related matters and to join in social and recreational activities. The proverbial grapevine conveys news and gossip.

Argyris states, "Specific individuals come to be recognized for their power even though they do not carry formally delegated authority. An informal organization develops to help satisfy the needs of individuals and groups."

Argyris presented the contrast in even more explicit terms.

| *Formal Organization* | *Informal Organization* |
|---|---|
| **1a.** At the outset interpersonal relations are *prescribed,* and they reflect the *organization's* idea of the most effective structure within which to achieve the *organization's goals.* | **1a.** At the outset interpersonal relations *arise* from members' interaction and reflect the *need* of *members* to interact with each other in order to fulfill their needs. |
| **1b.** The *leadership* role is assigned to the person the *organization* feels can best perform *organizationally* defined duties. | **1b.** The leadership role is delegated to the individual the *members* believe will best fulfill their needs. |
| **2a.** The formal behavior in organization manifested by an individual is "caused" by the individual's acceptance of *organizationally* defined reward and penalty (sanctions). | **2a.** All behavior of individual members in the group is caused by the attempts of individual members to *fulfill their needs.* |
| **2b.** The dependency of members upon the leader is *accepted* by members because of the existing organizational sanctions. | **2b.** *Dependency* of members upon the leader is created and accepted by members because they believe it will fulfill their needs.[4] |

Figure 7–4 illustrates how the concepts of formal and informal structure may be applied to a school organization.

| Formal | Structures | Informal |
|---|---|---|
| Designated administrative positions | Authority | "Old Boy" process doing favors |
| Job Descriptions | Roles | Role elaboration |
| Official evaluation system | Control mechanisms | Influence, charisma, seniority, personal power |
| "Secondary" groups such as departments or teaching teams | Grouping patterns | Primary groups, friends, cliques |
| Memos Announcements Bulletins | Communication | Rumor |
| Official line and staff relationships | Organization chart | Actual work practices |

FIGURE 7-4.   Formal and Informal Structures in a School Organization

## LEADERSHIP

Because the aim of the Partnership Model is to assist in *changing* schools, the question of leadership is crucial. Moreover, because the individual school is a conservative organization, local administrative leadership needs to be augmented to make change efforts succeed. Viewed from this perspective, a partnership is a mechanism to strengthen local leadership for change through collaboration. Members of the partnership share in this leadership function.

The concept of collaborative leadership for local school improvement is complex. Each collaborator represents a separate organization, each with its own goals, conditions, and elements. Therefore, highly complicated forces are at work in partnerships. The usefulness of the Partnership Model rests on the assumption that the analysis of school improvement processes requires such a level of complexity. School improvement is not a simple process, and it can succeed only when many complex forces are taken into account.

Modern leadership theory and research emphasize the situational aspects of effective leadership.[5] Therefore, in order to study leadership style in partnerships it is important to first review the nature of organization change process in a school.

A typical organization evolves through a series of periods of unrest, which produces anxiety in the people of the organization. This anxiety may motivate improvement and/or change. The change produces a period of comfort and then the cycle starts over again. This is initiated again by some stimulus which creates the impression that things are not all right.

The traditional strategy connected with this change theory phenomena has been associated with a single leader. This leader, a person in some power role with some degree of charisma, induces interventions designed to stimulate the existing order. This may be done in a unilateral dictum from the boss, shouting, "Some heads are going to roll around here," or it may be done more subtly utilizing a recent management technique learned at "motivation school."

In schools, this leader role is not always as successful as in business. In the first case, bureaucratic policies inhibit firing, and make it unreasonable to expect action from threats of unemployment. Also, schools have tried to operate in democratic fashions and have generally played down the principal as power figure who creates change by dictum.

Second, even though there may be more participatory administrative practices in evidence in sophisticated districts, the nature of staffing patterns in a school building is unique compared to other organizations, such as business enterprises. In organizational perspectives, there is a preponderance of people fulfilling "like-roles." This means that a principal in an elementary school with thirty teachers forms the most severe type of flat organizational structure depicted by a very large span of control. Communication typically does not follow a series of subordinate-superordinate roles more common in nonschool organizations. For example, in the matter of employee control, most management theories recommend a supervisory ratio of one to seven, not one to thirty. It appears to be difficult to control a school by dictum due to the unique structure of the organization; yet schools need leadership. From where does it come and in which direction (type of change) does it go?

When an organization is in a state whereby "What Is" (real) does not coincide with "What Should Be" (ideal), this can be labeled as a discrepancy which, in turn, can be used to establish goals for planned change. The change, if it happens, usually occurs through a natural evolutionary phenomenon or from planned interventions as mentioned before. Figure 7–5 depicts this idea.

In a school, the secret of converting discrepancies into goals and eventual new practice depends upon the intervention. If the intervention is made skillfully, then the goal can be reached. This initiative can come from the principal, a teacher, an external consultant, or some higher authority. The initial intervention (the act or word or change in structure) that begins to create the uncomfortable feeling that everything is not as well as it should be is a very sensitive one. That is the leadership function.

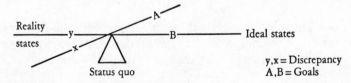

FIGURE 7–5.  Discrepancies and Goals

## BUILDING ADMINISTRATOR LEADERSHIP

The importance of this role, while reported by many authors, is perhaps best portrayed by a report of a Danforth project[6] which delineated the success of the NASSP Model Schools Project.

> The single most influential factor in all of the schools in determining the degree of progress or lack of it in achieving the model was the effectiveness of leadership in the various schools, mostly by the principals. Of the original thirty-four principals in the project, only thirteen of them were in the same school when the project officially terminated June 1975. Eighty percent of those who changed went on to a larger position in terms of school enrollment, or to a higher rank in a school system or other professional position.
>
> More than half of the programs deteriorated when the principals who started the model schools and worked with the staff to implement the prescriptions went on to a different new position. Most of those principals continued to work toward the model in the school to which they were appointed or as professors of education and in other positions where they worked to interest other persons in the ideas.
>
> The findings reinforce the conclusion that generations of persons have discovered; that the principal of a school more than any other individual determines the nature and the success of the school program. . . .

The importance of strong leadership has been documented in legendary ways. But is a strong, charismatic principal the only style of leadership? If it is, how do we reconcile the mobility of this type as described by Trump? The effect of the charismatic, strong leader leaving the innovative school can have serious consequences like problems of continuity.

The style of leadership necessary for partnerships is best described as "participatory" or "shared." Each person in the leadership role must provide an open style that exerts energy and strengths, but one that does not need dependent subordinates in order to execute. Leadership that promotes interdependency is extremely crucial in providing for the continuity of governance that is so important in organizational development projects. While the leadership continuity problem may not be as strong in the teacher union, college, and state department of education as it is in the principal position, the same style of leadership is preferred.

## TEACHER ASSOCIATION LEADERSHIP

In reviewing a large innovation diffusion project, Douglas A. Paul states:

> Unanticipated findings that emerged during interviewee descriptions of multi-unit school capability included the physical environment and teacher unions. Since the instructional and administrative design of individually guided education and the multi-unit school requires variable size student groupings and frequent staff cooperation and interaction, an open-space physical environment was described as a facilitating factor. Teacher unions

were described as an inhibiting force in some districts. Since some districts pay unit leaders an additional stipend, and since some districts pay unit teachers who are unwilling or uninterested in becoming involved in the multi-unit school, teacher unions have an interest in the implementation of the innovation. Either implicitly or explicitly, unions may exert considerable influence on the implementation procedures for the multi-unit school.[7]

It is no longer enough to include teacher representatives in planning and decision making. It is necessary to incorporate the leadership from the professional organizations (unions or associations) into the total organization's development. To ignore or deny the teachers' unions a chance to assume a share of the responsibility for program change is to be short sighted. For administrators to resist these kinds of changes is to insure survival pains of the greatest order.

## LEADERSHIP FROM HIGHER EDUCATION

In the same research report, Paul points out the need for collaborative leadership from teacher education institutions (TEI).

> Perceptions of the roles of the resource, mediating and user systems may reveal conflicting expectations, misperceptions and/or a lack of communication. By explicating the multiple role perceptions it may be possible to contribute to a greater understanding of the difficulties involved with inter-organizational cooperation and linkage. Attitudes of researchers, academics and practitioners may be another fruitful area to explore in view of the assumption that these groups should interact and work together effectively. The concept of legitimacy may also contribute to an understanding of the factors involved when one or more organizations intervene in the operations of another organization. For example, precedents for frequent TEI and local school inservice programs may facilitate the diffusion of innovations that involve TEI faculty. The presence or absence of complementary resources may also play an important role in facilitating or hindering interorganizational linkage. On the one hand, multi-unit schools that perceive needs being fulfilled by the TEI or another organization may be more likely to value and maintain a high level of interaction. On the other hand, teacher education institutions that perceive needs being fulfilled through involvement with local education agencies or other organizations may be more likely to enter into cooperative agreements for furnishing assistance. If the needs of the organizations are similar, then competition rather than cooperation is likely to arise.[8]

## STATE DEPARTMENT OF EDUCATION LEADERSHIP

In speaking for leadership from the state departments of education, Mark Shedd, Commissioner of Education, Connecticut, says it eloquently:

> Ironically, much of the problem of federal encroachment into state and local school governance can be laid at the doorstep of the state and local educators

themselves. The strong federal role in school governance has grown out of an overwhelming need for resources that state and local governments could not generate, and for leadership that they did not develop.

I believe, with many of my colleagues, that the solution lies with the state departments of education. Regrettably, the task has been made that much harder because state departments of education have not built a particularly good reputation for themselves in years past. Rather than exercising political leadership, they have established political bureaucracies; rather than aiding in the collection of disbursement of funds they have entangled them further and siphoned off needed dollars; rather than cutting red tape, they have added additional layers.

The state education agency can be the key to a new dynamic federalism—a system of school governance that recognizes not only the value of local democratic control, but the importance of the broader perspective and powerful resources of the national government. It will require the firm commitment and tremendous energies of each and every educator. But it can happen.[9]

## SCHOOL IMPROVEMENT LEADERSHIP

One way to look at the more individualistic approaches to leadership is to study Figure 7–6, which describes the theories of Tannenbaum and Schmidt.[10]

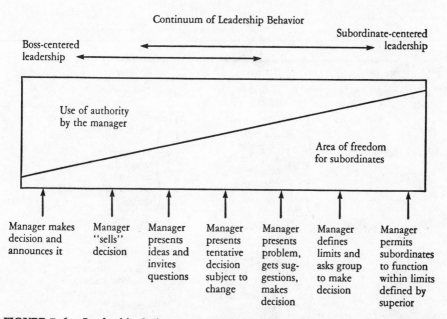

**FIGURE 7–6.  Leadership Styles**   Herbert Hicks and C. R. Gullett, *Organizations: Theory and Behavior* (New York: McGraw-Hill Co., 1975), p. 305. Adapted from Robert Tannenbaum and Warren H. Schmidt, "How to Choose a Leadership Pattern," *Harvard Business Review* (March-April 1958): 96. Copyright © 1958 by the President and Fellows of Harvard College; all rights reserved.

With this concept the leader can choose which leadership style is best for him or her based on personal motivation, the characteristics of the followers (subordinates), and the organizational environment. We believe that leaders involved in our model should direct their behavior so that it falls toward the *right* as depicted on this chart. We believe an arena of professional freedom and collaborative effort is necessary to partnership schools, if not all schools!

In order to understand how an organization might work under this style of leadership, we must look at motivation. The leading motivation theorists are Maslow, Herzberg, and McGregor. Hicks and Gullet[11] have summarized the three theories of these men in a way that has meaning to the leadership assumptions important to partnershipping.

> The theories of Maslow, McGregor, and Herzberg all seem to approach motivation from a different perspective. But when these theories are compared in Figure 7–7, it can be seen that they all emphasize similar sets of relationships. Maslow views the rarely satisfied higher-level needs as the motivating force behind the worker. Herzberg sees "satisfiers" as motivating after the hygiene factors have neutralized dissatisfaction. McGregor approaches motivation through his Theory Y which is based on assumptions concerning the motives of workers. Therefore, all three theories are relevant to studies of motivation, and particularly external motivation.
>
> The three lower-level needs in Maslow's hierarchy of needs theory, physiological, safety and social, are all relatively satisfied in our industrial society. Therefore, they are no longer strong, driving forces. They cease to be motiva-

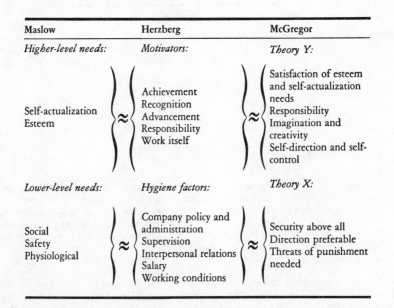

| Maslow | Herzberg | McGregor |
| --- | --- | --- |
| *Higher-level needs:* | *Motivators:* | *Theory Y:* |
| Self-actualization Esteem ≈ | Achievement Recognition Advancement Responsibility Work itself | ≈ Satisfaction of esteem and self-actualization needs Responsibility Imagination and creativity Self-direction and self-control |
| *Lower-level needs:* | *Hygiene factors:* | *Theory X:* |
| Social Safety Physiological ≈ | Company policy and administration Supervision Interpersonal relations Salary Working conditions | ≈ Security above all Direction preferable Threats of punishment needed |

**FIGURE 7–7. Motivation Theories**   Herbert Hicks and C. R. Gullett, *Organizations: Theory and Behavior* (New York: McGraw-Hill Co., 1975), p. 290.

tors, and they now assume the role of hygiene or maintenance factors as described by Herzberg. Conversely, the two higher-level needs, esteem and self-actualization, are rarely satisfied and therefore act the same as the motivators conceptualized by Herzberg.

McGregor's Theory Y can be compared to both Maslow's and Herzberg's theories of motivation. Theory Y assumes that the employee desires satisfaction of his esteem and self-actualization needs, desires responsibility, exercises self-direction and self-control and is imaginative and creative. Maslow's higher-level needs and Herzberg's motivational factors make the same assumptions. Therefore, a manager may choose either higher-level needs, motivational factors or Theory Y assumptions to motivate his employees. All emphasize the same set of relationships.

The set of relationships emphasized by these authors seems very close to the assumptions about motivation that leaders must make about partnership school improvement projects. We believe that when the leaders act on assumptions of human nature as suggested in the upper portion of Figure 7–7, that the change process will be optimized.

## ENDNOTES

1. Jacob W. Getzels, "Administration as a Social Process," in *Administrative Theory in Education,* ed. Andrew W. Halpin (Chicago: Midwest Administration Center, University of Chicago, 1958), p. 156.
2. Rensis Likert, *New Patterns of Management* (New York: McGraw-Hill Book Co., 1961), p. 103.
3. Clarence A. Newell, *Human Behavior in Educational Administration* (Englewood Cliffs, N.J.: Prentice-Hall, Inc., 1978), p. 117.
4. Chris Argyris, "Organizational Leadership," in *Leadership and Interpersonal Behavior,* ed. L. Petruelo and B. Boss (New York: Holt, Rinehart and Winston, Inc., 1961), p. 339.
5. F. E. Fiedler, *A Theory of Leadership Effectiveness* (New York: McGraw-Hill, 1967).
6. J. Lloyd Trump and William Georgiades, "What Happened and What Did Not Happen in the Model Schools," *NASSP Bulletin* (May 1977): 72.
7. Douglas A. Paul, "The Diffusion of an Innovation Through Inter-Organizational Linkages," *Educational Administration Quarterly* 12 (Spring 1976): 18–37.
8. Ibid.
9. Mark Shedd, "The State-Federal Partnership: Making It Work for Schools," *The School Administrator, AASA* 34 (May 1977).
10. Herbert G. Hicks and C. Roy Gullet, *Organizations: Theory and Behavior* (New York: McGraw-Hill Co., 1975), p. 305.
11. Ibid., pp. 289–290.

# Chapter 8

# The Process of Change:
# A Discrepancy Model

The recurring theme of our study is that through collaborative partnerships the process of change in a school can be directed toward significant goals in systematic and cost-effective ways. Even in a period of diminishing resources, this approach to successful, planned change is viewed as a realistic proposal for continuing progress toward educational goals that are mutually accepted by members of an individual school community.

Although the literature on organizational change is substantial, there is a great gap between the theory and the practice of organizational change. Despite failures, however, solid information about school improvement does exist. In this chapter, for example, basic conceptions of the process of change, especially as applied to cultural change, prove to be a helpful way to view changes in an individual school organization. Drawing upon these general ideas as background, the concept of disequilibrium is used to describe the starting point for organizational change. The practical result is a proposal to use discrepancy analysis as a primary tool in bringing about successful, planned change in an individual school.

## CONCEPTUAL BASIS FOR SUCCESSFUL, PLANNED CHANGE

The process of change may be viewed either as a natural phenomenon over which individuals have little control, or as one over which individuals may exercise conscious direction. While some cataclysmic events (floods, volcanoes, etc.) may appear to be beyond human control, even these natural phenomena can be influenced. Flood control projects may prevent damage; volcanic eruptions may be anticipated. Many times such natural forces can even be directed toward beneficial ends, such as hydroelectric power from water stored by flood control projects.

The focus of this book is on *planned change*. Planned change differs from the natural concept of change in that the change is anticipated, directed, and made to occur. The end product of the successful, planned change effort is the attainment of a predetermined objective within a specified context of space and time. In other words, change that is planned reflects a conscious effort to alter the existing environment in order to create a desired set of outcomes.

Historically, one of the most powerful and widespread views of change is that it results from motion created by opposing forces acting upon each other. Examples of this concept of change are found in the writings of many ancient and modern scholars. To illustrate the progression of change theory throughout history, three examples (Heraclitus, Hegel, and Linton) will be discussed to enable the reader to place change theory in a broader perspective. While each of these scholars was concerned with a different aspect of change, each uses the concept of motion generated by opposing forces to explain the change process.

Heraclitus, an Ionian Greek who lived from 536–470 B.C., was the first known scholar to devote a majority of his intellectual energies to the study of change. Heraclitus believed that the only permanence in nature was perpetual change. Everything in nature was constantly flowing toward some new synthesis. One popular expression of his was, "You cannot step twice into the same river, for fresh waters are ever flowing in upon you."[1]

The importance of the ideas expressed by Heraclitus to our study is that the appearance of permanence is actually a temporary equilibrium that exists between opposite forces flowing toward a new synthesis. Thus, change has previously occurred, and the ever-flowing cycle of change continues. There is no such thing as status quo!

The concept of continuous motion contained within the "opposing forces" posited by Heraclitus formed the core of what has become known as *Hegelian dialectic*. The essential elements of the dialectic are those of *thesis*, *antithesis*, and *synthesis*. These elements are used to describe human thought as a process of perpetual change.

According to Hegel, thought moves from : (1) a *thesis*, contradicted by (2) an *antithesis*, leading to (3) a *synthesis*, through which the totality of the opposites combine to form a new and unique view of the universe. Hegel's view of change has had a profound impact upon modern thought, especially as adapted by Karl Marx to predict the "downfall" of capitalism and the "rise" of socialism.

The concept of change as the combination of opposing forces has also been used to explain cultural change. An interesting example is a theory of cultural change developed by Linton.[2]

The phenomenon of cultural change, according to Linton, is generated from friction existing among the *universals*, *specialities*, and *alternatives* within a particular culture. *Universals*, according to Linton, represent those elements of the culture, both material and nonmaterial, that are accepted by all members of the adult population. These elements form the cement or cohesive glue that holds the society of a particular culture together. *Specialities*, on the other hand, represent those cultural elements accepted by specific subgroups within the adult population and are normally associated with occupational, professional, or social class groupings. *Alternatives* are those innovative elements of a material or nonmaterial nature derived from discovery, invention, or infusion from a foreign culture that are accepted and pursued by some individuals within the society. The relative stability of a culture at any given period, according to Linton, is a function of the ratios existing between universals, specialities, and alternatives. As the number of alternatives and specialities increases in proportion to the universals, the degree of stability of goals and values within the society decreases.

Thus, while Hegel envisioned three stages in the movement of thought (thesis, antithesis, and synthesis) as an impetus for changing people's knowledge and perception of ultimate reality, Linton perceived changes in our culture as being induced by the causal agents of universals, specialities, and alternatives.

While the initial intent of Hegel and Linton may have been directed toward the solution of quite different problems, the end product of both efforts results in a similar statement of the force or motion for change.

Linton's theory of cultural change may be applied to a local school. The individual school community is a culture in which universals, specialities, and alternatives exist in the form of differing educational values and beliefs that are held by various groups and individuals. In this situation, the administrator and teachers become involved in the ebb and flow of the forces created by traditions, innovations, and special-interest groups who desire to have their particular perception of the school program become dominant.

In this context, school personnel may experience a loss of direction about the fundamental goals of the educative process. Without community consensus, school administrators and teachers may be pressured by powerful special-interest groups. A well-defined, systematic approach to planned change involving all components of the school community is an effective deterrent to this disruptive situation.

These basic concepts of change, especially cultural change, are consistent with the more familiar concepts of need theory in psychology. From this point of view, all human responses result from tensions or needs within the human organism. The human organism functions as a totality, or "action-whole," and responses by the organism result from needs arising from either physical, mental, social, or emotional systems. In this view, all human action is purposeful or goal-oriented. Change is seen as an attempt by the organism to reduce tension by achieving that which will return it to a state of equilibrium.

It must be stressed that human needs are expansive, not just directed at maintaining a "steady state." Human beings naturally desire new experiences, new understanding, and higher levels of self-realization. Thus, human needs are dynamic, and need theory is consistent with the concepts of continuous change in which equilibrium is a temporary condition in a never-ending process.[3]

Implicit in the work of Heraclitus, Hegel, Linton, and the need theorists is a unique perception of change that serves as the conceptual basis for the approach to successful, planned change presented here. Its main features may be summarized as follows:

1. Within nature the only permanance is the perpetual process of change.
2. Equilibrium is a concept employed to describe a *momentary* balance existing between two or more opposing forces.
3. Change occurs as a result of an imbalance existing between opposing forces.
4. The state of perpetual change reflected in the physical universe also exists in the movement of human thought.
5. Action in the human organism is the result of need, which is a disequilibrium existing within the individual.

6. All behavioral responses exhibited by the human organism are purposeful and directed toward the fulfillment of some need and the reestablishment of equilibrium.
7. Rising aspirations and expectations in the human organism alter the quality, nature, and type of goals sought in order to satisfy a need.
8. The human organism possesses the capacity for planning and directing its behavior toward the achievement of goals that will reestablish equilibrium.

## CREATING AND CONTROLLING DISEQUILIBRIUMS

From the previous discussion, the concept of equilibrium emerges as a central theme in our model of successful, planned change. Equilibrium, in our study, is defined as the conscious effort in individuals or groups to eliminate tensions that emerge within their life-space in order to return to a condition of well-being. Due to rising aspirations and expectations, the conditions necessary for reestablishing equilibrium are never the same, and growth or change is always present.

The process of schooling, within the context of American society, was established primarily to perpetuate our cultural heritage. Because of the complexity of society, however, the core values (universals) of the society have become increasingly impossible to identify.

As Brameld has noted, the goals of the school must include the assimilation and/or integration of emerging core values if it is to remain a useful institution. He states:

> Education, in sum, is the chief institution through which culture, entirely the creation of men, maintains dynamic continuity. It stabilizes the patterning of social experience and, in this sense, always reflects that patterning. But education also makes possible the great or small innovations, the cumulative readjustments without which, in the long career of cultures, stability either degenerates into sterility or finally explodes into chaos and destruction.[4]

A major problem facing schools in contemporary society is a lack of consensus relative *to their role and function.* In local school districts throughout the nation, the institution of education is in trouble. Members of the adult population are divided as to what goals and priorities the process of schooling should be designed to facilitate.

Another way to view the lack of consensus about schools is to view it as a situation in which many *specialities* and *alternatives* exist to challenge *universals.* According to Linton's analysis, this is a situation where conflict may be high, but also a situation in which forces for change are great. These are productive forces if properly channeled; they are the very impetus for organizational change. What is often lacking in schools is a successful forum where universals, specialities, and alternatives are brought to bear in fashioning local school change. While existing mechanisms of school governance (e.g., local school board elections and meetings, collective bargaining sessions) provide such forums, they often fail to produce local school action plans that lead to a new synthesis (new universals) in terms of the local school organization and program.

In light of the lack of consensus about the role and function of schooling within our society, it is imperative that school authorities develop better strategies for changing schools. Such strategies need to be developed through a process of collaborative decision making that involves all members of the school community. As Dewey has noted, ". . . it is well to remind ourselves that education as such has no aims. Only persons, parents, teachers, etc., have aims, not an abstract idea like education."⁵

In the past, schools in our society have often failed to reflect the *emerging* needs of the society they were designed to serve. Goals and priorities reflecting the thinking of yesterday's heros or of today's most vocal subgroups tend to control the theories and practices of our educational enterprise. As a result, collaborative decision making about the quality of schools is often absent. In such a climate, educational leaders from all levels of the profession must assume responsibility for bringing about some integration of the conflicting elements of the culture. In this context the schools must function as instruments of change and the consolidation of conflicting ideas of the purpose of schooling.

In creating a design for change that is appropriate for schools, we return again to the concept of equilibrium. From the viewpoint of organizational development, the efforts of the institution to find effective means for achieving its goals and for rapidly adjusting to emerging needs may be described as a search for a new equilibrium. The search begins in a sense of disequilibrium, and the objectives for planned change are derived from mutual or complementary needs of members of the school community. Existing conditions in the school are seen as problematic in that the school community is prevented from reaching important goals or objectives. If there is no routine solution, a process must be designed to satisfy the needs and thus return the institution to a state of well-being, or equilibrium. Essentially, this process involves the following elements:

1. A detailed analysis of the need to be met.
2. The establishment of an objective as an end product to be attained.
3. The development of process strategies for implementation for attaining the desired end product.
4. A study of the potential that each alternative strategy possesses for attaining the end product and the possible negative consequences of each alternative strategy under consideration.
5. The selection and implementation of the alternative strategy possessing the greatest potential for the successful attainment of the desired end product and the least number of negative consequences.
6. The design and implementation of a system of formative and summative evaluation for the purpose of monitoring the degree to which the selected alternative strategy is attaining the desired end product and for manipulating resources and the strategy to attain the desired end product.

This process of planned change may be viewed as a *discrepancy approach* to change. The essential element in this approach is the determination of the differences existing between *what is* and *what is desired*. Planned change utilizing a discrepancy approach is, therefore, a process employed to reestablish a state of equilibrium—the desired level of performance determined by collaborative decision making and described in the objectives to be attained by the cooperatively developed program.

The desired level of performance emerging from each successive change effort will, of course, differ from previous objectives. As noted earlier, this successive change in goal orientation is a function of changing needs, rising expectations, and emerging alternatives within the culture. Thus, the discrepancy approach, while directed toward the restoration of equilibrium, is growth-oriented in terms of the structure, technology, and individuals within the school.

It should also be stressed that the discrepancy approach to change is best where all those affected are involved in selecting specific objectives, strategies, and tactics for change. Involvement provides the best chance for bringing about a desired state of equilibrium, which is an integration of diverse needs, aspirations, and beliefs into a mutually acceptable school program.

## ENDNOTES

1. Quoted in Bertrand Russell, *A History of Western Philosophy* (New York: Simon and Schuster, 1964), p. 45.
2. Ralph Linton, *The Study of Man* (New York: D. Appleton-Century Company, 1936).
3. For a classic exposition of need theory, see Abraham H. Maslow, *Motivation and Personality,* 2nd ed. (New York: Harper & Row, Publishers, 1970).
4. Theodore Brameld, *Philosophies of Education in Cultural Perspective, Prospects for American Education* (New York: Holt, Rinehart, and Winston, 1955), p. 388.
5. John Dewey, *Democracy and Education* (New York: The Macmillan Company, 1916), p. 125.

# Chapter 9

# The Organization Development (OD) Macro-Model

Every planned change project needs a master strategy that places key organizational variables into an action plan. Our master strategy, or macro-model, is *organization development through partnerships.*

## BACKGROUND OF ORGANIZATION DEVELOPMENT (OD)

Historically, change in organizations has been associated with authority. Traditional authority was based on power, autocracy, a heavy emphasis upon efficiency and control, superordinate/subordinate line relationships, and paternalism. Despite rhetoric to the contrary, change was typically imposed upon employees. This imposition often led employees to feel resentful, impotent, hostile, or passive. The result was a low level of employee morale and resistance to change. Usually, changes introduced in this way could be continued only with high levels of direct supervision and incentive. In the last several decades, however, a shift has occurred from reliance upon traditional authority to a more participative management style.

Three movements in particular have contributed to the new emphasis upon participative organizational governance. They are *sensitivity training,* the development of the National Training Laboratories, and the advancement of *management science.* Sensitivity training, including T-Group and laboratory training, became an extremely successful device to help persons become more aware of themselves and group processes. In its many variations and offshoots, laboratory training uses small group procedures for therapy, personal growth, or organizational improvement.

According to Bennis, laboratory training began in 1947 at Bethel, Maine, where the National Training Laboratories made their early headquarters. Building on the work of pioneer social psychologist Kurt Lewin, the originators made sensitivity training a major component of programs of the National Training Laboratories. The original emphasis on personal change shifted after the late 1950s to an emphasis on organization development.[1]

The development of laboratory training methods at the National Training Laboratories was accompanied by an interest in management science. Drawing on sociological theories of organizations and insights from social psychology, behavioral scientists created an applied science that came to be widely used in the management of large corporations. Summarizing these developments, Bennis noted the following basic assumptions of this management science:

1. All organizations from small groups to communities have similar tasks: integration of personal and social goals, collaboration, adaptation, and revitalization. Organizations can be understood in terms of these common processes.
2. Behavioral scientists should assume a practical focus so that the improvement of organizations becomes a respectable scientific pursuit.
3. Utilization of knowledge is a central problem of behavioral sciences. How such knowledge becomes the basis for action is an important area of study. Closer collaboration is needed between the producers and the users of knowledge to improve knowledge use.
4. Both scientists and practitioners must place higher value on the renewal of organizations and institutions.[2]

These developments combined to make a discipline of Applied Behavioral Science, which in one form is called Organization Development, or OD. OD has already proven itself as a system for creating change and improvement in organizations, particularly in human service organizations. OD deals with the organization as a totality and emphasizes the need to involve members of the organization in solving organizational problems. Despite its wide variety of styles and approaches, OD is a substantial movement which has a strong record of accomplishment. A sampling of the abundant literature on OD is included in the bibliography.

## DEFINITION OF OD

Organization development is a process, usually conducted by a specialist, that helps groups develop more effective ways of operating. Such organization development specialists, working as consultants to organizations, have made significant contributions in many organizations—creating change, developing innovations, and improving efficiency.

A distinction should be made between organization development specialists and management consultants. Management consultants usually provide specific services or make specific recommendations regarding the products, tasks, or operations of an organization. Typically, they specialize in a selected area, for instance, personnel, finance, or marketing. The contract with a management consultant is usually for a specific job over a short period of time. Once the consultant leaves, the organizational hierarchy can accept or reject the consultant's ideas and recommendations. This is an important kind of consultant to organizations, and educational institutions are no exception. Schools need expert advice about management problems and also about curriculum, instruction, and other matters.

The organization development consultant, on the other hand, approaches clients from a different perspective. The OD consultant looks at the total organization—its goals, its structures, its processes, its problems. He or she assists members of the organization in diagnosing problems and creating new structures and processes to accomplish organizational goals. Usually, the consultation occurs over a long period of time. The consultant's skills are working with people, helping them see their own problems, and working with them to create and implement new organizational structures and procedures.

OD consultants may be either external or internal. The external consultant brings a fresh, objective perspective to an organization and its problems. Such objectivity can be a significant contribution to those "caught up" in the organization itself. On the other hand, the external consultant may find it difficult to comprehend the total organization, or find that interventions are rejected as those of an "outsider." Also, external consultants may be unable to spend the amount of time necessary for changes to become integrated. Thus, many organizations have employed internal consultants, whose principal job is to assist the organization in self-renewal. Both the external and internal OD consultants use similar methods for making interventions in the organization.

Because organization development is relatively new and because there are many versions, it is difficult to describe OD in language that is both acceptable to the expert and understandable to the novice. Several brief descriptions are provided to help the reader obtain a general impression of OD.

One of the most popular definitions of OD was provided by Beckard: "Organization development is an effort (1) planned, (2) organization-wide, and (3) managed from the top, to (4) increase organization effectiveness and health through (5) planned interventions in the organization's 'processes,' using behavioral science knowledge."[3]

French and Bell define OD as " . . . a long-range effort to improve an organization's problem-solving and renewal processes, particularly through a more effective and collaborative management of organization culture . . . with the assistance of a change agent, or catalyst, and the use of the theory and technology of applied behavior science, including action research."[4]

Specialists in the application of organization development to schools at the University of Oregon have described OD as follows.

> Organizational development is a conceptual framework and a strategy to help schools meet the challenges of a changing pluralistic society. It encompasses a theory and a technology to help schools become self-renewing and self-correcting systems of people—receptive to clues that change is required and able to respond with innovative and integrated programs and arrangements. Organization development helps schools as they attempt to increase the amount of understanding, committment and involvement of professionals, parents, students and citizens.

Organizational development specialists desire to help people in schools learn productive ways of working on the problems they encounter, improve their organizational capabilities so that new ways of interacting can be initiated despite frustrations and become confident in their ability to understand themselves, assess their circumstances, identify their goals and perform the functions to which they commit themselves.[5]

Because of the extensive experience of the Oregon group with OD in educational settings, we will draw extensively upon their work in later chapters.

Those interested in OD can also profit from writings intended for consultants themselves. For example, the following guidelines for OD were adapted from Robert T. Golembiewski's recommendations to professionals.

1. OD efforts should rest on an appropriate concept of humankind. This means an adequate conception of the fully-functioning individual, including motivation, life-style, and values.
2. OD should always involve a two-way social contract in which the consultant and members of the organization have reciprocal obligations.
3. The consistent bias of OD should be toward participant choice instead of change by itself.
4. OD activities should be adaptable to alternative models of the change process; there is no single best method for all organizations.
5. OD activities need to be adjusted to the decision making conventions of each organization. (An OD adage is never to surprise the boss.)
6. In an OD intervention the appropriate contract, model of change, and decision-making conventions depend on the level in the organization at which the intervention is focused.
7. OD emphasizes that changes introduced in one part of the organization affect the total organization; all levels or parts of the organization need attention to integrate change.
8. Stress on integration means bringing together people and responsibilities; organizational structures and processes become integrated to the extent possible in given conditions.[6]

## COMMON ELEMENTS IN OD STRATEGIES

From the OD literature we have drawn some common themes that characterize the work of organizational development specialists.

**Participation by Organization Members.**   A central feature of organization development is the active participation of the clients in the process of change. Members of the organization at all levels need to be involved in the analysis of problems, the consideration of alternative solutions, and decisions about changes to be made.

**Participant Choice.**    Participant choice is valued more than change itself. Without support from the individuals involved, changes made in structure will be superficial and short-lived. The integration of process and product comes from resting decisions on participants' choice.

**Action Research.**    Action research techniques are an integral part of the process of organization development. This action research involves the constant use of feedback from surveys and evaluations to participants in the change process. Using techniques from the behavioral sciences, this research is focused on the need to diagnose organizational problems, weigh alternative action plans, monitor implementation efforts, and gain new knowledge about organizational processes. The focus of action research is on a particular organization, providing continuous feedback on organizational processes and products to guide institutional self-renewal.

**Organizational Process.**    The focus of organization development is on recurring patterns of behavior that reflect the tasks and the processes of the organization. OD takes particular note of organizational process because process is so often ignored. Some examples of key process variables are the degree of openness and ease of communication; the degree of trust and mutual support among members of the organization; and the willingness of individuals to take risks while searching for new behavior patterns.

## AN EXAMPLE OF ORGANIZATION DEVELOPMENT THROUGH PARTNERSHIPS

With some of the principles of OD in mind, it is important to show how these principles might be applied to our concept of partnership. Reminding the readers that we see OD as an organic, evolving process, the following is offered as a preliminary example of specific strategies that are elaborated later. The individual roles could be switched around to suit the expertise available.

The OD framework is a natural setting for the partnership approach. Partnership theory attempts to bring people together in productive collaborations to improve local schools. OD is based on the integration of people and their roles and relations with others in the organization. OD works on the structure of an organization in terms of role prescriptions (i.e., formal job descriptions) and role elaborations (what people make of their jobs). Both of these must change in order for the organization to change. Examining that role structure is, therefore, one of the goals of OD.

How would this work? One pattern would be to use the different members of the partnership to be facilitators for the change of roles in a local school. This is a logical pattern so long as the initial priorities have been established by the school. There are several roles that could be played by any partner, but, for example, a state department staff person could serve in the capacity of a process consultant. OD consultants often spend much of the time in process facilitation. They observe, diagnose, train, intervene, record, question, and give feedback to groups within the organization. All of these behaviors are designed to facilitate the OD process and answer "how" and "when" questions. A college faculty member could, of course, perform the same function. Or, the college could supply training to selected school personnel to be OD internal consultants.

Robert Jones,[7] an OD consultant, works with the ideas of the OD Loop: Assessment, Diagnosis, Action Plans, Implementation, Review and Revise (ADAIR). The outside consultant normally makes those interventions. Local employees could be trained in the separate techniques of each step. In other words, a few teachers could become adept at the assessment or sensing stage and could be used when needed in that capacity. The techniques are not difficult to learn and maximum involvement could be obtained by starting at ground level. One of the problems of implementing change is that leaders do not start involvement of others soon enough.

These training programs could be offered as graduate courses and applied to degree programs for teachers. What better way is there to acquaint the teaching staff with the OD process? A side benefit of such training is that it should hasten the teachers' readiness for change, which is a crucial factor for success in planned change projects.

State department staff members or college educators may also become involved as experts in specified content areas. They might concern themselves with the technology of instruction, resources, curriculum updating, legal implications, and the basic structure of the organization particularly as it relates to the local or state laws.

Teacher association or union representatives may be particularly useful at certain places along the OD loop. The development or screening of action plans would be an excellent way to utilize the teachers, for example. The teachers' association should be involved at decision points, thus having access to facts gathered at the assessment stage. The teachers' association would be encouraged to take a share in the responsibility for decisions about school improvement.

A scenario is presented here to illustrate how the OD process might work in a partnership school. A teacher in School "A" senses a disequilibrium in the school organization. The teacher believes that the school organization is weak because it isolates teachers in graded, self-contained classrooms. He or she talks to several other interested teachers who express their concern that there is a lack of cooperation and communication among teachers. This small group of teachers goes to the principal and expresses concern.

The principal listens and agrees that changes are desirable. The principal has recently been made aware that the State Education Department and the nearby college of education are interested in establishing partnerships to improve schools. A call is placed by the principal and a meeting is established.

At that first meeting the following people are in attendance: the principal, the teacher who started the intervention, a representative from the building teachers' association, a representative from the State Education Department, and a professor from the local college of education. The district office is represented by the director of elementary education. This group constitutes a task force with a one-year commitment to the newly identified project.

The principal requests in-service money from the district office to pay an external consultant to get them started in the OD process. The consultant is familiar with the concept of the "Jones OD Loop" and starts the process by following these steps:

1. *Analysis:*   Data are collected from the school staff via an interview technique (specifics of organizational analysis and diagnosis are explained in the next chapter). The task force conducts the interviews probing for teachers' attitudes about their school's structure and organization and their concept of how things might be changed for the better. For example, using the organizational variables outlined in Chapter 7, the task force could analyze the goals, conditions, and elements of the organization and how they might be altered. The data is collected, summarized, and disseminated to the faculty. The entire faculty is invited to participate in the diagnosis but it is the primary responsibility of the task force.

2. *Diagnosis:*   As the "interventionist teacher" suspected, the data reveal that there is general need for change and at least some confusion about organization. The diagnosis is that there is, in fact, a majority of teachers who are willing to look at new organization options.

3. *Action Planning:*   The task force asks for volunteers from the staff to serve on a subcommittee for planning in order to increase the level of involvement. A parent is invited to participate. The subcommittee reports to the task force, not the principal. Although the principal maintains veto power, he or she is perceptive enough to use it prudently. The planning committee follows an action research model, assisted by the professor from the task force.

   A theory for reorganization is developed, which contains a team approach utilizing a multigraded structure. Action plans are developed, including the specifics necessary to make the plan operational. The plans include dates for installation, how to promote the new idea, and an evaluation proposal. The evaluation is designed to periodically check on the new structure and the resulting shifts in process. The evaluation is written in the context of the original problem: improving communication patterns in the staff. The plan is then given to the task force.

   The reorganization plan is explained to the total staff through the task force. Several months are allowed for preparation and the implementation phase is ready. The teams are organized and, on an in-service day, the external consultant returns to act as a trainer and leads each team in some team-building exercises.

4. *Implementation:*   The task force implements the plan through the principal and establishes a system to receive constant feedback on how it is working. This feedback must look at organizational goals (teaming) and

individual needs; the task (is the plan, in fact, operating?); the process (what are the new attitudes?); the elements of the organization in terms of the formal structures (now changed through the OD intervention); and the informal structures (will the primary social groups change and how is staff morale?).

Other assessments such as student achievement, parents' feedback, and administrative observations (including district office) are made. In this implementation period, extra budgetary considerations are not involved, so that does not become a factor of evaluation.

5. *Review and Revise:* The formative evaluation process has been going on through the implementation period, but at the end of the year the task force must design and critique a formal, summative evaluation of the new structure and the resulting new processes. Did, in fact, the communication patterns improve?

In this case, the answer is "yes, but." The "but" implies that the multigraded approach was creating too much of an instructional-planning problem for the majority of the teachers. This was gleaned from an anonymous questionnaire designed for that purpose. Now, the task force must make a decision for next year. They can abandon the project, continue it as planned, or modify. They decide to modify in order to bring the individual needs of the teachers closer to the goals of the school (to reduce the discrepancy). This is accomplished by leaving the team concept intact, but by dropping the multigraded part of the reorganization. New teams are formed. (Readers who desire more information on the process of reconciling individual and organizational goals are referred to Barrett.)[8]

Consequently, the task force sets the new revised plans for next year and receive principal and district office approval. Parents are informed as well as students. The OD Loop, however, continues. This is not a single innovation, but a dynamic, organic process designed to establish a continual process of analyzing, diagnosing, planning, implementing, and reviewing.

## CONCLUDING THOUGHTS

For too long, we have had warring camps and power struggles over the control of schools. Administrators, because of their reluctance to delegate, have caused much of the teachers' motivation to question governance. Teachers have been reluctant, in many cases, to assume responsibility because they felt it was really the administrator's job; but more than that, teachers felt they could not gain any real reward for extended involvement. There are exceptions, of course, and careful diagnosis of the successful "change" schools has shown that they, in fact, were often ones in which authority and responsibility were delegated to lower levels. Participation has pay-offs. In the Partnership Model, individuals can participate on a much more equal basis if they have a framework in which to participate. OD can provide the framework, for it is through OD that schools with a concern for goals, conditions, elements, and leadership variables can make change theory a reality.

Furthermore, OD methods such as these have proven to be successful in schools. There is ample documentation of successful OD projects in the many references in the bibliography. Also, specific research studies on OD are regularly reported in *Group and Organization Studies: The International Journal for Group Facilitators.*[9]

Part III summarizes several significant bodies of research, theory, and practice related to OD in schools.

## ENDNOTES

1. Warren Bennis, *Beyond Bureaucracy* (New York: McGraw-Hill Book Co., 1973), pp. 119–120.
2. Ibid., pp. 207–208.
3. R. Beckard, *Organizational Development: Strategies and Models* (Reading, Mass.: Addison-Wesley, 1969), p. 9.
4. W. French and C. Bell, Jr., *Organization Development: Behavioral Science Interventions for Organization Improvement* (Englewood Cliffs, N.J.: Prentice-Hall, 1973), p. 15.
5. Richard I. Arends, Jane H. Phelps, and Richard A. Schmuck, *Organization Development: Building Human Systems in Schools* (Eugene, Ore.: Center for the Advanced Study of Educational Administration, no date), p. 10.
6. Robert T. Golembiewski, "Some Guidelines for Tomorrow's OD," in *Theory and Method in Organizational Development: An Evolutionary Process,* ed. John Adams (Arlington, Va.: NTL Institute for Applied Behavioral Science, 1974), p. 85.
7. Robert Jones, Consultant, University Associates, Publishers and Consultants, 7596 Eads Avenue, La Jolla, California 92037.
8. Jon H. Barrett, *Individual Goals and Organizational Objectives: A Study of Integration Mechanisms* (Ann Arbor: Institute for Social Research, University of Michigan, 1970).
9. N. Margulies, P. Wright, & R. Scholl, "Organization Development Techniques: Their Impact on Change," pp. 428–448; and L. Pate, W. Neilsen, & P. Bacon, "Advances in Research on Organization Development: Toward A Beginning," pp. 449–460. *Group and Organization Studies* 2 (December 1977).

# Chapter 10

# Into Action

A basic strategy for improving schools in an Age of Slowdown has now been introduced. The focus of change is the local school building organization in terms of its individual and group goals, products and processes, and formal and informal structures. To overcome the natural resistance to change in the local school organization, we have recommended organization development techniques making use of partnerships between the local school management, teachers, a local college, and a state department of education. Now we turn to the question of translating these recommendations into action. First, steps for forming partnerships will be discussed. Next, procedures for performing an organizational diagnosis will be presented. Finally, the three stages of planned change—initiation, implementation, and integration—are introduced.

## FORMING PARTNERSHIPS

Although the circumstances and procedures will differ in each individual case, there are some obvious steps to be taken in implementing the strategy of organization development through partnerships. The first of these is to investigate the formation of a partnership to initiate the process of planned change.

Any interested person can start the process, but those who hold responsibilities in one of the cooperating institutions are the most logical initiators. Sometimes, elements of a partnership already exist in the form of a teacher center, a school building planning committee, or an in-service education program. Otherwise, the occasion for establishing a partnership may arise from some local problems, such as low achievement scores, desegregation, or retrenchment. Or, an opportunity may come from federal, state, or school district initiatives or programs.

Whatever the starting point, the partnership must gain serious commitments from its members and the organizations they represent. Such commitments can begin in a simple willingness to explore possibilities, but soon must move to commitments of resources, at least in terms of time and energies of key people. Remembering that collaboration succeeds when members reach either individual or mutual goals, those forming the partnership must search for a solid reciprocal arrangement among the partners. Each partner must have a genuine expectation not only of contributing but also of *gaining* from participation. Among the possible goals individuals might have in forming a partnership are:

1. School building administrator
   a. Obtain a more effective and/or efficient school
   b. Solve persistent problems in the school

    c. Improve staff relationships

    d. Satisfy demands of parents or students

    e. Secure staff training resources

    f. Direct staff training toward school improvement goals

    g. Establish a mechanism to exert personal leadership

    h. Update curriculum expertise

2. Teacher or teacher organization

    a. Improve teaching conditions (quality of work life)

    b. Improve relationships among teachers or between teachers and students

    c. Improve relationships between teachers and school administration

    d. Solve persistent teacher problems

    e. Secure in-service training

    f. Have a voice in planned change

    g. Secure time and resources for teachers to improve programs

    h. Job advancement

3. College educator

    a. Secure a place to try out new ideas

    b. Obtain opportunities to do research

    c. Obtain students for courses and programs

    d. Obtain sites for student teachers or interns

    e. Develop new ideas for research

    f. Gain first-hand knowledge of the schools as they are today

    g. Recruit applicants for administrative training

4. State department personnel

    a. Pilot new materials or methods for the state

    b. Implement new programs with high priority at the state level.

    c. Obtain local reactions to state policies and programs

    d. Implement federal programs that are coordinated at the state level.

    e. Build good relationships with local school personnel

    f. Inform local educators about state regulations and resources

    g. Discover problems needing attention at the state level.

    h. Provide leadership for exemplary educational programs in the state

As potential partners and the basis for their participation are identified, the roles and responsibilities of each need to be determined, at least in a preliminary way. A common procedure is developing a written partnership agreement that outlines the goals of the partnership and the roles and responsibilities of each member. It may be that nothing fancy or legal is required, but just enough to secure discussion and mutual agreement at the start. On the other hand, a formal agreement signed by each party may serve to clarify matters and secure definite commitments from each participant. This is often the case in establishing teacher centers, where matters of governance are at issue. Such issues are best clarified at the start. A sample of such an agreement is given in Appendix E.

Our suggestion for a partnership group or committee calls for meetings not just of bodies but also of minds. Therefore, opportunities must be provided for members of the partnership group to become acquainted with one another, to share views, and to develop working relationships, group goals, and norms. As indicated in later chapters on tactics, we believe that organization development processes can find application in the partnership group itself. In fact, a good start for a partnership group might be an orientation to group process and organization development strategies.

Another crucial step in forming a partnership is establishing an advisory committee. Sometimes a school advisory committee already exists. If not, one should be formed. Such a group should represent the various different groups of parents and students in the school, not just one element. The specific role of the advisory group should be made clear at the start. Advisory committees take a long time to organize and become a functioning group. Therefore, an early start is needed to give the members of such a group the feeling that they have been involved from the beginning. Many times, advisory groups are formed at the last minute during a crisis, and the participants may believe they are serving as a "rubber stamp." This must be avoided.

## ORGANIZATIONAL DIAGNOSIS: PRELUDE TO ACTION

As a partnership group becomes oriented to its task and begins to function as a group, it must soon grapple with the question, "What kind of an organization do we have?" Because successful change projects arise from organizational needs (i.e., disequilibrium), successful planned change begins with attempts to assess needs and problems. Also, as has been argued, significant change means a change in the organization. Therefore, a preliminary analysis of the organization serves as a background for planning strategies to meet organizational needs and to move toward new equilibrium states. This procedure is referred to as organizational diagnosis.

Organizational diagnosis, as the beginning of an organization development effort in a local school, reflects the importance and value of action research. Above all else, organizational diagnosis involves research on the local school organization that is directed toward decision making and action. It is directed toward identifying a need or problem and developing a theory to help meet the need or solve the problem. The theory, in the form of an action plan, leads to an intervention in the organization. Information about the results of the intervention are then collected, analyzed, and evaluated. On the basis of this new information, the original diagnosis and theory may be revised and the intervention modified accordingly. This OD Loop, which was discussed in the previous chapter, is a continuous process during organization development.

To start the process, an organizational diagnostician turns to data survey and feedback techniques. There are four major methods in common use: questionnaires, interviews, observation, and documentation.[1]

*Questionnaires* collect quantifiable data about the organization. They are generally easy to administer and, because they are interpreted quantitatively, may provide convenient data for decision-making purposes. They may be previously prepared or constructed on site.

*Interviews* are the best method of making judgments about specific individuals and their perceptions of the organization. They uncover information, feelings, attitudes, and complaints that might not otherwise surface when using questionnaires.

*Observations* can be helpful particularly in earlier stages if the observer is trained and can be objective. We suggest that the role of any observer be explained to the faculty and that the observer be clearly identified.

*Documentation* is the process of reviewing and synthesizing information that appears to have meaning to the organization development procedures. Usually, documentation includes a review of existing historical records as well as current information. Demographic data, for example, is often available and pertinent.

Earlier we spoke of the importance of the variables of the organization in school improvement (goals, conditions, elements, and leadership). Organizational diagnosis in a partnership school should focus on these same variables. Three procedures for collecting data about the variables will be explained: prepared commercial instruments, locally-constructed questionnaires, and locally-conducted interviews.

**Prepared Questionnaires.**   A partial list of commercially-prepared instruments is included in Appendix B. The advantages of prepared instrumentation are that they have been tried and found useful. In some cases normative information is available to use in comparing the school with others. However, many of these instruments do not provide good comparative data and, because the instrument may not match the needs of the local organization, change agents are usually advised to construct their own or use an interview technique.

**Locally-Constructed Questionnaires.**   The advantage of the locally-constructed questionnaire is that those who design the questionnaire tend to value the results. It is therefore easier to implement action plans based on the data collected. Also, in generating local instruments the partnership school can concentrate on the variables that are crucial to the change process in the local setting. The following are sample categories and topics that could be formed into specific questions on a locally-prepared questionnaire.

*Individual Goals/Needs*
- long-term personal goals
- short-term (annual) objectives
- perceived discrepancies between individual goals and organizational goals
- prescribed roles and role elaborations
- relationships with my working team

- relationships with other peers
- motivational aspects such as salary, facility, equipment
- sources of stress in my work life
- my chances of advancement
- how do I know if I am doing a good job
- am I growing professionally

### Organizational Goals
- long-term organizational goals
- short-term (annual) objectives
- desired product outcomes
- perceptions of effectiveness
- evidence of effectiveness
- structural mechanisms
- relationship to the outside environment
- future directions for the organization
- what needs changing

### Process Variables
- efficiency
- relationships; subordinate/superordinate
- morale
- conflict management
- boredom/excitement components
- decision-making practices
- signs of fights for turfdom
- trust
- loyalty
- communication systems
- school climate
- emotional tone
- energies

### Task/Product/Structure Variables
- efficacy
- school site, building, grounds
- equipment, facilities, supplies
- standardized test scores
- financial state
- budget considerations
- grade point average
- personnel procedures
- signs of student achievement
- policies
- student awards and recognitions
- rules

- cycles, seasons, timing
- schedules
- employment records
- job descriptions
- college admissions
- committees
- parent satisfaction
- student/parent involvement

Once the diagnostician, in collaboration with the partners, selects the topics, an instrument or questionnaire can be created that speaks to the needs of this particular school. The steps in creating an instrument can be worked out for each organization.

Jones[2] recommends a series of small steps that increase ownership and validity in the instrument.

1. Establish a theory base.
2. Interview sample.
3. Write an open-ended form.
4. Administer, collate.
5. Write an "objective" form.
6. Administer form to sample.
7. Interview respondents.
8. Write a "final" form.
9. Survey, administer.
10. Feed the data back.
11. Revise the form.

This questionnaire construction process follows an action research methodology. One starts with a theory or an assumption about the organization. This theory base might be general or quite specific—as in the case of a problem to be solved, such as discipline.

Jones also recommends initial formal chats with people to get a sense of some of the expressed problems and, from this information, open-ended questions can be written. These are administered, usually to a random sample because collating may be time-consuming on open-ended questions to a large group. For example, asking why students misbehave may produce some rather lengthy responses.

Once the responses to the open-ended form have been analyzed, the diagnostician should feel free to construct the first objective form, which should serve as a pilot form. However, it may be feasible to administer this form to the faculty immediately. After respondents have completed the questionnaire, the data must be analyzed. It is possible that the form will be revised continuously.

Once the questions have been determined, a format for scaling questionnaire responses should be adopted. Some major scaling formats are summarized by Jones,[3] and some examples of each follow:

1. *Likert.*  The discipline in the school is the most important issue we face.  Strongly agree ( )   Agree ( )   Undecided ( )
   Disagree ( )   Strongly Disagree ( )
2. *Points.*  Indicate the relative seriousness of the following discipline problems by dividing 10 points among them.

   ____ hall behavior                         ____ school bus behavior
   ____ cafeteria behavior                     ____ classroom behavior

3. *Ratings.*  On a scale of 1 to 10, with 10 being the highest possible rating, how do you rate our discipline system?

   1  2  3  4  5  6  7  8  9  10

4. *Rankings.*  Rank the following punishments that you think are the most effective with (1) being the least effective.

   Spanking
   Detention
   In-school detention
   Grade reduction
   Calling parents
   Conference with teacher
   Conference with counselor

5. *Semantic Differential.*  How would you describe the principal's approach to discipline? (Place an "x" in the appropriate space.)

   Weak____:____:____:____:____:____:____ Strong

6. *Check Lists.*  Our parents support the school discipline policies (check one).

   100%____                                    20%____
    80%____                                     0%____
    50%____

**Interviews.**  Perhaps the most important method of collecting data is the *sensing interview.*

The sensing interview can be accomplished by internal or external consultants, or by trained employees, or combinations of the three. Either selected (random or representative) personnel or everyone in the organization can be interviewed. The latter is recommended and can easily be accomplished by training teachers to interview other teachers. Interviews should be thorough, guided by basic questions, and kept anonymous. However, summary results are made public. Some of the steps to consider are as follows:

- Deciding what questions are going to be asked
- Training the interviewers (if necessary)
- Informing the employees of the purpose of timing of the interviews
- Preparing the client
- Setting the stage
- Collecting the data
- Closing the interview
- Synthesizing the data
- Publicizing the results
- Developing action plans

The prepared questions are designed to collect open-ended responses, and the interviewer should feel free to explore areas that might be important even if they were not part of the question outline. In general, the questions should center around the variables—goals, conditions, and elements of the organization.

After the data are collected (regardless of method) there needs to be an analysis and diagnosis of the data and a follow-up. There are three major ways of disseminating the data. They are the waterfall, top-down and simultaneous methods.[4]

The *waterfall* method gives everyone in an organization all of the information but at different times. For example, the principal sees it first, passes it along to the partnership group, assistant principals, teachers, parents, and students, in that order.

The *top-down* process follows a hierarchical system as in the waterfall but at each step the information is screened and selected for the next step. This method is most expedient for large organizations but is not recommended for a partnership school.

In the *simultaneous* method everyone sees all the information at the same time. Although the simultaneous method is preferred, it entails logistical problems of presenting data in a form that is understandable to everyone. This method may also present some unnecessary information to certain groups and thus tend to be boring or contain wasted effort.

When data have been shared, they need to be analyzed and a tentative diagnosis of organizational needs and problems made. Both analysis and diagnosis should involve as many members in the organization as possible so that the diagnosis "belongs" to everyone. A variety of procedures may be used for this purpose. If possible, consensus procedures should be followed to identify areas of wide agreement. Ample opportunity should be provided for minority viewpoints to be expressed and taken into account. Opportunities should be provided for reactions to group decisions so that no one feels "railroaded."

The partnership group in our model may be particularly useful in pulling together the data, the group analysis, and reactions. For one thing, members of the partnership group include persons internal and external to the organization. Also, the partnership group can secure input from parents and students. In presenting the summary of the organizational diagnosis to members of the organization, they can speak from a variety of perspectives. Usually, the results of an organizational diagnosis should be put in writing and presented in a formal meeting to members of the organization with opportunities for comment and discussion. As indicated earlier, the diagnosis is tentative, a theory to be tested, and the organization is merely beginning a process of continuous feedback about its efforts to renew itself.

## STAGES OF PLANNED CHANGE

When an organization has formulated a statement of its own needs or problems, it has already begun the process of planned change. This process, if successful, will result in an organization that is new and different in some significant way. Although the specific outcomes of the process are always uncertain, there appear to be certain stages in this self-renewal process. A brief introduction to these stages should be helpful at this point.

After an extensive review of available literature (see Bibliography), we have selected over twenty-five descriptive theories of the process of organizational change. Although the theories vary in detail, there is agreement that stages do exist and that such stages are significant to those seeking to foster change. To summarize the views of these theorists, we have identified three major stages of planned change: initiation, implementation, and integration. Although different terms are used by different theorists, almost everyone recognizes these broad stages in the change process.

**Initiation.** During the first phase of organization development, needs are assessed, problems identified, and goals established. Many theorists emphasize, as we do, the need for research and data gathering as a basis for organizational diagnosis. Often, this is a stage where organizational priorities must be established.

The stage of initiation is also the place where action plans are developed and decisions made about how problems are to be solved or improvements made. In discussions about educational innovation this may be referred to as "adoption," in which case a particular innovative practice is selected for use. In any event, decisions are made about what and how to change.

**Implementation.** As has been noted, a common problem in educational change is that decisions to change are not backed up by effective implementation activities. Some concepts of planned change emphasize the need to try out or pilot new practices, often on a small scale, before widespread use. During a trial phase the new practices and procedures may be altered to fit the local setting. Also, personnel may need a development phase in which they can acquire the skills needed to install a new practice. Because educational innovations are usually complex and people-oriented, the local school organization itself may need to change in order to accommodate a new practice or procedure. Thus, the implementation stage may be viewed as a stage of mutual adaptation, in which a new practice and the existing school organization both change.

**Integration.**   The third stage of planned change usually denotes a time in which a new practice becomes "standard procedure." In experimental projects, this may come as a decision to continue trial procedures that have been found to be successful. Often, this decision arises at the end of a period of special funding when a grant terminates. Or, the integration stage is a stage where the organization reaches a new equilibrium with new structures, roles, and norms in place. This point may be indistinct because changes often are evolutionary in nature. Some aspects of an action plan will prove successful and remain; other aspects of the plan will disappear or be discarded.

Theoretical models of the change process often emphasize the role of evaluation at this stage. Have the new practices proved to be successful? Have the goals been achieved? Sometimes, reports of formal summative evaluations are considered with a clear decision about continuation. More often, the accummulated impressions of success or the degree of acceptance of the new practices by members of the organization determine the extent to which a planned change effort is integrated into the long term life of the organization.

As indicated in Figure 10-1, the three stages form a cycle of planned change with a new initiation phase growing from the end of the previous stage. The diagram is meant to emphasize the "ever-flowing stream of change" in which an organization passes through successive equilibriums—growing, changing, and evolving.

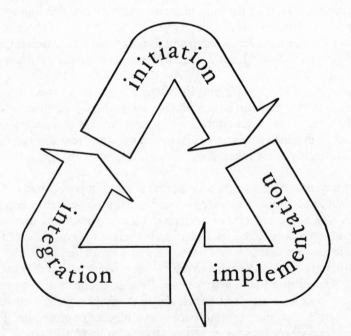

**FIGURE 10-1.   Stages of Planned Change for School Improvement**

It should also be noted that these stages of planned change represent broad generalizations about a process that varies greatly in each particular application. Likewise, those who study organization development have proposed somewhat different strategies to be employed in helping organizations use this process for self-renewal. Therefore, we have avoided making a single prescription for change, deciding instead to select four alternative models that seem promising as guides for organizational development through partnerships. These are presented in Part III.

## ENDNOTES

1. D. G. Bowers and J. L. Franklin, *Data Based Organizational Change* (La Jolla, Calif.: University Associates, 1977).
2. John E. Jones, "Clinic IV, Organization Assessment and Diagnosis," (unpublished clinic materials, University Associates, La Jolla, Calif., 1975).
3. Ibid.
4. Adapted from presentation by Anthony J. Reilly, Consultant, University Associates, at an Organization Development Clinic in September, 1975, Boston.

## SUMMARY OF PART II

A general model of organization development through partnerships has been presented. Emphasis is given to the individual school organization as the optimum focus for change because: (1) the diversity of school communities makes each school unique, (2) the individual school operates as a social unit, (3) traditions of local control of schools continue to be strong, (4) successful innovation requires a local implementation process, and (5) change targets larger than the local school building may spread resources for change too thin.

Changing the local school requires close attention to certain key organizational variables, including (1) individual and organizational goals, (2) process and product conditions, (3) formal and informal organizational structures, and (4) leadership.

General concepts of intellectual, social, and individual change were discussed as a background to the *discrepancy model,* in which organizational change is viewed as arising from a discrepancy between *what is* and *what is desired.* This is the beginning step in the process of planned change. Sensing and defining organizational needs in these terms becomes the basis for choosing systematic strategies to meet organizational needs.

Concepts of Organization Development (OD) were presented as a general framework from which to view change. OD was described as a set of practices characterized by the following common themes: (1) active participation by members of an organization in the total process of organizational change, (2) high priority given to choices made by individuals within an organization, (3) emphasis on action research to provide objective data to be considered by members of the organization, and (4) focus on organizational process as a key element in successful change.

Recommendations were given for using the OD macro-model in connection with partnerships for local school improvement. Suggestions were made for forming a partnership and conducting a preliminary organizational diagnosis. The stages of planned change—initiation, implementation, and integration—were described as a prelude to a discussion in Part III of alternative strategies that may be used to move a local school organization through stages of change.

# PART II  DISCUSSION QUESTIONS

1. The concept of school site management means that considerable autonomy must be given to the individual school. What are some economic, cultural, and educational problems that can best be solved at the level of the local school site?

2. Organizational efficiency and effectiveness necessitate that a delicate balance be maintained between the goals of the organization (nomothetic) and those of the individual (idiographic). What techniques can be employed by the school principal to facilitate the goals of the school and, at the same time, create a climate conducive to the self-actualization of members of the teaching staff?

3. Theories of change based on the concepts of equilibrium-disequilibrium have been challenged by some as "nongrowth" models since the direction of change is viewed as "back toward a state of well-being or well-functioning." How can "equilibrium" models explain growth?

4. A key factor in OD is the internal or external change agent who facilitates the renewal process within the organization. What personal characteristics (knowledge, skills, attitudes) should a change agent possess to be effective?

## SUGGESTED READINGS

Beckhard, Richard and Harris, Reuben T. *Organizational Transitions: Managing Complex Change.* Reading, Mass.: Addison-Wesley Publishing Company, 1977.

French, Wendell L. and Bell, Cecil H., Jr. *Organization Development,* 2nd ed. Englewood Cliffs, N.J.: Prentice-Hall, Inc., 1978.

Lassey, William R. and Fernandez, Richard R., eds. *Leadership and Social Change.* La Jolla, Calif.: University Associates, Inc., 1976.

Leonard, George B. *The Transformation: A Guide to the Inevitable Changes in Humankind.* Cambridge, Mass.: Schenkman Publishing Company, 1972.

Varney, Glenn H. *Organization Development for Managers.* Reading, Mass.: Addison-Wesley Publishing Company, 1977.

Zaltman, Gerald and Duncan, Robert. *Strategies for Planned Change.* New York: John Wiley and Sons, 1977.

# PART III

# ORGANIZATION DEVELOPMENT STRATEGY OPTIONS

# INTRODUCTION TO PART III

An excellent resource exists for educators in the record of recent efforts to improve American schools. From this record the authors have chosen four bodies of experience that fit current conditions. Each is summarized in a model that suggests strategies for moving a particular school or group of schools through the stages of organization development. Each model rests on a significant body of research, theory, and practice, and is well described in published sources.

Ronald G. Havelock's Linkage Model represents a synthesis of educational change efforts through the 1960s. The work is based on a review of over 1,000 published sources and extensive original research. Innovation is described as a process of linking knowledge producers to knowledge users. A variety of tactics are recommended at different stages of the change process, which is described in terms of steps in problem solving by a "user system."

Richard A. Schmuck's Organization Development in Schools includes a systematic program of theory, research, and practical application in trying to build self-renewing schools. The self-renewing school, according to Schmuck, is a humanized school characterized by feelings of trust, warmth, openness, and informality. Schools may become more humanized through OD interventions conducted by process consultants. A variety of laboratory training techniques are used with school personnel to help bring about this change.

John I. Goodlad's Responsive Model of Educational Improvement summarizes extensive efforts to join local schools in networks whose purpose is to encourage each member school to become self-renewing. Leadership for a network is often provided by a college, but the emphasis is on developing capabilities in each school for solving local problems. This model is the basis for an extensive national effort to implement Individually Guided Education.

The fourth model is the Rand Change Agent Study Model, which grew from a comprehensive research study of federal programs in support of educational change. The Change Agent Study Model places particular emphasis on local implementation efforts as a necessary ingredient in successful school improvement. The model contains specific suggestions for policies and procedures that can be used at the local level to encourage planned change.

Each model is discussed in relationship to current educational conditions and to the Partnership Model proposed in this book.

# Chapter 11

# Ronald G. Havelock's
# Linkage Model

Beginning in 1966, Ronald G. Havelock and his colleagues at the Center for Research on Utilization of Scientific Knowledge (CRUSK) at the University of Michigan undertook major studies of educational innovation and change. After an exhaustive survey of literature, Havelock summarized and integrated information from 1,000 key sources in his report to the U.S. Office of Education.[1]

## THREE STRATEGIC ORIENTATIONS

Havelock identified three principal "strategic orientations" toward innovation in education: (1) research, development, and diffusion (RD and D), (2) social interaction, and (3) problem solving.

The *RD and D* orientation was characterized by an emphasis on a systematic and controlled process of innovation with an orderly sequence from basic research through product development to mass dissemination. Substantial investments in basic and applied research were worthwhile, in this view, because a high quality product would improve the educational efficiency of a great many educational consumers.

A second strategic orientation identified by Havelock was the *social interaction* orientation. This perspective, which emphasized the process by which new practices are diffused through a social system, was supported by extensive work in rural sociology and agricultural extension. The social interaction orientation focuses on individual users or adopters of an innovation. Adoption or use is heavily influenced by an individual's place in a network of social relationships. Therefore, informal personal contacts and group memberships are especially significant to the innovation process, which proceeds slowly at first but more rapidly as an innovation "catches on" in particular groups. Characteristic strategies of this orientation are attempts to influence opinion leaders, mass dissemination of innovative practices, and the development of communication networks.

The third strategic orientation is *problem solving,* which includes those in the group dynamics and organization development frameworks. The emphasis in this orientation is on the problem-solving process of the user. Innovation begins in a need or problem of the user who seeks outside resources in diagnosing problems, designing solutions, and applying solutions. External consultants or change agents are often used in this approach. Many of the suggestions in this book fall into the problem-solving category proposed by Havelock.

## THE LINKAGE MODEL

Havelock found a common theme in the various strategic orientations in the concept of *linkage*. As pictured in Figure 11–1, educational innovation involves both user and resource systems. The starting point for educational change is in the problem-solving process of the user. Crucial to the process of change is the ability of the user to search for and find relevant knowledge that can be applied to the user's problems. The availability of useful information, in Havelock's view, is dependent upon a resource system that is effectively linked to the user system. The resource system must have information about user problems in order to retrieve or develop appropriate knowledge. Also, the resource system must be linked to the user to transmit possible solutions to the user's problems. A successful resource system is able to simulate the user's situation, proceeding through a cycle of diagnosis, search, retrieval, fabrication of solution, dissemination, and evaluation. Thus, knowledge is created that applies to the problems of users.

Notice that the basic process is one of knowledge transfer, in which knowledge producers are linked to knowledge users. It is a two-way process of linkage so that knowledge production is guided by user problems and knowledge use is facilitated by relating knowledge to problems of the user. Analysis of the knowledge transfer process is made in terms of *who* transfers *what* knowledge *how* (by what channel or medium) to *whom* for *what purpose*.

In applying his linkage model, Havelock suggested that a change agent draw upon the several strategic orientations to suit the particular situation, including the characteristics of the change agent, the client system, the innovation itself, and the available media for communication.

Detailed suggestions were developed and presented in *The Change Agent's Guide to Innovation in Education*,[2] which is a highly recommended source for readers of this book. Various strategies and tactics are related to the stages of change, as follows:

1. *Building a relationship.*  The first stage is establishing a good relationship between the change agent and the clients, or users. Good relationships include reciprocity, openness to new ideas, realistic expectations, clarity, equal power, low threat, and willingness to confront differences.
2. *Diagnosis.*  The change agent helps the clients identify problems and opportunities with particular attention to understanding the client as a system. What are the system's goals? Are there adequate structures for achieving goals? Are communication channels open? Does the system have the capacity to achieve desired goals? Are members rewarded for working toward system goals?
3. *Acquiring relevant resources.*  A crucial step in innovation is acquiring information and other resources related to each step of the client's change process. These include resources for diagnosis, awareness, evaluation before trial, trial, evaluation after trial, installation, and maintenance. Emphasis is given to building a permanent capacity for resource acquisition.

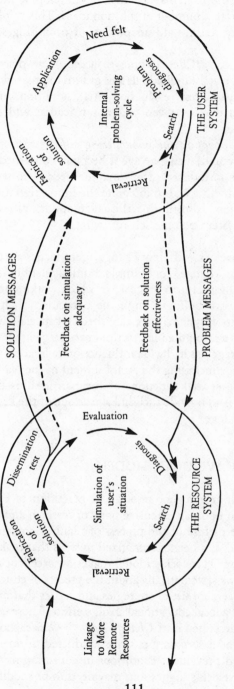

**FIGURE 11–1. Havelock's Linkage View of Resource-User Problem Solving** Ronald G. Havelock, *The Change Agent's Guide to Innovation in Education* (Englewood Cliffs, N.J.: Educational Technology Publications, 1973), p. 166.

111

4. *Choosing the solution.*   This stage includes developing implications from research to generate a number of solution ideas. This is followed by a period of feasibility testing and adaptation of promising solutions to the local situation.

5. *Gaining acceptance.*   Clients come to accept new practices gradually. Change agents can assist individuals and groups to proceed through awareness, preliminary interest, evaluation, trial, adoption, and integration. Special attention may be given to opinion leaders and to problems in group acceptance.

6. *Stabilizing the innovation and generalizing self-renewal.*   As a new practice becomes accepted, a change agent becomes concerned about the stability of changes introduced. Steps may be needed to secure continued support for the changes and to integrate the innovation into the structure of the organization. Also, during this stage opportunities are present to help the client system become self-renewing.

According to Havelock, different change agent tactics are appropriate depending on the stage of change. For example, human relations laboratory training might be especially useful in Stage 1, in which working relationships are established. Or, network building might be particularly helpful at Stage 3 when resource acquisition systems are established. Of special interest is the importance of *linkage* as a recommended tactic at *each* stage of Havelock's model. This emphasis on linkage has had wide influence on federal programs to stimulate educational change including the establishment of the National Diffusion Network. One of the central functions of the partnerships that are recommended in this book is to provide such linkage as one of the key ingredients in successful planned change.

## EVALUATION OF HAVELOCK'S MODEL

Havelock's Linkage Model is a good resource for practitioners. Havelock and his colleagues have drawn upon an extensive body of research and practice to present a comprehensive picture of the process of planned change in education. Furthermore, the work has been summarized in ways that make it convenient for practitioners to use. Havelock's model makes an excellent introduction to those who wish to think systematically about the process of educational change, and it contains a convenient list of strategies and tactics that may be useful in the different stages of a local educational change effort. Those using Havelock's model, especially as described in *A Change Agent's Guide,* should remember, however, that the model summarizes work conducted during the 1950s and 1960s. As emphasized previously, conditions in education have changed dramatically, so that Havelock's suggestions may need to be modified to suit new conditions.

For example, a major contribution of Havelock is the emphasis on linkage. The importance attached to the connections between user problems and resources for solutions is *still* critical, perhaps even more so than during the former period. In fact, one might criticize Havelock's model for being weak on practical suggestions to improve such linkage. The model appears to assume a forceful (and usually external) consultant plus a client system that is prepared to organize and sustain a complex series of actions. These important ingredients may be missing. Such problems are particularly pressing now when educational resources are scant and retrenchments are common. Hiring an external consultant to work over an extended period of time may be difficult or impossible. Likewise, many schools are especially weak in the organizational qualities that are necessary to devise, support, and sustain the complex program of innovation. The formation of a partnership group is recommended to remedy these difficulties by linking local schools to knowledge resources and by providing leadership for change. Successful change does not rest on a single external consultant or on substantial supplementary funds.

One strength of the Havelock model is the specific, practical advice on how to encourage schools to adopt specific innovative practices or products. This is particularly helpful to those working in the initiation stage of school improvement. The model is less helpful, however, in the stages of implementation and integration. Much of the literature that Havelock summarized dealt with the *adoption* of specific innovations in agriculture and industry. Much of the focus in that work was on the decision to adopt a given new practice. Since then, implementation has come to be recognized as a special problem in educational change efforts. Therefore, other strategic options may be more helpful at these later stages. For example, more emphasis may be needed on general structural changes in a school organization to accommodate new practices. Thus, a substantial effort in organization development may be needed. In general, Havelock's advice to change agents is short on strategies and tactics to make the local school a self-renewing organization.

Another weakness in the Havelock model might be called the "missing link" with students and parents. Although there is room in the model for consultation with these groups, the published recommendations do not emphasize this side of the innovation process. This is a serious omission; acceptance and support of new educational programs and practices by parents and students is crucial. In fact, parent cooperation may be required in order to implement desired changes. Therefore, linkage to parent or student groups throughout the change process is an essential addition to the Havelock model.

## A PARTNERSHIP EXAMPLE OF HAVELOCK'S LINKAGE MODEL

An example of how a partnership group might adapt Havelock's Linkage Model may be useful. Remember, this example is only suggestive; each local situation needs its own adaptation. Suppose a partnership group had formed and came to believe that Havelock's approach was compatible with the local situation. First of all, a partnership group might arrange a workshop to familiarize itself with Havelock's materials. One or more members of the group might take responsibility for devising such a workshop. Next, the partnership group might develop its special adaptation of the Havelock recommendations, devising a tentative plan of action for moving through Havelock's steps and choosing strategies and tactics from his suggestions. Quite possibly the partnership group could accept the change agent role, assigning elements of the role to different members of the partnership group.

An early priority, as suggested in this model, would be to establish relationships of confidence and trust between the partnership group and school personnel. Possibly, the partnership group would arrange an orientation to Havelock's model for the school staff and for an advisory committee of parents and students.

As the partnership group assisted the school organization to move into a diagnosis stage, the built-in linkages of the partnership to the school district administration, the teachers' organization, the local college, and the state department of education could provide a variety of perspectives to be documented and fed back to the total school community. The special expertise of each member of the partnership group could be utilized in the process. For example, the college professor might be helpful in designing an instructional model or instruments to gather data; the teacher representative might be particularly good at interviewing faculty members; the state education agency representative might have access to state-wide data systems; and the school-building administrator could arrange communication procedures to feed results back to the school community.

The partnership concept is especially useful in Havelock's stage of choosing solutions. Because of its diverse membership and linkages to resources, the partnership group could conveniently assemble implications from research, generate a wide range of solution ideas, and plan for feasibility testing of the most promising solutions. Members of the partnership group possess the abilities to monitor the results of pilot work and plan adaptations for wider utilization. Likewise, they should be in a good position to encourage acceptance of the proposed solutions by all members of the school community.

Finally, the partnership group combines the advantages of an internal and an external change agent. Because members of the organization itself belong to the partnership group, internal change agent resources are developed. These can provide a continuing presence that can help changes to become integrated in the organization and help the organization itself to continue self-renewal processes. Because others in the partnership are not members of the local school organization, the presence of "disinterested" parties is also helpful. This can provide an important source of objective feedback on local progress and maintain linkages to knowledge sources.

Taking Havelock's point of view about educational change as a process of knowledge transfer, the partnership group brings together knowledge producers and knowledge users in a way that fits Havelock's Linkage Model precisely, perhaps even better than in Havelock's own recommended tactics.

## ENDNOTES

1. Ronald G. Havelock, in collaboration with Alan Guskin. *Planning for Innovation Through the Dissemination and Utilization of Knowledge* (Ann Arbor: Institute for Social Research, University of Michigan, 1969).
2. Ronald G. Havelock, *The Change Agent's Guide to Innovation in Education* (Englewood Cliffs, N.J.: Educational Technology Publications, 1973).

Chapter 12

# Richard A. Schmuck's Organization Development in Schools

A major effort to apply organization development strategies in schools has been organized and conducted by Richard A. Schmuck and his associates. Spanning more than a decade, this work, which includes theory, research, and practical application, is documented in a variety of published sources. Principal works encompass a source book for OD work in schools that includes materials up to 1970,[1] *A Handbook of Organization Development in Schools,*[2] and *The Second Handbook of Organization Development in Schools.*[3] A convenient introduction to Schmuck's views are contained in Schmuck & Schmuck, *A Humanistic Psychology of Education.*[4] The work has continued at the Center for Educational Policy and Management at the University of Oregon, Eugene, where a variety of technical reports have also been published.

The central objective of organization development, according to Schmuck, is to build self-renewing schools. Such schools are continuously adapting to changes within the student body, the community, and the world, modifying procedures and organizational structures to provide effective education. Thus, the self-renewing school will be constantly monitoring and responding to changes in its environment and will be identifying and using a variety of resources to respond to these changes. Visitors to a self-renewing school should be able to see school personnel and students communicating openly, collaborating to solve problems, and making decisions cooperatively.

The emphasis in Schmuck's work is, therefore, on the school as an organization: its norms, goals, roles, communication networks, and patterns of power and influence. Furthermore, the self-renewing school organization is a humanized school that is characterized by feelings of trust, warmth, openness, and informality. A self-renewing school is person-centered. The goal of OD, according to Schmuck, is to change the culture of a school to be more self-renewing in these terms.

> OD offers the kind of consultation that encourages the members of a school to collaborate with one another to solve their own problems. In emphasizing system change rather than mere attitudinal changes in individuals, OD aims at modifying the culture of the school, and not just some of the feelings of the staff and students. To accomplish this cultural change, OD involves the school participants themselves in the assessment, diagnosis, and transformation of their own goals, a development of their own newly acquired group

117

skills, the re-design of their own structures and procedures for achieving the goals, the alteration of the working climate of their school, and the assessment of results.[5]

## OD INTERVENTIONS

Organization development in schools is conducted through one or more "OD interventions," which are managed by external or internal consultants. Usually, an external consultant begins the process, working directly with members of the organization to explore problems, design solutions, and implement changes. Often, according to Schmuck, OD interventions move through three sequential stages.

1. *Communication training.* Members of the staff participate in training sessions designed to increase open and effective communication, building such skills as restating another person's message, describing behaviors without interference, communicating feelings, and giving feedback. Opportunities are provided for members of the organization to practice communication skills in regular work groups and to apply them in problem-solving and decision-making activities.

2. *Development of norms for problem solving.* Once communication skills are improved, the OD training emphasizes the development of humanistic norms to support collaboration among staff and students. Members of the school organization are taught problem-solving steps that are applied to current school problems. In the process, new collaborative norms are encouraged.

3. *Changing organizational structures.* The result of problem-solving activities is the implementation of changes in practices and policies in the school. The OD intervention has, therefore, been completed only when new structures are integrated into the school organization.

Special emphasis is given in Schmuck's model to *process consultation*, as opposed to *content consultation*. In content consultation an expert may be hired to advise on methods of teaching reading, mathematics, or other subject matters. Or, a specialist may train school personnel in specific procedures, such as behavior modification. Although content consultation is invaluable, according to Schmuck, it does not replace the need for process consultation that is focused on organization development. The emphasis in OD is on the *how* of interpersonal relationships instead of the *what*, or content. The process consultation is designed to make members of the school more aware of the processes of communication, problem solving, and decision making. Then, these can be evaluated and improved. A central contribution of the consultant is to provide objective data for this evaluation so that members of the organization may "confront themselves." Discrepancies can be identified between processes as they currently exist and processes as organization members would like to see them. This is a fundamental lever for organizational change. Hence, process observation is a key component of this model.

Schmuck and Schmuck have described the qualities of interpersonal effectiveness that make for good process consultation. First, trust and rapport are important because a consultant must confront clients with discrepancies between actual performances and ideals. Social distance, on the other hand, is undesirable because it is usually accompanied by client defensiveness. The interpersonal behavior of a process consultant should be like a friend who understands, but who also cares enough to give honest, constructive criticism. Process consultants must therefore be skilled in conveying acceptance, support, and encouragement to the client. This may require the consultant setting aside personal preferences and desires in favor of those of clients.

Process consultants must themselves have the skills that are the objective of the organization development training. They must be experts in listening, probing, questioning, interviewing, clarifying, and confronting. Process consultants must also exemplify the values of a humanistic school, being guided by the assumptions that each person desires to develop more adaptive ways of coping with life and that all members of the school community have legitimate needs for personal growth within the school organization.

## LESSONS FROM OD INTERVENTIONS

Schmuck and his colleagues have conducted such OD interventions in a substantial number of schools, including elementary schools and junior and senior high schools. Several district-wide interventions have also been reported. Drawing upon their own experience and the experiences of colleagues elsewhere, Runkel and Schmuck[6] summarized some lessons that have been learned from this work. Among their conclusions are the following:

1. To improve the self-renewing capabilities of a school requires a well-organized conception of the change process and a workable plan of action. Both of these can be provided by consultation in organization development.

2. The results of field experiments indicate that OD can help school faculties to become more skillful in interpersonal communication, more helpful toward one another, and more willing to take personal risks. Not only can OD improve the quality of school meetings, but it can also increase the number of innovations attempted in a school. Evidence exists that OD interventions can improve decision making, as perceived by teachers, and raise school morale.

3. Organization development can also be ineffective, especially if there is a failure at the start to establish good relationships between the OD consultant and key authorities in the school. Likewise, care must be taken in the early stages to develop openness and trust between a school faculty and an OD consultant, making sure that clients fully understand the goals and procedures of the OD process. A full school year is an appropriate time period for a school to enter an organizational change program.

4. Success in organization development in schools depends upon bringing entire subsystems into the consultation (e.g., departments or school buildings) and upon support from the school district office for the efforts of individual schools. Support from the school building principal is an essential ingredient in OD interventions; without it, failure is likely.

5. Successful OD interventions are more likely when participants are willing to express disagreements, desire collaboration, and are agreed that the OD intervention is desirable. After entering the period of intervention, a school can make significant changes within a year, provided that substantial amounts of time are devoted to the process. Runkel and Schmuck recommend approximately 40 to 80 hours before school opens with an additional 80 to 120 hours distributed during the school year. Often, training activities can double as regular work sessions, but many additional hours are needed to make organizational changes.

6. The results of OD intervention are lasting. Changes in the operating norms and procedures in successful cases last at least several years. A successful cadre of internal consultants trained in OD work can maintain and enhance these changes for longer periods.

Also of interest are the observations of Schmuck, Arends, and Arends,[7] about the special attributes of school organizations that must be taken into account in applying OD strategies to schools. They note that many OD interventions have mistakenly assumed that training strategies successful in industrial settings can be directly applied to schools. Instead, three differences appear to be crucial. First, the goals of school organizations are markedly different from those of industrial firms. Many goals of school organizations may not be explicitly stated. Also, educational goals are diverse, with a constant shift in external pressures to emphasize one or another goal. Finally, explicit goals of schools take a long time to achieve, such that feedback on goal attainment is difficult to obtain. Unlike business firms whose profit goals may be singular, clear, and easy to measure, schools have many problems in the organization development process in identifying discrepancies and measuring goal attainment.

Another feature of schools that must be taken into account in OD interventions is the lack of differentiation in organization roles. Unlike industrial organizations, where well-differentiated teams of workers collaborate under the leadership of a middle manager, school staffs are organized into loose groupings (e.g., grade level or subject matter) of relatively autonomous roles at the same bureaucratic level. Norms of collaboration which may exist in industrial firms may not exist in schools. Teachers are not accustomed to having their daily work monitored, nor do they receive much feedback from peers or supervisors. These factors, which are crucial to success in implementing the OD strategy, require special attention in OD work in schools.

A third problem for OD intervention in schools is a tendency to manage schools in a "crisis orientation." Schools are quite vulnerable to short-term demands, often responding quickly to the latest fad or pressure. Education professionals appear to lack a base of professional status and expertise strong enough to sustain long-term development plans.

Schmuck, Arends, and Arends[8] proposed a number of guidelines for OD interventions in schools to provide for these special characteristics. The following summary has been adapted from their work in terms of suggestions to a consultant. The consultant should:

1. Continually reemphasize the goals of the OD intervention.
2. Build readiness for OD by helping to develop norms for collaboration.
3. Emphasize the need for sustained effort over many months to make OD interventions work.
4. Assess progress regularly and plan for recycling to reemphasize the processes of trust-building, goal-setting, and diagnostic information gathering.
5. Emphasize collaborative relationships with key authorities and involve all participants in the development of the intervention plan, making clear from the start the role of the consultant.
6. Emphasize from the beginning that a formal diagnosis will precede any training and that objective data on current conditions in the organization will be a primary ingredient in the OD process.
7. Use both formal and informal methods of data collection for diagnosis and feedback to clients who can then use it for further planning.
8. Adapt the content of training, data feedback, confrontation, and process consultation to the local situation, avoiding personal bias and preference in the design of training.
9. Create an overall design for the intervention to include short- and long-term intervention goals with opportunities for flexibility.

## EVALUATION OF SCHMUCK'S OD MODEL

If the analysis presented in this book is correct, organization development strategies are among the best avenues for school improvement at the present time. Therefore, Schmuck's OD in Schools deserves the most careful study by educators. Schmuck and his colleagues have collected the best theories and techniques from organization development work in a variety of institutional settings and adapted them to the particular characteristics of American schools in a systematic program of research and development. The fruits of this work are clearly described in published sources that give detailed suggestions to those engaged in organization development work in schools. *The Second Handbook of Organization Development in Schools*[9] is highly recommended to members of partnership groups.

When considering Schmuck's OD in schools as a strategy option, one should keep in mind its particular points of emphasis. The model's strength lies in attention to process dimensions of school organization: in interaction, in the formation of effective working teams, and in consultant interventions. The strategy emphasizes collaboration and places high value on openness of communication, trust, and faith in individual responsibility. The Schmuck model is especially well suited to schools that prize such humanistic values and desire to move in that direction.

Naturally, some schools might find other approaches more compatible. For example, some schools may want a model that emphasizes how a particular new practice may be adopted. Others may want strategies that place more emphasis on how conflict, power, risk-taking, and negotiations may play a part in change. There are other situations, too, in which the Schmuck model may not be useful; for example, a change in structure might not always be necessary or desired. Another problem is the heavy reliance on consultants. Certainly a well-skilled, respected, charismatic consultant can do wonders with a school when there is agreement as to OD outcomes. In the Age of Slowdown, however, there may not be money for projects such as those Schmuck describes. We believe that in-house consultants from a partnership may be more practical.

Despite its limitations, however, the Schmuck model is one of the best resources for OD work in schools, including the partnerships for school improvement that are recommended in this book.

## A PARTNERSHIP EXAMPLE OF SCHMUCK'S OD MODEL

How might Schmuck's organization development strategy be adapted to the Partnership Model? First, the partnership group itself can take on the role of process consultant if members have or can obtain the necessary skills and expertise. In this case, different members of the partnership group may be able to assume different aspects of the consultant role. Perhaps one member is experienced as a laboratory trainer in communication skills. Perhaps another is particularly good at devising action research instruments. Sometimes, of course, members of the partnership group are lacking in the experience and expertise necessary, and may undertake a program of training or seek to supplement their resources by using faculty from local colleges or the State Department of Education.

The partnership group can play a major role in working with the process consultant. This should be an aid to the external consultant because he or she has a ready-made steering committee with access to a variety of participant groups and resources. In such cases, the consultant might utilize the partnership group to build readiness for the OD intervention, participate in the organizational diagnosis, help develop an overall training design, and monitor the overall process in cooperation with the consultant.

Because the central goal of Schmuck's OD model is humanizing the climate of schools, the partnership group might begin by developing such a climate in its own operations. Thus, members of the partnership group might utilize a consultant to develop communication process, collaborative norms, and cooperative methods of decision making for the partnership group. In addition, attention could be given to developing interpersonal behaviors that are effective in helping relationships, so that the partnership group can provide better assistance to the client system.

Following Schmuck's OD intervention strategy, after a period of readiness development, an OD intervention would be made in the particular school. The training would be conducted in the three sequential stages: (1) communication training, (2) the development of norms for problem solving, and (3) attempts to change organizational structures. The partnership group could utilize published materials from Schmuck and his associates for specific ideas about training options and pitfalls to avoid. Contacts could be established with schools that had gone through OD interventions of this type to get first-hand advice on the process.

One modification of Schmuck's work that is suggested by the Partnership Model is the involvement of community input. Our analysis emphasizes the value of an advisory committee that includes parents or community representatives. The advisory committee to the partnership group might be an excellent device to build both parent and student involvement early in the OD intervention. Also, the committee could supply a continuing mechanism for obtaining progress feedback from these groups.

Schmuck's work may also be related to our three stages of organization development—initiation, implementation, and integration.

**Initiation Stage.**    The procedures for the initiation stage that need to be emphasized are:

1. Improving communications through repeated discussions and the use of consensus techniques for decision making.
2. Changing norms through problem solving and group development training.
3. Interventions in the interactions of people.

For example, in most successful situations, the initiation intervention comes from a charismatic leader—one who has power and control. This can still be a *modus operendi* in a partnership school, but the partnership members also represent authority and influence. Power struggles are reduced because the typical resistors to change, people who represent affiliations with various groups affected by such change, become part of the leadership. These affiliations are usually grouped as follows:

| *Group Resistors* | *Partnership Representation* |
| --- | --- |
| Teachers | Professional Organization |
| Parents | Local School District Citizen Advisory Groups |
| Administrators | Local School District Hierarchy |
| Students | Local Building Representation |
| School Board, State Dept. Personnel | Dept. of Public Instruction Personnel |

Representatives of these groups need to form leadership groups who provide intervention strategies. That is the most viable way to satisfy both individual and organizational goals. In fact, Schmuck recommends the use of similar leadership groups. He prescribes their duties as coordinating educational programs, keeping communication lines open, and maintaining contact with resources outside of school. A partnership/leadership team composed of representatives of the aforementioned groups could have considerable influence. Not only would their linkage be more comprehensive, but their interventions would have greater impact. We recommend leadership teams who have OD training and who are given intervention authority (not decision making in regard to actual changes). They can follow the Schmuck advice by sensing the readiness of the system for change, observing process, representing the subsystems (partners), and being responsible for the initiation stage of the change process. Clearly, the extent to which the intervenor represents the partners is related to the success of the project as perceived by the representatives of the partnership and the target school in general.

**Implementation Stage.**    The procedures in the second stage entail:

1. Completing interventions in the structure of the organization and in the differentiation of individual roles.
2. Establishing group agreements about solutions to problems because success is strongly influenced by client readiness and group cohesiveness.
3. Practicing new modes of interaction, emphasizing trust and truth.

Implementation involves increasing interaction levels and restructuring processes. From an organizational management point of view, schools have an unique boss-worker relationship. The typical elementary school has one principal and twenty to thirty teachers (autonomous decision makers in teaching and learning processes). The teachers are all on the same hierarchical level, have the same job descriptions, and enjoy a great deal of autonomy. Unlike many organizations there is very little job-oriented interaction that takes place. The conversation that does concern the organization tends to be on "trivial" matters. This supervisory ratio is unthinkable in business management theory. It is generally recommended that there be no more than seven workers to one boss. All of these unique features of the typical school-building organization are natural impediments to communication about real, professional educational concerns. Schmuck expands on this in his treatment of the differences in school OD and other kinds of OD.

Involving the staff in decision making, differentiating the staff roles, and developing staff teams are highly recommended ways of increasing the work-related human interaction in schools. This interaction will focus attention on teacher behavior and thus increase the chances of changing that behavior.

Partnerships are a useful way to develop transactions between organizations and people. The school as an organization can improve its "intra-transactions" through the partnership leader group suggested previously. The committee or task force offers an arena for conversation, planning, debate, conflict, and brainstorming—*interaction*. This could be envisioned as a center for operations managed by some prescribed combination of the various people in the organization. The group task could vary from attending graduate college seminars to a decision-making function. *The point to stress is the importance of providing the partners with an arena for interaction.*

The other kind of interaction that is so essential to school improvement is "inter-transactions." This applies to transactions between people and their parent organizations. This need for a people-to-people link is essential in a time of educational divisiveness. The teacher in an individual school needs and should demand linkage to his or her professional organization (AFT-NEA) that supplies welfare and worker-rights expertise. The same is true for administrators. A partnership affiliation extends to the representative professionals access to information, updating of skills, collaborative activities, staff development projects, and support for educational change. *If the individuals in a partnership school know that their professional ties are connected to a supraorganization that is also cooperating, their readiness for change will improve.* This is shown in Figure 12-1.

The partnership concept can be instrumental in encouraging and maintaining the various structural role changes that are highly recommended by Schmuck and others and are important in the implementation stage. Specific examples might be teaming and differentiating the staff. The subsystems of the teaching units need to be accessed by the partnership representatives. Changing to smaller work units provides this access because different jobs are created, one of which can have the special assignment of linking to other authority bases. Once the individual professional is given a forum for sharing with a team, access to new and more exciting techniques and schemes is on the way.

Partnership activities can help in this area by providing support. For example, most states have some form of unit allotment system to allocate teachers to a district or school based on the number of students attending that district. The state department of education, knowing the specific needs of differentiated staffing patterns, can arrange for special approval and sanctions for alternative staff allotment procedures which will increase differentiation. In most states, the state department of education policies for allocating impedes experi-

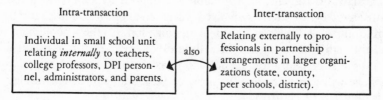

FIGURE 12-1.  Linking Interactions

mentation in staffing patterns. The state, county, or district personnel responsible for staffing assignments need to be involved in the school's planning. Once involved and committed, they can influence policy making and legislators to develop and approve optional patterns.

The teachers' unions and associations must obviously be involved. Many teacher organizations have resisted teaming and differentiated staffing because of the fear that it was a ploy to undermine union strength through "merit pay." If union or association representatives could be involved in planning, this concern could be eliminated.

Colleges of education can play a very supportive role in teaming, differentiated staffing, and other role changes by training personnel in the methods and techniques involved. They can also plan their teacher education programs around diverse staffing patterns by providing a range of undergraduate aides, junior-senior student teachers, senior-fifth year interns, graduate assistant team leaders and administrative interns for unit leaders and division directors.

**Integration Stage.**    Actual changes occur as a result of the previous steps. These specific changes are found in curriculum instructional techniques, pupil personnel policies, evaluation procedures, etc. The duration of these changes is directly related to several variables such as: (1) district office support, (2) the degree to which changes are fused with existing structures, and (3) the degree to which the new idea has been internalized.

The integration stage places emphasis on district office support. If external and internal change agents leave the school, the impetus dies and so will the innovation or change if not "carried on" by the more established authority of the district office. The innovation should start in the individual school but must be supported at the district level for long-term effects.

In the final stage of the partnership OD process, the school must concentrate on *integrating* the projects with the existing structure. In order for the integration stage to reach equilibrium for a "successful run," there is a need for melding the new with the old. Integration occurs when the idea is no longer visable or receiving special attention.

In order for a system to achieve the internalization of an idea, innovation, or project, it needs support from the total community. While district office and school board support is crucial for changes to have lasting impact, the same is true, perhaps to a lesser extent, regarding support by state education agencies and college personnel who lend credence to the projects.

Partnerships can insure reasonable integration by supplying a four-part support base: (1) the teachers involved will receive continual moral and psychological support from their professional organization, (2) the school board represented through its administration will be more apt to continue financial support, (3) the state education agency will be committed to the project, and (4) the college will lend continual support of personnel and of technology. This plan is depicted in Figure 12–2.

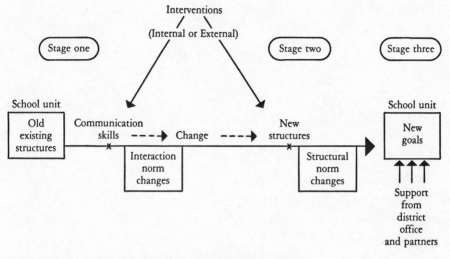

**FIGURE 12-2.    A Partnership Example of OD in Schools**

# ENDNOTES

1. Richard A. Schmuck and Matthew B. Miles, eds., *Organization Development in Schools* (Palo Alto, Calif.: National Press Books, 1971).
2. Richard A. Schmuck et al., *Handbook of Organization Development in Schools* (Palo Alto, Calif.: National Press Books, 1972).
3. Richard A. Schmuck et al., *The Second Handbook of Organization Development in Schools* (Palo Alto, Calif.: Mayfield Publishing Co., 1977).
4. Richard A. Schmuck and Patricia A. Schmuck, *A Humanistic Psychology of Education. Making the School Everybody's House* (Palo Alto, Calif.: National Press Books, 1974).
5. Ibid., p. 267.
6. Philip J. Runkel and Richard A. Schmuck, *Findings From the Research and Development Program on Strategies of Organizational Change at CEPM-CASEA* (Eugene, Ore.: Center for Educational Policy and Management, September, 1974).
7. Richard Schmuck, Jane Arends, and Richard Arends, *Tailoring Consultation in Organization Development for Particular Schools* (Eugene, Ore.: Center for Educational Policy & Management, October, 1974).
8. Schmuck, Arends, and Arends, *Tailoring Consultation,* pp. 6–22.
9. Schmuck et al., *The Second Handbook.*

# CHAPTER 13

# John I. Goodlad's Responsive Model of Educational Improvement

Another major strategy option has emerged from the work of John I. Goodlad and his colleagues in the Research Division of the Institute for Development of Educational Activities, Inc. (/I/D/E/A/), an affiliate of the Charles F. Kettering Foundation. From 1966 to 1972 they maintained a close relationship with eighteen schools in southern California in a League of Cooperating Schools in order to develop a change strategy focused on the total culture of the individual school. The results of this work, documented in a series of publications and films, contain excellent suggestions for those who are searching for ways to improve schools.

## BEHIND THE CLASSROOM DOOR

The League of Cooperating Schools grew out of Goodlad's long interest in the process of school improvement, and especially from an observational study of 158 classrooms in 67 elementary schools that he and his colleagues conducted in the late 1960s.[1] Expecting to see in school classrooms the results of educational reform efforts of the 1950s and 1960s, the researchers were dismayed and disappointed. Life in classrooms appeared not to have been affected at all by such educational innovations as individualized instruction, discovery learning, or new curricula. Even when school personnel thought they had introduced changes, there was a great gap between rhetoric and actual classroom events. Moreover, there was no evidence in schools of processes for bringing about desirable changes.

> What bothered us most was the apparent absence of processes by means of which the schools and the people in them might have some reasonable prospect for self-renewal. With the possible exception of four schools among the sixty-seven, they simply did not contain groups of responsible parties diligently at work on the problems teachers and principals said they faced. And there was not in any school, so far as we could see, a critical mass of people—principal, teachers, parents, children—committed to continuous analysis of what their school was for and what should be done to make it a better place of study and work today, next week, and the years to come.[2]

Drawing upon his earlier experiences in working with the Englewood School in Florida and the UCLA University Elementary School of which he was the Director, Goodlad developed the basic hypothesis for the Responsive Model:

> *That an effective change strategy is one through which the alternative best suited to the needs of a given institution come to the attention of those in it and are used in a continuous process of improvement.* Or, stated differently, an effective change strategy is one through which those within a given institution become responsive to what is required to assure institutional renewal and to outside resources most likely to expedite that renewal.[3]

In Goodlad's view, school improvement must focus on two complementary processes in a local school culture. An "inner" process must be developed so that members of the school culture are sensitive to the needs of the institution and recognize problems or discrepancies between ideals and realities. Also, there must be an "outer" process that can identify and utilize outside resources to solve problems, meet needs, and achieve goals.

## THE LEAGUE AND DDAE

The League of Cooperating Schools was established in 1966 to explore and refine Goodlad's working hypothesis. The UCLA School of Education, of which Goodlad was Dean, entered into an agreement with a variety of local school districts under sponsorship of /I/D/E/A/. The Central League Office at UCLA brought together the principal and other staff members from individual schools within each cooperating school district. Principals were brought together by Goodlad and his staff to develop a working program for the project. The result was a partnership in which college educators could conduct research and the individual schools could receive help in making local school improvements. What developed was a kind of "buddy" system, which Goodlad likened to a wheel. The League Office at UCLA was the hub with spokes reaching out to each of the participating schools. The rim of the wheel was a strong bond of mutual support among cooperating schools.

An important outcome of the League's activities was a system that could be employed to develop each school's ability to be self-renewing. Central to this process was a problem-solving process in which staff members addressed the needs and goals of their individual schools.

It should be emphasized that the League did not select any particular innovation in school organization or curriculum. Rather, the League promoted a particular process which was developed and refined over time. The process came to be summarized as DDAE, standing for dialogue, decision making, action, and evaluation.

*Dialogue* is a continuing process of interaction in which the entire school staff participates in discussions about the school organization, curriculum, and instruction. This dialogue occurs both formally and informally as the chosen method for dealing with concerns, issues, and problems.

*Decision making* is a process based upon staff involvement in dialogue. Alternative courses of actions are identified, weighed in terms of evidence, and selected for implementation.

*Action* is the process by which decisions are implemented, leading to more dialogue. In a self-renewing school such actions ought to affect basic characteristics of the school program.

*Evaluation* is a data-based process in which the staff assesses how well the school is carrying out its role. Explicit criteria are used to measure the results of decisions.

Four characteristics of the DDAE process came to be important indicators that a school was receptive to change. These were:

1. *Scope.* How widespread was the dialogue? How many people were participating in decisions? How extensive were the actions and evaluations?
2. *Importance.* Was the DDAE process simply window-dressing or were the dialogues, decisions, actions, and evaluations important to staff members?
3. *Relevance.* Was the dialogue part of integrated, continuing staff deliberations about the issues faced in operating the school or was the DDAE process fragmented, only dealing with matters peripheral to the main business at hand?
4. *Flexibility.* Was the DDAE process carried on in an atmosphere of experimentation? Were decisions flexible? Did evaluation contribute to the modification of future practice?

Although at first staff members from the Central League Office acted as consultants to help school staffs use the DDAE process in their schools, in the later stages of the League, school staff members helped one another to develop the DDAE process. The role of the Central staff became one of assessing local schools by means of questionnaires, the results of which were given to the local school staff as feedback. Thus, more and more the "rim of the wheel" provided the stimulus for developing the DDAE process in member schools. The Central office, or hub, thus became an intermediate agency to bring together local schools having something to offer one another and also to be a link between these schools and knowledge resources.

The part played by the League of Cooperating Schools in the process of improving each local school is instructive. The League grew away from the external consultant strategy to emphasize more and more the role of peer group support and idea exchange. A key concept in this process was "The Magic Feather Principle," a subtitle chosen for one of the League reports.[4] Remembering the story of Dumbo, the flying circus elephant, it seemed to be the case that local school staffs became self-renewing in a way similar to the way Dumbo learned to fly. Dumbo, who was born with oversized ears, began to fly only after a small mouse gave Dumbo a "magic feather" to convince Dumbo that the ears could be used as wings. Dumbo believed in the magic feather, tried his "wings," and flew. Later, when he dropped the feather, he found that he could still fly without its magic.

The League of Cooperating Schools as an organization encouraged "fliers" which was an important ingredient in its success. The support came not just from external consultants but, very importantly, from peers.

Looking back at the League of Cooperating Schools, Goodlad summarized the lessons learned as follows:

> First, it became strikingly clear that, to make any difference to what happens in the school-based learning of students, all the projects, research, work of specialists in state or local offices of education, and so on, ultimately must come to roost within the finite dimensions of a school day, week or year. Second, most of what goes on outside of and in the name of schools has little to do with their functions and never comes to roost there. Third, a good deal that does come to roost there is so irrelevant or inappropriate that it does more to impede than to aid school functioning. Fourth, with help and guidance from an informed, caring outside resource, school staffs can become extraordinarily aware of what is required to improve and discriminately selective in what they reach out for and bring into the school. Fifth, most inner-oriented change is directed to doing better what is assumed to be required of the school and, consequently, is well suited to refinement of practices. Sixth, the incentive to make fundamental changes seems to require awareness of pronounced discrepancies between existing programs and rather clear alternatives. Seventh, seriously attempting to do something about such discrepancies requires legitimization by a supportive surrounding infrastructure.[5]

## EVALUATION OF GOODLAD'S RESPONSIVE MODEL

The Responsive Model of Educational Improvement recommends itself particularly because it combines Goodlad's comprehensive scholarly knowledge about school reform with an intensive experimental project seeking to bring about change in schools. As such, the model summarizes more than two decades of systematic work on school improvement.

One strength of the model is its recognition of the difficulty of bringing about substantive change in school organizations. Furthermore, the limitations of external agencies who seek to install selected new practices in local schools is well understood and underlined. In particular, the Responsive Model recognizes the reality of the local school-building organization and its fundamental conservatism. The absence in the local school organization of structures to identify problems, seek alternative solutions, decide on action plans, and implement and evaluate plans is a fact of fundamental importance in understanding schools. That school improvement efforts need to develop such structures and processes is an absolutely crucial insight for change agents. Using the metaphor of "culture," Goodlad and his colleagues have suggested the character of changes that are required to transform a local school into such a self-renewing organization.

A related strength of the Responsive Model of Educational Improvement is the demonstrated power of external linkages to stimulate the necessary changes in a local school culture. College educators *can* provide dynamic leadership in local school improvement. Local districts *can* support idiosyncratic change in a local school. Networks of local schools *can* be created to give mutual assistance and support. The concept of a voluntary organization to provide mutual support is shown to be a feasible strategy for school improvement. The League of Cooperating Schools has been successfully replicated in the /I/D/E/A/ Change Program for Individually Guided Education (IGE). As mentioned in later chapters, hundreds of schools have joined such leagues, brought together by such intermediate agencies as colleges, state departments of education, or research and development units.

The Responsive Model of Educational Improvement is strong also in its flexibility. The League of Cooperating Schools developed its own programs of action, permitting adaptation of school improvement programs to local conditions, local personnel, and local needs.

Some limitations in the model do exist. For example, the League of Cooperating Schools was dependent upon special funding from /I/D/E/A/. Although the money must have been modest in comparison to many large federal programs, nevertheless a local school might have difficulty in finding the extra resources. Also, it is apparent that Goodlad himself was a central force in stimulating the success of the League. Persons with his expertise and commitment to practical change in schools are exceedingly rare. Even Dr. Goodlad recognized the need for a strong spark of enthusiasm and guidance as a rallying point for school staffs, especially in the beginning.

A final problem with using the Responsive Model is the lack of specific guidance on how to proceed in a given case. Although the DDAE process is very helpful, it is suggestive only in broad terms. Many persons will prefer a more explicit and detailed set of procedures as a guide for moving through the stages of school improvement.

## A PARTNERSHIP EXAMPLE OF GOODLAD'S RESPONSIVE MODEL

One application of Goodlad's model would be to create a League of Partnership Schools. One could imagine a college of education and a state department of education forming such a League. They might consider adding a representative from the state or local teachers' organization. Individual school principals could be brought together to set such a league in motion. One could see such a league moving in many directions, possibly toward the creation of a teacher center with emphasis upon regional service and self-help. Of course, the /I/D/E/A/ Change Program is itself an example of this partnership strategy for school improvement.

Another possibility for applying Goodlad's model exists in the local partnership structure that has been recommended in this book. In such a case, a local partnership groups concerns itself with a single school. The function of the partnership group is to stimulate self-renewal processes in the local school culture. The local partnership group might use the concepts and strategies developed in Goodlad's League of Cooperating Schools. Thus, the DDAE process might become the focus for change. The partnership group could perform such functions as introducing the process (or securing consultants to introduce it), providing support and encouragement for the school staff to engage in the process, and collecting data and giving feedback to members of the school staff on how well the process is functioning.

As the DDAE process goes forward, the partnership group provides linkages to knowledge resources that are used by the school staff in the problem-solving cycle. The focus, however, is on developing the necessary structures and processes in the local school culture that will enable the local school to be self-renewing.

Goodlad's model is especially strong in its emphasis on the role of links to other school staffs. A representative of the State Department of Education might play a particular role in this regard to identify other schools who could be linked in mutual support to the partnership school. Also, it should be noted that the League of Cooperating Schools emphasizes support at the school-district level and the involvement of parents and students in self-renewal efforts. The Partnership Model provides structures to accomodate these crucial ingredients.

## ENDNOTES

1. John I. Goodlad, M. Frances Klein, and Associates, *Looking Behind the Classroom Door* (Worthington, Ohio: Charles A. Jones Publishing Co., 1974.)
2. John I. Goodlad, *Dynamics of Educational Change: Toward Responsive Schools* (New York: McGraw-Hill Book Co., 1975), p. 71.
3. Ibid., p. 19.
4. Mary M. Bentzen and Associates, *Changing Schools: The Magic Feather Principle* (New York: McGraw-Hill Book Co., 1974.)
5. John I. Goodlad, "What Goes On In Our Schools?" *Educational Researcher* 6 (March 1977): 5.

# Chapter 14

# The Rand Change
# Agent Study Model

A fourth strategy option is a model of successful, planned change that was developed in connection with the Rand Change Agent Study.[1] The Change Agent Study was conducted from 1973 to 1978 under the sponsorship of the United States Office of Education to review four major federal change agent programs: Elementary and Secondary Education Act, Title III (Innovative Projects); Elementary and Secondary Education Act, Title VII (Bilingual Projects); Vocational Education Act, Part D (Exemplary Programs); and The Right-to-Read Program. The purpose of the study was to identify factors that promote or inhibit innovations in schools.

The Rand investigators began with a review of available evidence, developing a conceptual model of the factors affecting change in local educational practices. This model is of particular interest because, having been developed more recently than the models considered previously, it incorporates the disappointing results of educational change efforts that were reported in the early 1970s. In fact, a major purpose of the Rand Study was to identify limitations of earlier models that might explain the lack of success.

The review of previous literature on educational innovations led to the following conclusions:

1. Research on the effectiveness of schooling and the possible causes of absolute and differential effects provides little guidance on how to change educational practices.
2. Impact-oriented studies of innovative projects have not produced generalizable findings because they fail to deal with the interaction of the project with its institutional setting.
3. Implementation problems dominate the outcomes of change processes in the educational change system.[2]

The Rand researchers were particularly critical of Havelock's Linkage Model because of its preoccupation with the adoption process; that is, what happens *before* decisions to change existing practices. Furthermore, the primary barriers to change did not appear to be, as assumed in the Havelock model, deficiencies in the amount of information being communicated. Rather, the chief barriers to change seemed to be in the organizational dynamics of a school *after* a decision had been made to adopt a new practice.

Thus, the Rand Change Agent Study Model emphasizes organizational variables that facilitate or inhibit change at all stages of the process, but especially at the implementation stage. The model stresses ways to overcome the "dynamic conservatism" of the school system with its natural tendencies to resist change.

## CHANGE AGENT STUDY MODEL

The Rand Model hypothesized three stages in the change process: (1) initiation, (2) implementation, and (3) incorporation . These three stages, which correspond to the three stages presented in this book, may be summarized as follows:

1. *Initiation.* The first stage in a change program is to secure support; that is, the personal backing of individuals (e.g., superintendent, principal, teachers) for an innovative project and the commitment of resources to it. In the Change Agent Study, this was assumed to be a function of local school characteristics, federal and state policies, characteristics of the community, and characteristics of the proposed innovative program.
2. *Implementation.* Once support has been achieved, an innovative program enters a stage of implementation, in which both the proposed change and the local school organization itself are changed in a process of "mutual adaptation." The success of the local implementation process is assumed to be primarily a function of the characteristics of the proposed change, the nature of the local community, and the nature of the local school organization.
3. *Incorporation.* If the process of mutual adaptation is successful, the long-term changes in the local school organization are referred to as incorporation. Changes become a permanent part of the organization, either adding to or replacing previous patterns. This stage was assumed to depend upon the successful outcomes of the first two stages plus the effects of the new practice on student learning.

The Rand Model pictures change as a complex developmental process in which the school organization changes as a promising new practice gains support, is adapted to local circumstances, and becomes incorporated into the regular organizational functioning.

## CHANGE AGENT STUDY FINDINGS

The Rand Model was tested in a nation-wide survey of 293 change agent projects in eighteen states. Personal interviews were conducted with 1,735 people at all levels in participating school districts to explore the factors that influence change. Interviews were supplemented by field observations at twenty-nine projects to provide a comparison of similar innovations tried in different settings and in different federal programs. Also, Rand staff members interviewed a variety of federal and state officials. "Successful" projects were defined as those characterized by (1) fidelity of implementation (the degree to which original plans for change were carried out); (2) perceived success (the opinions of local staff members); (3) change in behavior (the extent to which school staff members changed); and (4) continuation (in terms of expected life after federal funds were terminated). Successful projects were compared with unsuccessful projects on the following factors:

1. *Project characteristics.* These included the type of innovation being tried, the amount of money committed to the change project, the scope of the change effort, and the implementation strategy.
2. *Institutional setting.* The organizational climate of the school, including the morale of the teachers, the support of school administrators, and the willingness of staff to spend extra time. Also, the characteristics of the school, district, and staff.
3. *Federal policies.* Characteristics of the different federal programs in terms of their objectives and management strategies.

The findings of the Rand Change Agent Study contained a number of surprises.[3] First, considering project characteristics, the success of federal programs in support of change seemed not to be a function of the type of innovation nor of the amount of money available to support a particular change. Instead, success appeared to be related to the scope of change. For example, the fact that an innovation was perceived as central to the priorities of the school district was an important factor related to success. Also, projects which were initiated with a view toward solving local problems succeeded much better than those undertaken "opportunistically" to acquire federal funds.

Extremely complex innovations that involved many grade levels or all classrooms in a particular grade level appeared to be difficult to implement. Such projects appeared to break down from lack of coordination. On the other hand, narrow projects that attempted isolated changes did not appear to last. An intermediate type of change appeared to be most enduring, where innovations involving a comprehensive area of curriculum requiring an overall change in teacher behavior were most likely to produce change. Whether or not the values and goals in a particular change project matched those of project participants was an important factor in success. Projects that lacked this consonance were not likely to succeed.

The most striking finding of the Rand Change Agent Study was the significance to success of a local implementation strategy that promoted the mutual adaptation process. Successful projects were characterized by an implementation strategy that included the following elements:

1. *Adaptive planning.* In successful projects, provisions were made for continuous planning to adapt a proposed change to a local setting. Such planning consisted in regular meetings to review goals, monitor progress, and solve specific problems occasioned by the changes.

2. *On-line staff training.*   Successful projects also provided for flexible staff training tailored to the needs of local school personnel. In making changes, the need for a new knowledge and skill became apparent during the implementation. A resource person at the local school site could meet such needs as they arose.

3. *Local material development.*   The process of adapting materials to a local setting was also an important aspect of successful projects. Rand investigators hypothesized that local material development helped local school staff members to understand the proposed changes and learn first hand about their use.

4. *Critical mass.*   It was clear that a group of innovators was required to give mutual support and stimulation to one another if an innovation was to succeed. Although the actual number of personnel comprising a critical mass was not determined, it was clear that school improvement is a group process for the kinds of changes being supported in these federal programs.

The Rand investigation also found a relationship between project success and the organizational climate of local schools. High morale of teachers, the active support of principals, general support of district officials, and teachers' willingness to spend extra effort all increased the chances of success. A receptive institutional setting appeared to be a necessary condition for success, although without a successful implementation strategy, it was not sufficient to guarantee success.

Finally, the Rand Change Agent Study found no important differences among the different federal programs under investigation. Federal programs appeared to differ little in the degree of success achieved. The Rand investigators summarized their findings as follows:

> In summary, our data show that a receptive institutional setting is a necessary but not sufficient condition for effective implementation. An implementation strategy that promotes mutual adaptation is critical.
>
> The main factors affecting innovations were the institutional setting, particularly organizational climate and the motivations of participants, the implementation strategy employed by local innovators to install the project treatment, and the scope of change implied by the project relative to its setting. Neither the technology nor the project resources nor the different federal management strategies influenced outcomes in major ways. Thus, project outcomes did not depend primarily on "inputs" from outside but on internal factors and local decisions.[4]

Pursuing the findings of the Rand Change Agent Study, Berman and McLaughlin investigated school districts that differed in degree of success in planned change. They found marked contrasts which were summarized in terms of two distinct approaches to change. First, they found a *deficit model,* which assumes that school problems are caused by inadequate information, skills, and materials. School improvement programs, in this view, are remedial, supplying the missing elements through workshops, consultants, or the acquisition of materials. Staff development programs are typically designed at higher administrative levels to prescribe for the missing ingredients. Little staff participation occurs in the determination of objectives or format for training. Major incentives for participation are salary credits or released time.

In sharp contrast, they observed a *developmental model*, in which a school district takes a pervasive point of view about staff development. This point of view can be summarized as follows:

1. Responsibility for development is decentralized with considerable authority in the hands of principals and teachers. Discretionary funds are available for school improvement in the local school building.
2. Continuing education of principals is considered important in view of new roles for principals as school managers.
3. Sharing of ideas among teachers is encouraged, as in the case of teacher centers.
4. Staff development programs are not standardized across a school district but are developed by groups of teachers within local school buildings.
5. Local resource persons rather than outside consultants are preferred to provide leadership for school improvement. Joint governance between teachers and administration is seen as critical for staff development.
6. Released time is provided to teachers for training. Less emphasis is given to monetary incentives.

Berman and McLaughlin found school districts with the developmental model of school improvement to be far more successful in bringing about change than districts following the deficit model.[5]

## EVALUATION OF THE CHANGE AGENT STUDY MODEL

The Rand Change Agent Study Model is an extremely valuable contribution to knowledge about educational change. First, it builds upon previous efforts to understand the change process, incorporating the experience of extensive efforts to change schools during the 1950s and 1960s. In particular, the Rand Model highlights two lessons learned from earlier experience: (1) a receptive local school organization is a necessary condition for change, and (2) successful change efforts must go beyond decisions to adopt new practices to the matter of organization development.

The Rand Model is also important because it summarizes the experience gained in an important array of federal programs that utilized change agent strategies. The synthesis of this enormous body of practical experience is extremely valuable to those interested in school improvement.

Third, at a practical level, the findings of the Rand Change Agent Study give important guidance to local efforts to improve schools. Particularly helpful is the suggested developmental strategy for a school district in which school improvement is decentralized to the local school site. Recommendations for an emphasis on staff training are extremely practical in terms of making change. The emphasis on strengthening local leadership is good.

Certain limitations in the Change Agent Study Model should be noted, however. It should be remembered, for example, that the Rand Study was limited to federal programs in support of local change. In these programs, federal monies were available through various grant procedures to support a variety of projects. In some cases (for example, Right-To-Read), the strategies were prescribed. One cannot know whether the findings that come from a study of such federal programs might apply to other kinds of change efforts. Another limitation of the Change Agent Study was the reliance upon questionnaire and interview data for staff perceptions of success as a measure of change. A stronger test of successful change (e.g., improvements in student learning) would have been desirable. Also, many factors that might be involved in successful change were not included in the study. Therefore, the Rand Change Agent Study should not be taken as the last word on the subject of change. Rather, its findings should be considered as tentative, especially when one asks whether or not the quality of education was improved in projects labeled as successful.

A weakness of the Rand Model for those who are seeking to stimulate change in a local school is the absence of convenient published materials to guide a change agent. The primary documents are technical reports of research rather than practical guides for a local change agent. Other models appear to be more helpful in suggesting specific steps in a school improvement cycle and more helpful in discussing organizational variables that might be utilized to change a school into a self-renewing model.

## A PARTNERSHIP EXAMPLE OF THE CHANGE AGENT STUDY MODEL

The Rand Change Agent Study Model fits easily into the concept of organization development through partnerships. In the Rand Model, the focus is upon the local school building organization as the focal point for change with the principal and the teachers in the school as primary agents in the change process.

Consistent with the Rand Model, the concept of a partnership group places the principal in a central leadership role with a continuing comitment to the change process. Following the Rand Model, he or she might use the partnership group and its advisory committee of students and parents to build receptivity to any given program of change. In fact, the partnership structure provides for the involvement of all interested parties in the identification of local needs and the selection of a solution strategy, thus building in the local problem-solving orientation identified in the Rand Study.

Another crucial factor in the Rand Model is the local implementation strategy that is recommended. To follow this strategy, a local partnership group could be a mechanism to plan and monitor the necessary implementation process. The arrangement of regular staff meetings with local materials development could be included. The continuous, on-line planning that characterize successful change projects could be periodically reviewed and arrangements for the necessary on-going staff training could be made through the partnership group. The presence of a college educator and a State Department of Education representative might be particularly useful in this regard, especially because they are familiar with the local setting and the specific training needs.

Other suggestions for partnership groups following the Rand Model would be to work for the conditions that characterize developmental districts, such as discretionary funds for local change efforts, released time for teachers to engage in implementation efforts, or a teacher center where mutual support and exchange of ideas among peers could take place.

## ENDNOTES

1.  Paul Berman & Milbrey W. McLaughlin, *Federal Programs Supporting Educational Change, Vol. VIII: Implementing and Sustaining Innovations* (Santa Monica, Calif.: The Rand Corporation, May, 1978.)
2.  Paul Berman & Milbrey W. McLaughlin, *Federal Programs Supporting Educational Change, Vol. I: A Model of Educational Change* (Santa Monica, Calif.: The Rand Corporation, September, 1974.)
3.  Paul Berman & Milbrey W. McLaughlin, *Federal Programs Supporting Educational Change, Vol. IV: The Findings in Review* (Santa Monica, Calif.: The Rand Corporation, April, 1975.)
4.  Ibid., p. 23.
5.  Milbrey McLaughlin & Paul Berman, "Retooling Staff Development in a Period of Retrenchment," *Educational Leadership* (December 1977): 191–194.

## SUMMARY OF PART III

Four strategy options for organization development through partnerships were presented. Each model suggests alternative ways to help an individual school move through the stages of planned change. Together, they comprise an extensive array of tested techniques that may be adapted to change efforts in a local school.

Ronald G. Havelock's Linkage Model emphasizes the importance of knowledge transfer within and between "producer" and "user" systems. The model includes a variety of tactics appropriate to steps in a problem-solving process that can lead to planned change in a local school.

Richard A. Schmuck's Organization Development in Schools focuses on OD interventions to make schools more self-renewing. Process consultation is used to increase levels of trust, warmth, openness, and informality within a school organization. Skills of communication and cooperative problem solving are learned and applied to important school problems. In the process the school organization itself changes and becomes more self-renewing.

John I. Goodlad's Responsive Model of Educational Improvement emphasizes the creation of networks of local schools who support one another to make each member school self-renewing. With leadership from a college or other agency, the network helps each school organization to develop problem-solving processes by which it may become more responsive to its own environment. The model has been implemented on a broad scale in the /I/D/E/A/ Change Program for Individually Guided Education.

The Rand Change Agent Study Model incorporates the findings of research on a variety of federal programs in support of change. Successful change occurs when an important local problem is the starting point for change and when strong efforts are made to adapt new practices to the local setting. External support for this local implementation process is also an important aspect of the model.

## PART III DISCUSSION QUESTIONS

1. School improvement can be approached through the use of many different models of change. Identify and compare the key elements in the change models advocated by Havelock, Schmuck, Goodlad, and the Rand Study. Which model (or combination of models) appeals to you most?

2. The retraining of teachers and other school personnel is a prerequisite to a successful educational change effort. What provisions for retraining are evident in the four change models presented in this chapter?

3. The concept of "mutual adaptation" presented in the Rand Change Agent Study Model recognizes the importance of local school goals, climate, and human resources. What problems can arise when local school personnel make drastic changes in a program or practice that has proven to be successful elsewhere? Give an example if you can.

4. Collaborative problem solving is recommended practice in each of the four models. What difficulties arise where a school board or a district-level administrator decides unilaterally to institue a new program or practice in an individual school?

## SUGGESTED READINGS

Berman, Paul and McLaughlin, Milbrey W. *Federal Programs Supporting Educational Change, Vol. VIII: Implementing and Sustaining Innovations.* Santa Monica, Calif.: The Rand Corporation, May, 1978.

Bushnell, David S. and Rappaport, Donald, eds. *Planned Change in Education: A System Approach.* New York: Harcourt Brace Jovanovich, Inc., 1971.

Friedmann, John. *Retracking America: A Theory of Transactive Planning.* New York: Anchor Press/Doubleday, 1973.

Goodlad, John I. *The Dynamics of Educational Change: Toward Responsive Schools.* New York: McGraw-Hill Book Company, 1975.

Havelock, Ronald G. *The Change Agent's Guide to Innovation in Education.* Englewood Cliffs, N.J.: Educational Technology Publications, 1973.

Schmuck, Richard A., et al. *The Second Handbook of Organization Development in Schools.* Palo Alto, Calif.: Mayfield Publishing Company, 1977.

# PART IV

# TACTICS FOR SCHOOL IMPROVEMENT

## INTRODUCTION TO PART IV

Having presented a general model of organization development through partnerships with alternative strategies to guide local schools through the stages of planned change, we turn now to a consideration of tactics. By tactics we mean those specific procedures that can be used to implement strategies, which are more general courses of action. Special consideration is given to the tactics that are crucial to the success of the Partnership Model for School Improvement.

First, change agent roles are discussed. Specific suggestions are made for all those who wish to play change agent roles, but especially for those with designated responsibility for change, such as members of a partnership committee or consultants.

Successful collaboration by members of the partnership group is an important requirement for the strategies recommended in this book. Therefore, specific suggestions are made for improving the dynamics of partnership groups, including procedures for making decisions and managing conflict.

Next, tactics for administering partnerships are reviewed with particular emphasis on governance, finance, personnel, and community involvement. Suggestions are made for written agreements about partner roles and responsibilities.

The problem of how to identify and use a variety of knowledge resources in a local school improvement process is then discussed. Recommendations are made for partnership groups to provide needed links between local problems and knowledge resources.

Another central process in local school improvement is staff development. Information about teacher education and certification is given as a background for recommended tactics to improve training programs for local school personnel.

A final set of recommendations about tactics is made with respect to evaluation, which is an important activity at each stage of the local school improvement process. Recommendations about evaluating partnerships themselves are included.

Part IV concludes with a description of several examples of collaboration in school improvement. Examples are drawn from a variety of sources, including personal experiences. Each example is discussed briefly in relationship to the Partnership Model.

# Chapter 15

# Change Agent Roles

Organization development efforts require particular individuals to perform in change agent roles. Such roles may be played by a wide variety of people—students, teachers, administrators, internal consultants, external consultants, state employees, professors, parents, or interested citizens. Some individuals, of course, are especially well-suited to function as change agents because their regular job descriptions include change agent duties, because they are temporarily assigned change agent responsibilities, or because they have special skills and expertise.

In this chapter we examine a number of change agent roles, giving particular attention to roles that can be assumed by members of a partnership group or may require the services of a hired consultant. Whatever the case, the various roles need systematic attention to see that they are defined in terms of local needs and that someone is designated to perform each one. This is an excellent task for a partnership committee, which has good knowledge about what is needed and about resources that are available.

## INITIATORS

Operationally, the change process starts with someone who expresses the need for change. This person may identify a specific problem or make general suggestions for change. Such a person is an initiator and consequently a change agent even if that is the only function served.

Initiators can be almost anyone in the educational community. External initiators can be individual students, parents, tax payers, or representatives of community interest groups. For example, a local minister might be upset about the lack of a sex-education program in the community and come to the school to initiate a change; or a student may make a complaint about program options.

Internal initiators are the paid professionals or school board members, and they may initiate the change in a variety of ways. Some of the methods are writing position papers, forming ad hoc committees, submitting proposals, or simply "speaking out." Both internal and external initiators may enter the scene from a negative standpoint, as irritants to the system, or they may take a more positive approach. In either case, initiators are needed to begin a process of change.

In keeping with the recommendations of this book, members of a partnership group are more apt to be recognized as initiators in a positive sense. In this case the initiator may continue in the change process far into the project. However, many times the initiator serves only as a catalyst and is not further involved.

The more successful change projects always have an initiation phase, which requires a person serving as a change agent. While in retrospect the initiator's role may be seen as minor, the initiation phase requires someone to serve as ''starter.''

*The important point is that every organization needs to encourage both internal and external initiators.* This encouragement is provided through appropriate structures and through an open atmosphere. Negative, as well as positive, suggestions for change need to be solicited. Structures for encouraging initiators and their complaints can be provided through special committees, forums, suggestion boxes, brainstorming sessions, etc. The attitude of teachers and administrators toward initiators is also important, and this is particularly true of the partnership committee. The attitude should be one that is open and nondefensive about suggestions, regardless of their source. Therefore, one important function of the partnership committee is to provide a structure and establish an attitude that is receptive to initiators.

## CONSULTANT ROLES

In organization development work, after a need for change has been expressed, internal or external consultants are often identified to help the organization change. Consultants usually play one of three basic roles: (1) researcher, (2) trainer, or (3) facilitator. One individual might play all roles or several people might be involved.

**Researcher.**   OD activities may involve both action research and basic research. The heaviest emphasis is usually on action research techniques such as evaluation, collection and dissemination of data, discovering new information, planning and developing, and various uses of assessment and feedback surveys. Any of the partners' organizations can supply researchers as long as people with the necessary skills and interest are available. Otherwise, a hired consultant can be selected with the needed expertise. The interventions that are made under the researcher role are those of providing information, making observations, analyzing data, testing hypotheses, and record keeping. These techniques are required during every stage of the OD process. If appropriate, basic research opportunities may result from these activities, but the *primary role of the researcher in OD is to provide the decision makers with as much useful and timely data as possible.*

**Trainer.**   Another consultant role is that of trainer. A trainer is one who assumes the responsibility for reeducation activities that lead to specific organizational and staff improvement. The trainer can be someone from within the school organization, one of the partners, or someone hired specifically for the job. Trainers may be a seminar leader, a subject-matter specialist, a teacher of specific academic methodology, a demonstration expert, a master teacher, a process observer, a parlimentarian, a parent coordinator, a student advisor, or anyone providing input in a specific area. All make interventions that are designed to create change in the organization through the training of individuals and groups. The trainer conducts specific training activities which may or may not be the same as that of the facilitator.

Facilitator.    The facilitator is someone who concentrates on the OD process itself. He or she can be internal (a member of the existing organization), or external (someone brought in from the outside). The internal facilitator obviously should be someone who wants to serve in that role, who has confidence and training in OD, and who can arrange for the time within the confines of the present job. Some organizations hire full-time internal facilitators as consultants to work on OD projects. We would certainly recommend a policy that calls for a full-time internal facilitator to guide the partners in their concepts, ideas, actions, and evaluations. School districts are beginning to see the advantages of placing medical doctors, lawyers, nurses, and facility engineers on some kind of retainer or permanent employment basis. Why not employ a person skilled in perhaps the most important activity—organization effectiveness? Other specialists are typically responsible for staff development, but these are usually limited to areas such as curriculum studies. School districts need full-time OD facilitators. However, the typical pattern is to employ external facilitator-consultants.

Figure 15–1 illustrates the options available to schools in their deployment of the various consultant roles in an OD intervention. It may be used as a check list, adding specific names when identified.

In any of the three consultant roles, facilitator, trainer, or researcher, the external consultant has somewhat different problems than the internal consultant. The need for effective interventions is always present, but there is increased pressure placed on external people centering around credibility issues. If possible, the "outsider" should represent one of the partners. If so, that will

|  | Internal | External |
|---|---|---|
| Initiator |  |  |
| Consultant |  |  |
| Researcher |  |  |
| Trainer |  |  |
| Facilitator |  |  |

FIGURE 15–1.   Change Agent Roles

make communication easier, and members of the target school will probably be more ready to accept the consultant. However, it is quite possible that the partnership committee has selected an independent consultant to work in the school for a specific reason. Again, this function may be researcher, trainer, or OD facilitator.

The following guidelines should be helpful to partners if they need to secure an outside consultant.

1. Be very explicit in outlining needs and goals.
2. Be as business-like as possible (without creating mistrust) about the contractual agreement.
3. Insist on evaluation built into the contract.
4. Insist that the consultant "never surprise the boss."
5. Check out the credentials of substitutes, co-trainers, aides, etc.
6. Investigate the possibility of a contract with contingencies that allow check points, at which time the task force determines if the consultancy should continue and for how long. Phasing the project may help.
7. Have critique sessions with the task force during the project so that two-way feedback is established and adjustments can be made as the project continues.
8. Don't try to cut corners on the consultant's time. Pay for planning, calls, evaluation, etc.
9. Double check materials and equipment needed for training activities.
10. Make every effort for good attendance records at meetings and interviews.
11. Provide adequate living and eating arrangements for the consultants.
12. Pay the consultant as soon as possible. Some school district expense and stipend procedures can be unnecessarily slow.
13. Ask for a written summary report from the consultant.
14. If the consultant does not provide devices for consultant evaluation, then the task force should do it. You have the right to ask for feedback and adaptation to style, process, timing, selection of activities, change of design, etc.

When an outside consultant is hired, a written contract should be drawn. Many consultancies have ended on a sour note for both parties because there was not a written agreement. This written agreement does not have to be legalistic, but stipends, duties, schedules, dates, and specifications for the work itself should be included.

One important consideration is the number of consultants hired for a particular project. Of course, budgets may be a determining factor. At least one consulting group states, "In fact, we have operated, almost without exception, with the guideline that no one should consult solo."[1] The advantages of co-consulting are that it encourages risk-taking, improves perception and accuracy, serves to generate more and better ideas, provides better continuity during unforeseen emergencies, and provides clients with alternative styles.

Schmuck[2] provides a provocative list of guidelines from the consultants' point of view:

1. Continually restate the goals of the consultation.
2. Be prepared to undertake procedures for increasing organizational readiness.
3. Make it clear that successful OD requires sustained effort over many months.
4. Assess progress at each stage to ascertain how much of earlier stages need to be recycled.
5. Be sure the macro-design includes micro-designs for recycling the process of trust-building, goal-setting, and diagnostic information gathering.
6. Establish collaborative relationships with key authorities.
7. Engage all participants in introductory demonstrations and contract building.
8. Clarify interpersonal relationships between consultants and clients.
9. Tell clients that a formal diagnosis will precede training.
10. Insist on collecting data on present conditions.
11. Use formal and informal methods of data collection.
12. Use diagnoses for feedback to clients and for further planning.
13. Don't let the consultants' personal biases get in the way.
14. Adapt the themes of training, data feedback, confrontation, and process consultation to the local situation.
15. Build the macro-design to encompass the mode of intervention, the focus of attention, and diagnosed problems.
16. Phase the work to meet short- and long-term intervention goals. Include time to renegotiate the plan.

## CHANGE AGENT TACTICS

What tactics are recommended for change agents in the Partnership Model? For one thing, a change agent's behavior should be based on an understanding of how people change as individuals within the organizational setting. For example, consultants cannot create real change by creating dependencies in clients, even though that is easy to do. Therefore, one priority should be to use techniques that encourage interdependence on the part of the individuals in the organization. Most OD consultants use evaluation instruments and organizational measurement devices. These can be standardized and brought to the organization. However, instruments that are constructed and administered at the local level are more useful because of client ownership.

There are other helpful guidelines that will increase the understanding of change. Kelman[3] has developed a theory of individual behavior that typically occurs in organizations that are in a change period. His thoughts may be beneficial in looking at the variety of ways in which institutions might reach greater potential for change through consultancies.

When looking at new ideas, there is a tendency for many to accept the new thing superficially because they want to *conform* to the change agent or the latest "in-thing." Once they start that acceptance, they can begin an *identity* phase, which brings them closer (through feelings of ownership and pride) to the final stage, *internalization*. It is the internalization of the change that we are ultimately seeking. Kelman's CII formula (conform, identify, internalization) can be observed operating in innovative environments. The formula is especially useful in assessing the progress of the organization in the degree to which people are accepting the desired change. In other words, the consultants can use the formula as an organizational climate barometer.

In a closed, traditional organization, the implementation of the formula might be thought of as manipulative or secretive. However, used in a partnership organizational setting it could be helpful in both diagnosis and feedback to staff members. In a very open climate, the consultants could establish assessment devices to monitor the stages the staff is undergoing. This may be done informally through random conversations, "sensing" the status of the specific change in question, or it could be assessed through sociometric instrumentation.

Goodwin Watson[4] describes the process of change in organizations. He sees change as a phenomenon that must be directed. Change has been successfully managed in many situations following the lines of Watson's SPA formula. Using this concept, the consultant, in connection with a Partnership committee, changes the *structure* of the organization, which in turn alters the *processes* or normal behavior, which in time will permeate an actual change in *attitudes*.

Watson claims that, in effect, what institutions are seeking through self-renewal projects is a change in attitudes. The process by which that attitudinal change eventually occurs, then, becomes a crucial factor. The SPA formula emphasizes the initiation stage by a change agent who provides a different "organizational mind-set" through a change in structure. This leads to different modes of behaving (daily, procedural, and process orientation) until the actual "organizational attitude" has assumed the new posture.

This theory applies to the concept of partnerships. The partners become initiators with the clients in full knowledge of the anticipated change to result from the strategy. Utilizing the partnership as the initiator has powerful implications. The structural change in the organizational pattern actually begins when a school community accepts the partnership plan. The structure is changed, which means that principals and teachers will begin to function in a different manner. Change agent roles can then be assigned to a special task force, the partnership committee itself or an outside consultant. The OD school does this in full knowledge of the anticipated results—sensing the stages of change as they occur.

Another important practice for the OD consultant is assessing and establishing the climate for change. As McMillan points out:

Roughly, this test should determine whether the subsystem in which employees, i.e., teachers, operate is conducive to change; whether participation is valued; whether individual initiative is recognized; and whether new ideas are rewarded by those in position of authority. It may well be that in an environment not conducive to change, participation in certain decision making processes will not have an incentive effect on performance and . . . work against the success of a change project.[5]

The partnership concept emphasizes shared decision making by its very definition. The aware consultant utilizes this concept in encouraging a climate for change.

An image used by Dan Lortie of the University of Chicago sums it up very well.

> Interventions into a school system are like putting your hand into a bowl of jello. While your hand is in the jello it moves the jello away but once your hand is removed the jello flows back again. It is helpful to the survival of schools that they are so resilient and surprisingly flexible, but it does not help in producing worthwhile lasting changes.[6]

Consultants must become part of the school, particularly if they do not already represent one of the partners. A partnership school "places its own finger in its own jello" and really never has to pull it out and leave. Because the consultancy is built-in, the chances of interventions leading to lasting change are definitely increased.

The tactics recommended for change agents may be contrasted with those of the more traditional consultant as shown in Figure 15-2. The usual management expert, curriculum consultant, or workshop leader has a particular "bag

| The Traditional Consultant's Way | Questions for Innovation | OD Change Agent's Way |
|---|---|---|
| Consultant and principal conspire to "move" people | Who | Partnership Committee decides to undergo OD process |
| Recent fad—specific innovation—consultant's "bag of tricks" | What | Changes occur as a result of the OD process. Change agents not pushing any one innovation |
| Anytime there is lack of resistance or federal money available | When | When planned by the school (partnership committee, faculty, parents, students) |
| Ego trip for consultant and administrators | Why | Needs assessment, action research, survey feedback indicates |
| Administrative decision plus persuasion | How | Concensus procedures |
| System-wide or in isolated classrooms | Where | The building level or teaching teams |
| Hit and run | How long | Continuing help |

FIGURE 15-2.   Change Agent Tactics Compared to Traditional Consultant Role

of tricks'' to display. Such consultants are often brought in by school administrators to convince teachers to adopt some specific practice. They present their wares and leave, returning only occasionally for reexhortation. Change agents in the Partnership Model, on the other hand, emphasize work with members of the organization to identify needs, select innovations that will meet local needs, and adapt innovations to the local setting in a continuous process.

## OLMOSK'S CHANGE STRATEGIES

Those who are taking consultant roles in the change process may also profit from considering seven change strategies identified by Kurt Olmosk.[7] Each strategy suggests an approach that might be taken by a change agent, although each strategy has its particular strengths and weaknesses.

**Fellowship Strategy.**    In this model, great emphasis is placed on social interaction; consequently, it is easily identified by the presence of coffees, parties, group dinners, etc. It is common in church groups, and has been successfully used in many schools by relationship-oriented administrators who accomplish their objectives through activities such as contacts during golf matches, dinner parties, etc. Conflict is generally avoided and, for this reason, the fellowship strategy is most effective in the early stages of a project when it is important to minimize threatening situations. This is important for the consultant. The weakness lies in the problem of keeping members committed to the project.

**Political Strategy.**    This strategy, well known to most, is based on getting influential people involved. It works on the informal power structure of an organization as much as it works on the formal hierarchy. This strategy is usually effective in implementing ideas once they have been planned and decided upon; consequently, it cannot be overlooked in the implementation stage. The problems associated with this strategy usually revolve around broken promises or commitments that were made as a short-term expediency and may eventually collide with basic value systems.

**Economic Strategy.**    The economic strategy has perhaps been more successful in the past then it might in the future due to the decline in financial resources. The most striking example is the federal program, Title IV, Part C, which literally pays for change. Obviously, the drawbacks are the limitations on finances, but the economic strategy is still potent through the allocation of existing operating funds. An example of this practice would be rewarding teachers for innovative practices through an in-house, mini-proposal system that takes money from the top of the instructional supply budget for this purpose. Teachers who are the most innovative receive a larger share of the instructional budget.

**Academic Strategy.**    The academic strategy is commonly used with administrators' attempts to influence teachers through a rational approach. Consultants may be even more successful at this because they may be seen as people who do not have a personal commitment to the idea; hence, the psychological threat is minimal. The consultant, during the implementation stage, can sit with groups and logically discuss the necessary action. It is our opinion that this strategy is particularly helpful in curricular change projects where research, demonstration models, local data about student performance, and other information sources can be used to discuss the topic. Teachers who live in an "idea world" generally like this approach. The disadvantages are the time involved to collect data and the lack of assessment of the emotional impact which is usually involved.

**Engineering Strategy.**    The basic premise here is that if the consultant can create changes in the environment, then change in individual people will occur accordingly. It is somewhat descriptive of the Goodwin Watson model discussed earlier. This concentration on structure may be particularly helpful in new organizations or unstable environments. The problems usually center on the lack of emotional commitment from individual people since there is a tendency to ignore personal feelings from the start. It may also create suspicion from the people that the consultant is in collusion with the administration. For those same reasons, however, it is quite successful for high-level management directed projects.

**Military Strategy.**    The name of this strategy is self-explanatory. Because it relies on force of one kind or another, it has very little use in our OD model; but it is included here because Olmosk includes it. It might have some use when there is serious disarray in an organization. For example, if there were threats of physical violence in a school desegregation project, temporary military enforcement might prevent physical harm to constituents, but the strategy has no real importance for a consultant.

**Confrontation Strategy.**    Like the military strategy, confrontation may be more useful to an administrator than a consultant. However, in situations where there is a high level of conflict (and it must be resolved before the group can really be productive), confrontation tactics, which might occur in a T-group or encounter training group, may be legitimate behavior to be encouraged by a consultant-facilitator. The disadvantage is that the conflict may escalate to a point that is counterproductive before being resolved through confrontation techniques. There are times, however, when the consultant simply has to facilitate through conflict.

In addition to the seven strategies described, Olmosk recommends an Applied Behavioral Science Model that is consistent with the thesis of this book.

## RUNKLE AND SCHMUCK FINDINGS

Some particularly valuable lessons for change agents have been summarized by Runkle and Schmuck on the basis of a comprehensive review of OD research in schools. Each of their findings is discussed in relation to change agent roles.

1. "OD helps faculties become more open and skillful in interpersonal communication, more helpful toward one another, and more willing to take risks in trying out new ideas." It has been our experience that this is, in fact, very likely. It is so much so that the consultant should really warn the administration about this possibility because many administrators do not want that kind of behavior. They think in terms of specific structural or systematic changes, not interpersonal. For example, on a practical basis this may mean that teachers will be more outspoken. Administrators should be prepared for this possibility before training starts.

2. "We have found that a year is a reasonable time to allow for the entry stage of an organizational change program." This is a very important concept for consultants to express to administrators. Frequently, training activities have been planned over a long period of time. A great deal of time and energy may have gone into funding requests, so that with initial activities alone, the expectations are so high the consultant has no chance. It is wise for the consultant to spend considerable time discussing the realistic outcomes and length of time needed before the actual work begins. In fact, visible progress generally takes so long many consultants are refusing contracts if they are not funded long enough to have a chance for success. The integration period is a long-lasting process.

3. "We believe that most existing schools fail to make use of enough of the abilities of their staff, students, and parents." The maximum use of the local human resources should be a major goal of consultants if they are to get involved in specific suggestions at all. This again emphasizes the continual approach to change common to OD experiences. Partnership theory dictates that maximum use be made of all available parties in the educational community. Collaboration will at first seem painful because of the difficulty of working in groups as opposed to solo change-engineering. But after OD training, most schools never willingly return to a situation calling for less involvement. *If the administrator is fearful of continued involvement, then the consultant should be very leery about a contract with this district in the first place.*

4. "OD consultants must have detailed scientific information on which to base their intervention designs; gathering systematic data about a school's facilitative or debilitating dynamics is vital to effective action." One way for the consultant to attempt to fulfill the needs of the client on a long-term basis is to teach the clients how to collect data, do action research, and use feedback surveys and other instrumentations. The use of hard and soft data will make the OD integration phase more credible, be more ob-

jective and keep the consultant out of the "depending business." The bibliography contains several sources of applied research techniques.

5.  "Consultation in organization development is more likely to have beneficial effects if members of the district office support the school in pursuing its own leads, or at least are permissive to it." Consultants need to work deliberately to keep school district officers informed and involved. Likewise, members of the school board may need to know about the work. Of course, the direct involvement of the board will vary depending on the size of the school district.

6.  "OD is more likely to help a school achieve an innovation if the decision to move into innovation is almost consensual." The evidence supports logical thinking, but consensus is more tricky than one might think. Therefore, the consultant should take a central role in helping the small planning groups and the school as a whole in that consensus. Hints for this process are as follows (to be facilitated by the consultant in most cases):

    a.  First, it is important to consider that Robert's Rules will probably be discarded. For example, simple voting may be a very *ineffective* means of assessing the feelings and thinking of the group. A one person, one vote rule does not consider the importance of the situation to individuals. Voting should only be used as a last resort.

    b.  If voting is the process for decision making, then experiment with weighted scales such as one hand for a yes or no vote, two hands for feeling very strongly for or very strongly against.

    c.  All consensus gathering should include an opportunity for everyone to express his or her opinion. Trained consultants should know ways to facilitate this. It includes placing importance on listening skills by everyone in the group.

    d.  A careful polling of everyone can then determine if most of the people are in favor or not (and you already know why).

    e.  Carefully check to see if anyone violently opposes the idea. If there is *one* person who is very hurt, adamant, or visibly nervous about the idea in question, then consensus "rules" say *do not proceed*. More discussion is necessary. Yes, a group can go ahead with a split decision, but since maintaining the change is important, long-term comfort with the decision is extremely important.

7.  The amount of time is a very important consultancy consideration. Runkle and Schmuck found the following:

    a.  Most successful projects last at least one year.

    b.  About 80 to 160 hours of staff time are devoted to OD work. They may be spread over a two- or three-year period.

    c.  Forty to eighty hours should be spent before school opens.

    d.  Less than twenty-four hours (three days) can have a negative effect.

    e.  On a weekly basis (during the school year) schools that normally spend about two hours a week in meetings will at least double them during OD periods.

8. "A school that deals purposefully, actively, and confrontively with conflict during a transition to a new structure is the more likely to achieve and stabilize the new structure." This is very important evidence for the integration stage. Conflict is natural in organizational life, and confrontation (the overt behavior resulting from conflict) is inevitable in organizations undergoing change and development. Experience tends to back up the Runkle and Schmuck findings; schools that deal appropriately with conflict and confrontation are more able to adapt to the innovation and continue it. In other words, change becomes integrated. A problem is that most people in our culture view conflict as a negative behavior. A smooth-running organization may create comfortable feelings about organizational climate, but too often there exist unrecognized undercurrents of dissent. When attempts to change are started, these suppressed conflicts may emerge and normal problems of change may be exaggerated. The intelligent, experienced facilitator understands the dynamics of conflict and knows how to help people handle it. Conflict management might be a good training activity for a school that is receiving OD interventions because conflict is an expected outcome. A good facilitator will be most helpful in this regard.[8]

## EVALUATION OF CHANGE AGENT ROLES

Whether a consultant serves as researcher, facilitator, or trainer—or all three—there should be an ongoing evaluation and feedback process. The type of evaluations available are numerous, but the most commonly used are survey feedback instruments that can be designed for daily, weekly, or longer periods. They should be designed to provide specific feedback to the consultant in question, although it is a good idea to include other topics for evaluation while collecting information on the consultant. All information should be made known to the consultant in question, the administrators in charge, and the whole group, if appropriate. Simple Likert Scales and open-ended questions are quite adequate, and the forms should usually be brief, to the point, and anonymous. Sample forms are included in Appendix A.

## ENDNOTES

1. R. Schmuck, J. Arends, and R. Arends, "Tailoring Consultation in Organization Development for Particular Schools." A CEPM Occasional Paper, October 1974 (Center for Educational Policy and Management, University of Oregon), p. 22.
2. Ibid., p. 6.
3. Herbert C. Kelman, "Compliance, Identification and Integration: Three Processes of Attitude Changes," Journal of Conflict Resolution 2, no. 1 (1958): 51.
4. Goodwin Watson, ed., Change in School Systems (Washington, D.C.: National Training Laboratory, NEA, 1967), p. 25.

5. R. McMillan, "Organizational Change in Schools," *Journal of Applied Behavioral Science* 2 no. 4 (1975): 446.
6. Daniel Langmeyer, "Surviving an Intervention: The Jello Principle," *Journal of Applied Behavioral Science* 2 no. 4 (1975): 456.
7. Kurt E. Olmosk, "Seven Pure Strategies of Change," *The 1972 Annual Handbook for Group Facilitators* (La Jolla, Calif.: University Associates, 1972).
8. Philip Runkle and Richard Schmuck, *Research and Development Program on Strategies of Educational Change at CEPM-CASEA* (University of Oregon: Center for Educational Policy and Management, 1974), p. 5.

# Chapter 16

# Group Dynamics Issues

Collaboration is a major theme in this book. This means at least one thing—partnership educators are going to spend hours in group meetings of one kind or another. The reaction of the reader might be, "Oh, no, not another committee meeting!" The problems associated with school committees have left a negative impression on almost everyone. For this reason, understanding group dynamics is important. This section summarizes some of the major generalizations about groups that might be used to make partnership groups and school committees more effective and more rewarding.

## THE ROLE OF LEADERSHIP GROUPS

In the first place, why use groups? What are the advantages of group governance and group roles? The most obvious advantage has to do with the quality of cooperative decisions. An excellent structured activity that is used in group training situations is called "lost on the moon." Designed for the astronauts' training program, the task is to prioritize items to carry with you if you are "ship-wrecked" on the moon. Most people, having limited knowledge about life on the moon, must rely on sound logic to discover the best answer. The activity is designed so that each individual first tries to work a solution to the problem. Next, groups of five to seven people are asked to solve the same problem. Invariably, the groups do better than any one individual, proving experimentally that "two or more heads are better than one." The activity also provides some interesting data in group interaction that a skillful trainer can use to help the group look at its own process and in turn learn about group behavior in general. It is an excellent way for a group of people to start a task force project.

Most people recognize the intellectual advantages of pooling ideas for the most effective solution to problems. This "combined knowledge effect" is particularly important in the Partnership Model.

A second advantage has to do with representation. Many institutions attempt to maintain ideals of democracy but fall short in practice. In many decisions, employees do not have the chance to represent their particular interests. Teachers particularly need to be represented in more of the decisions that affect them. Shared decision making is becoming more and more important in the institutions of our nation and the collaborative groups described earlier exemplify this principle.

The third advantage is in the learning that takes place in group experiences. For example, many curriculum committees have stated that the process of working on a project was more valuable than the end product achieved. Getting to know one another, receiving feedback on how one operates in a group, experimenting with behavior, trying new ideas, and listening to others' ideas—are all helpful in the professional growth experiences of individual participants.

The fourth advantage is in the possibility of improved communication. Organizational communication will improve if the following practices are adhered to in group meetings:

1. Minutes of meetings are posted or distributed.
2. Meetings are open (at least to faculty) or only closed for specific reasons.
3. A regular time, in addition to emergency meetings, is established.
4. Group participants agree as to what to say to constituents when asked about the meetings' accomplishments. (What are the levels of confidence?)
5. Membership in the task force is seen as an important position. Thus, the trust level and interest in the representatives will be high.

The fifth advantage involves responsibility and work. Group leadership spreads responsibility, relieving the administrator from some work load. Administrators are very busy people. Many of the long-term decisions and some of the day-to-day operation issues can be handled through group leadership, if the group's function is so declared. The sharing of responsibility for leadership can also raise morale.

The disadvantages of committees may be more obvious than the advantages because of experiences many people have had working in poorly managed groups. Most disadvantages center around inefficiency. Compared to the unilateral judgments of the efficient administrator, group decision making and group leadership will generally take more time. Also, the process may be very frustrating to many of the participants.

The very strengths associated with group leadership may be the problem areas in reverse. For example, representation of faculty groups is an advantage, but selecting and maintaining fair representation of faculty groups may lead to dissension and be another organizational "headache." Too many ideas, regardless of how good they are, sometimes complicate the issue. Spreading the work load may give teachers more responsibility than they can handle. Simple problems of location, timing, duration, and numbers of participants may create new problems.

Knowing that group leadership has these disadvantages may help the partners and their leaders recognize the problems and thus increase the chances of dealing with them successfully. We believe the "trouble" is worthwhile because of increased possibilities for bringing about school improvement.

## ORGANIZING GROUPS

There are many kinds of formal groups in organizational life. Consequently, the terms *group* and *group leadership* can mean different things to different individuals. We distinguish between two basic kinds of groups as they relate to the Partnership Model.

The more obvious are *task-oriented* work groups that are assigned a variety of activities with a definite purpose or goal to be attained, usually in a given period of time, and deal directly with the operations and functioning of the organization. These tasks might involve decision making, for example. Names used for this purpose might be committee, task force, presidium, senate, council, board, etc.

The other groups that should be functioning are *training groups*. They might be directed toward personal or professional growth, human relations training, sensitivity or T-groups, educational information, and/or skills workshops. Both of these kinds are essential to the Partnership Model.

In establishing and maintaining leadership groups, operational decisions regarding size, place, time, agenda generation, and evaluation need to be made. The specific situation and setting of the partnership community should dictate the answers to these questions. The variables of the local situation and the leadership styles are going to have (and should have) the greatest influence on the operational mechanics of the groups in question. The important point is that someone (preferably the group itself) must deal with and plan for the group process and procedures of size, place, meeting time, decision making, etc.

The following guidelines are offered to aid in the group's structure and process.

**Number of Participants.**   The number of participants in the leadership group is important. We suggest an odd number of people to facilitate voting and other forms of decision making. Too many people will make a group unwieldy, but one must always consider the representation factor and the effectiveness factor. We recommend a task force comprised of five, seven, or nine people. Any less than five really does not provide enough input and any more than nine prohibits interaction and makes consensus procedures difficult. Seven is probably an ideal number of people for a leadership/task-force group. There are research studies to support this guideline.

**Meeting Place.**   The importance of the place where the group meets must not be overlooked. The facility should be convenient, comfortable, and private. Furthermore, the group should occupy the most prestigious space available. The Partnership concept cannot operate with a "closet-group." If possible, the meeting room should be in the school building and at least be a place where the group will not be disturbed. It is possible that some meetings will be open to the educational community, so provisions for spectator seats should be provided.

**Meeting Time.**   There are two distinct occasions when a leadership group should meet. The first is to meet when needed. If an emergency arises, they should meet as soon as possible in order to deal with the immediate situation. Second, they should meet at a regularly scheduled time. Groups should meet frequently enough so that the meetings are not long. The frequency of the regular meetings must be decided locally, but we believe in the importance of regularly scheduled meetings.

**Membership.**    Along with scheduling is the problem of membership. Do you allow substitutes or alternates? Do you insist on the actual representatives? If so, do you still conduct a meeting with members absent? Do you follow Robert's Rules using quorums and by-laws or do you work more on a mutual respect, humanistic, consensus model? These decisions are important and must be answered for and by each partnership leadership group.

**Agendas.**    We believe the group should meet whether they have an agenda or not, but if there are known items for discussion, an agenda should be drawn and made public. The minimal requirement is that the group take time at the onset to share members' needs and concerns before proceeding. Agendas can be informal and friendly but they do contribute to effective group behavior.

**Meeting Evaluation.**    Every meeting must be evaluated! We have all been to so many poor meetings in our lives that we are familiar with the frustrations of ineffective, boring, unorganized, and/or threatening meetings. One way to enhance meetings is to evaluate every one that is conducted. The device for this can be a frank discussion in which process of the meeting is critiqued, or paper and pencil instruments can be used. Figure 16–1 is an example of an evaluation form.

The evaluation process can concern itself with any issues the group deems important, but minimumly, topics to receive feedback should include: levels of interaction, quantity and quality of group decision making and closure, length of meeting, expectation fulfillment, physical arrangements, and the management of conflict.

Different people in the group can take charge of the evaluation process on a rotating basis, or one person can be assigned for the year. This evaluator can be the chairperson or preferably some other designee, but someone *must* see to an evaluation of and feedback for the process of each and every meeting conducted. It is one way of increasing the chances of effective meetings.

## GROUP COHESIVENESS

Once a task force or committee has been created to work on school improvement, attention should be given to aspects of group process that may be crucial to the successful functioning of the partnership group. One of these is group cohesiveness.

The cohesiveness of a group is the degree to which members of a group develop loyalty, a feeling of belonging, and a willingness to work for the common good. It is a direct function of the extent to which each individual has made the group's goals his or her own. In that sense, cohesiveness is the sign of a strong and healthy group.

Cohesive groups are often relaxed and informal, spending time on social interplay and items of personal interest. Members of a cohesive group often

A.  How do I feel about this task force as of now?

    1.  Worst possible group
    2.  Almost worst possible group
    3.  Moderately poor group
    4.  Neutral

    5.  Slightly more good than poor
    6.  Moderately good
    7.  Almost best possible group

B.  How clear were the task force goals today?

    1.  Completely unclear
    2.  Almost completely unclear
    3.  Moderately unclear
    4.  Neither clear nor unclear

    5.  Moderately clear
    6.  Almost completely clear
    7.  Completely clear

C.  How did the group work today?

    1.  Work level was completely routine,
       dealt in automatic, passive, uninvolved
       fashion with what was before us
    2.  Almost completely routine and boring
    3.  Rather routine
    4.  About equally productive and routine

    5.  Quite productive
    6.  Almost fully productive
    7.  Work level was fully productive,
       creative, insightful, cumulative

D.  Were different views listened to and used?

    1.  No, they were completely ignored,
       disregarded, disallowed, rejected, or left
       as is
    2.  Almost completely disregarded
    3.  Disregarded quite a bit
    4.  Neither disregarded nor used

    5.  Used quite a bit
    6.  Almost completely used
    7.  Yes, they were completely discussed,
       examined, evaluated, and considered
       in an effort to use them in the
       group's work

E.  How effective was I at this session in helping the group reach its goals?

    1.  Completely ineffective
    2.  Almost completely ineffective
    3.  Quite ineffective
    4.  Neither ineffective nor effective

    5.  Quite effective
    6.  Almost completely effective
    7.  Completely effective

F.  How effectively did we manage conflict?

    1.  Completely ineffective
    2.  Almost completely ineffective
    3.  Somewhat ineffective
    4.  Neutral

    5.  Quite effective
    6.  Almost completely effective
    7.  Completely effective

Please make comments about the physical arrangements and the length of the meeting.

**FIGURE 16–1.  Daily Meeting Evaluation Form**

comment on the good qualities of the group, including past achievements and future potential. Members compliment each other and offer help. They feel free to disagree about group decisions, but support such decisions when made.

    Cohesiveness is not synonymous with group productivity. In fact, for many task-oriented groups, too much emphasis on social relationships may detract from the accomplishment of group business. On the other hand, it is clear that some minimum level of cohesiveness is necessary to have a group at all. In any event, this is a central dimension of group process, which should receive continuing attention in the maintenance of successful groups.

**Group Composition and Cohesiveness.**    Group cohesiveness is known to be a function of member characteristics. When group members are similar in age, sex, background, and experience, cohesiveness is likely to be high. Because members may differ in many ways, this may become a problem for partnership groups. For example, the interests, values, and priorities of teachers and school administrators may be quite different from those of a college faculty member. Likewise, school administrators or state department supervisors might see themselves quite differently from teachers. Awkwardness sometimes results from assumptions made about the differing social status of group members or from the fact that some are "management" and some are "labor." Deliberate attention to these potential obstacles to group cohesiveness is needed to develop a smoothly functioning partnership group.

**Cohesiveness and Member Needs.**    Another important factor in group cohesiveness is the extent to which each of the members feels rewarded for his or her participation. One obvious reward for participation is money, which is commonly delivered in the form of salary, with the expectation that a person's regular duties include committee membership. With the partnership group, this may be a central problem to be solved. Each member of the group, and each institution represented, might need to formalize the assignment of members to this activity. Other important rewards for such group participation include social recognition and prestige, which may require special attention in partnership groups. Deliberate provisions can be made for announcing membership, designating power or authority, and recognizing the importance of accomplishments. In the case of partnership groups, provisions must be made for such rewards in each member's home institution, as well as in the local school environment. Finally, each member of a cohesive group needs to feel like an important contributor. Thus, it is essential that an appropriate role be developed for each member in terms of his or her own talents and interests.

**Cohesiveness and Group Process.**    Each group has a life of its own and each group creates a unique history. Events in the life of a group constitute a tradition that has important consequences for subsequent group functioning. Members can contribute to the development of a group identity by dramatizing crucial events in group life. These common experiences are often symbolized in "fantasy" episodes. As indicated below, such fantasizing is an important mechanism for relieving group tension and developing the "culture" of a group.

## SOCIAL CLIMATE

Some of the most significant insights into group process have been provided by Robert S. Bales[1] who has proposed three critical dimensions of the social climate of small groups. Bales' interaction process analysis categorizes statements, comments, and gestures in such a way that a group can be described on each of the three dimensions.

**Solidarity versus Antagonism.**  A show of group solidarity is any statement or gesture that indicates a member believes the group to be important and that he or she will help the group collectively and other members individually. Antagonism is the opposite, in which case a member gives indications that the group is unimportant or that he or she is unwilling to contribute to group goals. Obviously, the amount of communication high on the group solidarity dimension is important to the development of group cohesiveness.

**Tension versus Tension Release.**  A certain degree of social unease and stiffness is present in every new social group. This "primary tension," which may be accompanied by extreme politeness, frequent silence, or apparent boredom, passes normally as members become acquainted. However, at times, direct recognition of this social tension is necessary to release it. Most groups will release primary tensions easily. On the other hand, "secondary tensions" may be a more difficult problem. These tensions arise from group functioning as the group works out a social structure and establishes a pattern of work. Competition among members or disagreements about the group task may create sufficient tension to interrupt efficient group work. Often such tensions are not faced directly because of the vested interests of individual members. Here, statements of tension release are especially important to successful group work. Group members may use laughter, conciliation, or confrontation to reduce group tensions. Each group seems to develop its own mechanism for tension release, often referring to the early experiences of the group. Alert group members can play a constructive role in group functioning by remaining aware of tension levels and seeking to relieve tensions when they seem to interfere with task progress.

**Agreement versus Disagreement.**  A third dimension of social climate is the extent to which group communication reflects agreement or disagreement. Of course, the amount of agreement and disagreement is a function of the task set for the group. In fact, disagreement may be an essential aspect of accomplishing the group task. However, as Bales has emphasized, the extent of agreement or disagreement has important consequences for the social climate of groups. Too much disagreement may damage the social fabric, reducing group cohesiveness and increasing tension to levels that interfere with group functions. Thus, a crucial aspect of group process is the handling of disagreements. Groups need special awareness and skills to resolve conflicts and disagreements, especially in partnership groups where different interests are represented and disagreements are likely. This problem is treated at length later in the chapter.

## TRAINING GROUPS

One of the earlier and still successful training techniques used by applied behavioral scientists is the T-group or training group. The T-group is a method where a small group of people deal with the immediate concerns and processes of the group.

Bradford, Gibb, and Benne describe the T-group as follows:

> A T-Group is a relatively unstructured group in which individuals participate as learners. The data for learning are not outside these individuals or remote from their immediate experience within the T-Group. The data are the transactions among members, their own behavior in the group, as they struggle to create a productive and viable organization, miniature society; and as they work to stimulate and support one another's learning within that society.[2]

Participating in a T-group can be a very enriching experience in personal growth and group dynamics. Standard group functions such as directive leader, an agenda, a set of operating principles, time-lines, and other normative group behaviors are reduced or are expendable, and the group is left to deal with itself and the social-interaction patterns that develop.

The experience can be very rewarding to a work group such as a task force who must spend hours together for specific task functions. The T-group can provide participants with personal data about themselves and others, and also learning experiences about the group as a whole so the group can function more openly, frankly, comfortably, and effectively.

Under the leadership of a qualified trainer, we recommend this team-building approach along with other team-building activities for each of the leadership groups that are formed. T-grouping is often a part of staff-development and OD projects. However, in addition to utilizing this technique for training, there is something to be learned from the behavior of people when in a T-group that has a great deal to do with the effectiveness of a task-oriented group. We call this the T-group analogy.

Most experts in group dynamics agree that typical, "successful" T-groups have at least two identifiable phases. In phase one, the participants are described as first acting dependently and then counterdependently. That is, participants first rely on the leader, the group, then friends for the group's activities. This is accompanied by frustration, high-level interaction, self-oriented activity, discussion of problems external to the T-group, aggression, subgrouping, and a concern for rules and authority. Then, behavior is apt to switch to revolt, trainer challenge, intense involvement in group tasks, pairing, and independent actions—which is labeled the counterdependent or independent stage.

The second phase is aptly described as an interdependency phase when participants begin to show concern for the group and spend less energy on their own needs. In this phase, behavior is characterized by assertiveness, understanding, acceptance, consensus, and what has been referred to as "group mind" or cohesiveness.

The task-oriented group many times will (or should) go through the same phases as they struggle to deal with each other and the group task. See Figure 16-2.

Since total commitment never occurs in this phase, individuals never "get out of their box." Individual efforts toward goals are limited because of dependent-independent conflicts. Many task groups do not resolve external problems because they do not deal with internal dynamics. See Figure 16-3.

Groups that have resolved internal problems are like T-groups in Phase II. Individuals act interdependently and use full energies to solve target problems. See Figure 16–4.

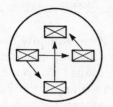

Typical group interaction scheme during planning, brainstorming session characterized by:

1. high level of verbal interaction

2. high degree of role clarification activity testing authority, mistrusting, claiming territory, checking credentials, etc.

3. low degree of commitment to group activity

4. medium degree of concern for ''Those I Represent''

**FIGURE 16–2.   Phase I of a Traditional T-Group**

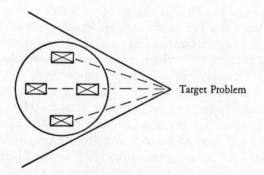

Target Problem

**FIGURE 16–3.   Problem-Solving Efforts Limited in Phase I Climate**

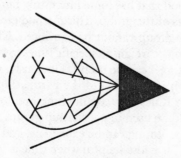

TARGET PROBLEM

**FIGURE 16–4.   Phase II of T-Group Climate**

## GROUP DECISION-MAKING METHODS

There are a variety of methods that can be employed for the process of decision making. Many groups do not understand or review those methods prior to implementing their assignment. An analysis of these options should help task force groups to avoid common pitfalls.

Of course, groups can allow one person in authority to make all of the decisions. This approach may be useful in satisfying administrator needs and may be practical when the issues concern routine matters, emergency situa-tions, or matters that are clearly not within the jurisdiction of the group's re-sponsibility in the first place. Another reason for authority-based decision mak-ing might be when time is a problem. The disadvantages are clear. One person is not a good resource for every decision, and even if one authority figure were, the advantages of group interaction are lost. The greatest disadvantage, how-ever, comes from lack of commitment to the decision by the group after the de-cision is made.

There is another method, that of relying on an expert, that resembles the authority model, except the "authority" shifts to whomever appears to be the expert or have the most knowledge about any particular issue at any particular time. The difficulty lies in determining just who is the expert. Also, the same problem of commitment may occur as in the authority model. Resources of the other members are ignored or are not utilized to the full extent. This method is expedient when one member of the group possesses advanced skills, knowl-edge, or motivation on a particular issue. Using the expertise of one member to make decisions is a superior method when other group-oriented methods could be classified or perceived as "sharing ignorance." Generally speaking, these methods have little application for Partnership settings.

A variation of the authority/expert rule method is to use discussion pre-ceding the ultimate decision by the authority or expert. Many advisory councils operate in this manner. The principal, for example, forms a group and calls the meetings to hear different points of view before making the decisions. One of the disadvantages is that it creates a tendency for members to compete for influence upon the leader. This situation usually does not allow equal partici-pation, even in discussion, since the most vocal will dominate the floor. There is also the possibility that the group will get the impression that the leader is merely pacifying the group or patronizing them with listening but not acting.

An infrequently used method that has some interesting ramifications is to average the opinions or thoughts of the group. This method can be applied to routine matters especially if the group cannot be convinced. There are situa-tions that may require prioritizing or weighing specific issues in which a mathe-matical averaging or "mean-taking" can be useful. Obviously, there is a defi-nite loss in the interaction which is so crucial to the partnership concept.

Voting, usually by Robert's Rules, is a common method for small groups to make decisions. Voting should be used in partnership groups only as a back-up method when consensus fails. Voting can be expedient, and it has the sur-face appearance of being "fair." It is also helpful when time is short, when the decision is not very important, when minority feelings will not be a hindrance, or when complete member commitment is not essential. The disadvantages are that, in fact, voting usually leaves a disenchanted minority that endangers implementation and future group effectiveness and cohesiveness. A major problem is the fact it does not allow for the weighing of issues. The single vote for each person does not allow for the fact that some people may feel very strongly about a particular point, and there is no "legal" way to express this.

One variation of voting that helps to alleviate the previous problem is to allow voting on a scaled basis. For example, the following could be arranged: two points—very strongly in favor; one point—in favor; minus one point—not in favor; minus two points—very strongly against. Members can be allowed a certain number of points to "spend" during any one meeting. The process works, but many people may perceive the procedure as unnecessarily complicated. However, this procedure can be used as a training device to illustrate the disadvantages of the accepted process of straight voting.

The preferred method for collaborative efforts is the process of consensus. Consensus is frequently misunderstood or misused and, for that reason, it is important to discuss the method thoroughly. The consensus model must include the following steps:

1.  All members must express their opinion on every issue. This means that leaders must take care to see that discussions allow for "equal" participation. If a member feels absolutely neutral on an issue, then he or she must explain why.
2.  As it becomes apparent that consensus is going to be difficult (there is a difference of opinion), each member professing ideas against the point must be allowed extra time to express their particular reasons.
3.  Once there is a thorough airing of opinions, the chairperson must confer with those that are opposed to determine if they will block the proposal (because they cannot "live" with the decision). If those opposed are extremely upset with the proposal, then the leader must declare that the issue is *not* resolved. A few people, then, can block the majority's wishes in a consensus model.
4.  Further discussion can occur, the proposal can be modified, or the issue can be dropped altogether; but the group, like a hung jury, cannot, must not, proceed on that particular decision.

The disadvantages of the consensus method are that it takes time, energy, patience, trust, and understanding. It can be divisive to a group that needs cohesiveness, but if the group understands the purpose and the leader is skillful, using the consensus model should build cohesiveness and trust within the group. The rationale for this method is that it tends to produce creative solutions to problems, develops high quality decision making for innovative projects, increases chances of implementation because of member commitment, uses the resources of all members, makes future decision making easier, and is most applicable for large, important, philosophical issues that concern the life of all people in the educational community.

If a group fails to discuss the alternatives of group decision making and fails to make a thorough study of the options available to them, then the group effectiveness will be seriously threatened. Robert's Rules are clumsy and do not facilitate consensus. The other permissive alternative is to allow the more vocal minority to intimidate the group so that very little participation is accomplished. Members may feel sorry for those that complain the most, cry the loudest, and seem to be most easily hurt. The result is that majority members do not speak out, and implementation of change projects is difficult. Partnershipping experiences dictate that groups of people work together in the decision-making process as part of governance. Groups must abide by valid and accepted patterns of good group process. Group decision making is crucial to the life of the partnership group. These issues of group life must be dealt with before, during, and after school improvement projects.

## CONFLICT MANAGEMENT

The management of conflict is an area of group life that is very important. No matter how careful small groups manage their decision-making process, there will be conflict. This is as true of the school organization itself as it is of small groups. For this reason, the last section of this chapter will be devoted to the issue of conflict management.

Conflict in organizations is inevitable—whether the group is managed by autocratic methods or democratic/participatory methods. Schools are no exception to this truism. Conflict is everywhere in the educational community, but it is only recently that conflict is being recognized as a natural source of organizational energy.

Evidence of this general shift of attitude about conflict is found in the literature and in the increased number of workshops, conferences, and graduate classes that deal with it. Perhaps a fair historical assessment of the general attitude toward conflict has been one of closed mouth, denial, cover-up, and guilt. Now, the attitude seems to be shifting toward openness, acceptance, exposure, and constructive problem solving.

This change is extremely interesting in light of our group leadership model for school improvement. Conflict is normally increased during change activities. Therefore, it is important to look at conflict management as it relates to our theme because the activities we are recommending will probably increase overt conflict and open confrontation. There is a wealth of information available to managers dealing with conflict. The following is a brief outline of management techniques that may be especially useful to partners. Some of these ideas have been adapted from Roland Barnes.[3]

1. As long as there is interaction there will be conflict. Conflict is part of the nature of human life and is to be expected in organizations utilizing group leadership.
2. The chance of conflict increases when drastic changes in the organizational and social structure occur. Changes or threats of change seem to increase aggression and confrontation.

3. Conflict has positive, constructive functions in organizations. It can keep small groups stimulated, active, and creative.
4. Conflict is a complex social/psychological phenomenon which is difficult to understand and an even more difficult one with which to cope, but one that generally should not be avoided.
5. Confrontations for leaders usually occur in the arena of an adversary versus the administrator, or in the form of two groups representing different interests which need arbitration.
6. An increase in involvement (group leadership) increases the opportunity for conflict, but also legitimizes a "stage" or an arena for it.
7. Events that lead to conflict are usually centered around the following:
    a. the event touches an important aspect of the life of the person in conflict
    b. the event treats different groups differently, or is perceived as such
    c. the event is viewed as something someone should or could do something about.
8. Typical content areas over which conflict occurs are:
    a. power and authority
    b. cultural values and beliefs
    c. personality conflicts
    d. "turfdom" or territoriality.

Three specific phases of conflict can be identified and managed through planning and training. *Crisis prevention* reduces the number of potentially destructive conflict situations. *Confrontation and conflict intervention* deal with the "here and now" of individuals or groups in disagreement. *Conflict resolution* involves long-range problem solving.

**Crisis Prevention.** While conflict is a natural force in organizational life, no one wants conflict to escalate to destructive proportions. Riots, demonstrations, sit-ins, strikes, walk-outs, organizational sabotage, and vandalism are examples of events that have occurred in schools at some time or another. They are crises that could have been prevented. If conflict is not managed properly, then the situation may develop into a crisis which is obviously a negative experience (at least temporarily) for the organization. However, there is significant difference between crisis prevention and conflict prevention. Too many administrators have concentrated on the latter, which has a stifling effect on employees and is an unreasonable expectation for the organization.

The problem facing groups in leadership roles is to expect and allow conflict, but to prevent or reduce the possibility of crisis. A crisis in a planning group may not be seen as catastrophic to the organization's members at large, but it can be very devastating to the life of the group and consequently to the organization development. Crises in small groups might include group disbandment, poor attendance, collusion, factions, extreme counterproductive behaviors, costly and purposeful delays, and/or physical violence. We could describe crisis prevention in task force groups as that portion of the group development energies that are devoted to reducing the conditions of poor interpersonal relations and conflict situations which negatively influence the groups' effectiveness. The following list may provide some specific suggestions for crisis prevention:

1. Early recognition of symptoms which, in part, can be achieved through feedback devices such as survey analysis.
2. Establishing within the group normative behavior which could be described as "approach behavior" as opposed to normative behavior described as "avoidance behavior"; group leaders can and should encourage this assertive style within the group. Team-building training activities will also contribute to the kind of trust relationships that condone confrontive behaviors.
3. Open-door policies on the part of the authority figures in the group who make serious attempts to be available and are receptive to subordinate members.
4. Leaders who admit mistakes and thus establish a vulnerable posture, which has the tendency to reduce defensiveness which, in turn, reduces the potential of confrontation escalation.
5. Inclusion of occasional activities which have the sole purpose of improving morale.
6. Using self-evaluation and introspective devices for group members—the sharing of self-evaluation and self-disclosure activities that usually accompany team-building training facilitate this goal.
7. Well-planned meetings with agenda items announced in advance especially for controversial subjects—this includes a careful consideration of the nonmember attendance policy.
8. Providing time for social interaction and informal chats as long as these do not exceed the limits of being perceived as avoidance behaviors.
9. Using suggestion boxes and other devices that enable members free and easy access to the decision-making process.
10. Reducing organizational structures and procedures that contribute to the territorial imperative syndrome—certain group member representation forms, competitive departments, hierarchical alignments, racial imbalances, seating arrangements, etc., can all contribute to "turfdom fights."
11. Conscious efforts to avoid overwork burn-out and other stress-producing situations.

**Confrontation and Conflict Intervention.** The immediate strategy used to deal with interpersonal or intergroup relations that have suffered due to a crisis situation is referred to as the *confrontation* part of conflict management. These situations are usually manifested in the following situations:

1. A long-term conflict is brought to the surface through an intervention that forces people to deal with the problem in the "here and now."
2. Two opposing factions within the group become polarized to the point of aggressive behavior.

3. Two individuals or two groups have a disagreement with each other that is manifested in loud, angry behavior and requires arbitration on the part of some third party.
4. Someone in authority is challenged by a subordinate and the dialogue is escalated in an aggressive manner.

In other words, confrontation usually occurs or can be identified when the behavior of at least one party becomes aggressive (as opposed to assertive). Anger is very much a psychological factor in these cases and must be dealt with directly. If one is in a leadership role (either individual or group) one must try to reduce the anger, satisfy the angry parties, and shift the dialogue to tones of problem-solving and conflict resolution. Barnes[4] suggested four steps as confrontation procedures: accessibility, reception, acceptance, and credibility. Figure 16–5 shows an elaboration of these concepts.

**Conflict Resolution.**   The third phase of conflict management in the small group setting is conflict resolution. It can be defined as the amelioration of current crisis symptoms through problem-solving activities that change the conditions which caused the crisis or conflict in the first place.

There are many systems established for problem-solving steps, but the following are recommended to partnership groups as one type of action planning for conflict resolution.

1. *Problem awareness.*   The admission of the problem without defensiveness is the first important thing.
2. *Cause/effect discrimination.*   The causal or symptomatic behavior should be identified without the group "pointing fingers."
3. *Problem focus.*   Alternative solutions must be identified and group energies must focus on same.
4. *Solution.*   At this point, anything but *in*action is desired. One solution is selected and planning activated.
5. *Implementation.*   The solution must be put into operation and given a chance.
6. *Review and evaluation.*   Since conflict is dynamic, the situation must be reviewed and evaluated constantly.

In summary, we cannot be too strong in advocating planned conflict management based on the premise that conflict is natural to groups and organizations, and must be dealt with, not repressed. Schools need to provide an open arena where conflict is legitimate. This means providing a structure as well as procedures to encourage conflict resolution. This theme is particularly important for groups and organizations during times of change. If the leadership group becomes cautious because there is conflict or because they receive criticism, then the innovation will not survive. Conflict and the resulting stress are both an integral part of school improvement.

|  | Remember, it will be a race |
|---|---|
| *Accessability:* | First make yourself accessible and available to the persons or groups involved. ("Come in, I'll talk with you right now.") |
| *Reception:* | Establish a friendly or neutral reception for the people under stress. ("I'm glad you came to me.") |
| *Acceptance:* | Show that you accept their feelings or their claims. This can be done without *agreeing* to their point. ("You feel very strong about this don't you?") |
| *Credibility:* | You must establish credibility as a group or as someone who is capable of and willing to take action regarding their claim. ("I'll have to check this out and I'll make a judgment about your situation by tomorrow noon and call you back.") |
| *Expression:* | You are entitled to express your views and personal beliefs if called for. The group members must be "real persons" who can express feelings and emotions. Be assertive—not aggressive in so doing. ("I know I don't like to be called names," or "I am feeling very upset about this.") |

**FIGURE 16-5.   Confrontation Procedures**

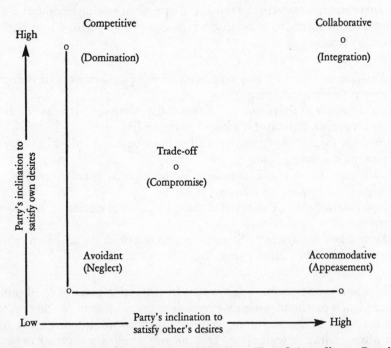

**FIGURE 16-6.   Five Conflict-handling Orientations, Plotted According to Party's Inclinations to Satisfy Own and Other's Desires.**   Adapted by Jeffrey Eiseman from K. Thomas, "Conflict and Conflict Management," in *Handbook of Industrial and Organizational Psychology,* ed. M. D. Dunnette (Chicago: Rand McNally, 1976). This diagram is built on the work of R. R. Blake and J. S. Mouton, *The Managerial Grid* (Houston: Gulf Publishing, 1964); and R. R. Blake; H. A. Shepard; and J. S. Mouton, *Managing Intergroup Conflict in Industry* (Houston: Gulf Publishing, 1964).

The Partnership Model is particularly strong in this regard. The leadership group can "field" conflicts originating outside of the group and deal with internal conflicts as well. The fact that the leadership group meets in the school building, conducts open meetings, utilizes high involvement tactics, and provides a reward system (it's alright to express conflict; something good comes from it)—all help to create a good atmosphere for conflict management.

Eiseman[5] has developed a schema that puts this collaborative strategy for conflict management in good perspective. Collaboration is explained by Eiseman as one of five basic stances that can be taken when faced with conflict. They are described in Figure 16-6.

## ENDNOTES

1. Robert S. Bales, *Personality and Interpersonal Behavior* (New York: Holt, Rinehart & Winston, 1970).
2. L. Bradford, J. Gibb, and K. Benne, "Two Educational Innovations," in *T-Group Theory and Laboratory Method,* ed. Bradford, Gibb, and Benne (New York: John Wiley & Sons, Inc., 1964), p. 1.
3. Roland E. Barnes, *Understanding the Nature of Conflict: A Neglected Dimension in Educational Administration* (Pittsburgh: Center for the Study of Desegregation and Conflict, University of Pittsburgh, 1974).
4. Ibid., p. 10.
5. Jeffrey Eiseman, "A Third-Party Consideration Model for Resolving Recurring Conflicts Collaboratively," *The Journal of Applied Behavioral Science,* NTL Institute for Applied Behavioral Science 13, no. 3. (1977): 303–314.

# Chapter 17

# Administrative Issues

Another set of tactics are needed to deal with administrative issues that arise in the Partnership Model of School Improvement. How can questions of governance and control be resolved? How can financing be arranged? How can personnel from different agencies be assigned? How can parents, students, and other members of the community best be involved? In answering these questions, we shall be searching for specific ways to reduce tendencies toward institutional territoriality and to strengthen tendencies toward collaboration. Also, we will be stressing processes of personal interaction in which partners experience a genuine sense of parity.

## GOVERNANCE, CONTROL, AND SHARED LEADERSHIP

The condition of parity refers to an operational equality in decision making relative to goal setting, program intervention, resource utilization, and evaluation. Conditions that enhance this concept of equality in a problem-solving group have been described by Petrella and Block.

> A group of people must be willing to address some very difficult human problems, if they wish to become an effective problem-solving team. They must be clear about and jointly committed to a common purpose or mission. They must confront and manage the distribution of authority, influence and power within the group. They must confront and manage conflict and aggression that arises in the group. They must also understand and manage the urge to take flight from this conflict and aggression. They must give support to one another and yet be critical of one another. This critical attitude must include facing and dealing with incompetence and failure.[1]

In the public school system the conditions identified by Petrella and Block are often missing. From the individual school in a local district through colleges, universities, and state departments of education, a climate of isolation has developed in which each institution blames others for current problems within the total educational system. In such a climate, the elements in the system often work, not together, but separately or at cross purposes. We have recommended local partnerships for school improvement to change the current climate and bring about better cooperation among educational institutions. One aspect of these recommendations is that local partnerships adopt the principle of parity in decision making.

Organizationally, these issues are confronted when a partnership group is established and representatives of each institution begin to meet. This group may be labeled a task force, a policy board, a governing body, a board of directors, or whatever. If possible, the group should consist of an individual from each participating agency capable of committing the resources of the respective agencies to the partnership effort. If policies are developed by representatives who do not possess this capacity, the success of the partnership will be meager at best.

Discussions should begin about goals, methods, and resources of the collaboration. The following may suggest some issues to be resolved:

1. Is the collaborative unit concerned with policy only, program only, or with both?
2. To what extent is the collaborative unit established to develop policy? Develop program? Implement policy? Implement program? Assess policy? Assess/evaluate program?
3. What process should be used in selecting/electing representatives to the collaborative unit? Is selection by the chief administrative officer of a constituent organization assurance that the constituency is represented? Should the membership of the constituency group elect its representative to ensure representation?
4. How can disparities that may exist between organized and unorganized constituent groups be resolved?
5. What is the role of the representative: (a) an advocate of the organization and its political interest, (b) protector of the constituency and its interests and territory, (c) an expert in a program area? Can one person be all things?
6. What is each representative's responsibility and authority?
7. Who determines each representative's responsibility and authority? The constituent organization? The collaborative unit? State, federal, or local standards/guidelines?
8. What are the statutory, regulatory, and policy responsibilities of the constituent organizations which must be recognized and which will set limits, protect agency prerogatives and jurisdictions, and are essential to independence and uniqueness?
9. How do groups with vested interests or special interests gain recognition and representation?

Once the policy board has worked through these questions and has established a definitive statement of purpose, program interventions, and resource utilization, a formal agreement should be established. Mico[2] has described the essential features of a type of agreement that should form the basis of a partnership effort involving educational agencies. This agreement has been labeled a *Memorandum of Agreement* or MOA.

> The MOA can have many parts to it, depending upon the complexities of the relationships between the parties and of the problem they are working with. Generally speaking, it describes the reasons why the parties are collaborating and how they will work together; it identifies the resources which each pro-

pose to use and/or share in the problem-solving effort; and it describes the "ground rules" under which the parties agree to abide. The MOA differs from a contract in a legal sense in that it is not binding once signed. In fact, it was part of our intent to devise an instrument which could be a basis for a "continuing process of negotiation." We think it is important that any party can request a renegotiation of an MOA if it feels one is needed, and that a mandatory review of the agreement is conducted if a fixed period of time—such as six months—passes in which a renegotiation has not been conducted.

It is our contention that ongoing confrontation and negotiation are essential between and among the parties involved in a social problem-solving effort, if conducted in settings conducive to collaborative, constructive decision-making.

Coleman and Cushnie,[3] in their work in the area of community development, have found the MOA to be an excellent tool for establishing positive working relationships between agencies involved in partnership efforts. Three of their findings are given:

Where MOA's and goals are set early, means of negotiating relationships and measuring progress are available.

Where MOA's were developed, they provide a helpful means of testing norms and standards of working together.

The MOA concept is a valuable tool for establishing working relationships and deserves continuing thought, development and adaptation to a variety of relationships.

Thus, following the establishment of a governing board and a delineation of policies, including statements of the goals, methods, and resources within the partnership, the MOA serves as an instrument through which each participating agency commits itself to the collaborative effort. These are essential ingredients for the governance, control and shared leadership functions of the partnership.

## FINANCE AND BUDGETING

As in every business enterprise, the educational partnership must be concerned with the efficiency of the operation in a rigorous attempt to achieve maximum gains at minimum cost. In respect to the financial efficiency of the partnership effort, two concepts stated in the preceding section of this chapter are important. First, the policy board must be specific in delineating the goals of the partnership and establishing priorities among these goals. Second, the MOA must specify the sources of funding and their limits. Since the MOA is to be reviewed and renegotiated at regular intervals, questions pertaining to finance and budget are never permitted to drift.

To be effective, a partnership effort designed to improve some aspect of the elementary/secondary schools must involve the expenditure of operating funds from each participating agency. Federal funding is usually for specific purposes, and partnership efforts relying solely on such funds are severely limited in scope. Thus, while funding should be sought from a variety of sources, a fundamental point to be remembered is that seldom does a true fit exist between the goal intent of another's money and that of the partnership. In the past, partnership efforts have been based on the availability of either federal or state funds. When the funding period ended, the partnership also ended. School improvement efforts based on such a haphazard system of collaboration tend to become sporadic and piecemeal.

Perhaps the most important elements to be remembered relative to financing and budgeting in the partnership approach to school improvement are (1) the policy board establishes and approves goals, priorities, and budgets; and (2) either the director of the partnership program or a budget officer approves expenditures. To the extent policy board members try to manage daily operations of the program, the program will drift because of an absence of daily monitoring and adjustment.

## PERSONNEL DEPLOYMENT

As with financial decisions, the utilization of personnel is determined by the policy board and described in the MOA. Specific personnel to be utilized in the partnership effort will vary from time to time, depending on the nature of expertise needed to achieve the specific goal or objective being pursued at a particular time. In reference to this aspect of partnerships, Petrella and Block state:

> In developing teamwork, what really is at stake is managing the process of decision making within a shifting power framework. As early as 1925, Mary Parker Follett was writing about the distinction of power over people and power with people and the "law of the situation." The law of the situation is that at different times and for different tasks, different team members must take the lead and be accorded greater influence. Further, it is rare—maybe we should rule it out altogether—that any one person has the capacity to make valid and wise organizational decisions. An interplay of ideas, feelings and experiences is required to meet the demands of given situations. This requires a management of team relationships which allows full participation of the membership or delegation to those members most capable to manage the problem. This means that the authority structure of a team is not in a condition of steady state with fixed rules of operation. Instead, a team must pursue a dynamic equilibrium which is established and re-established.[4]

An essential characteristic of successful partnerships, therefore, is flexible teamwork, in which personnel from each participating agency work together in an attempt to achieve the goals of the venture. As indicated in the previous chapter, systematic efforts to build teamwork are probably required.

Sometimes the assignment of personnel to work on school improvement can be simple and direct; each institution incorporates partnership work into the duties of existing personnel. At other times, more complicated administrative arrangements are needed. For example, a partnership may need to "buy" released time for personnel from one or more institutions. For example, money may be transferred to a local college to hire a part-time person who releases a regular faculty member from regular duties.

Special administrative structures may need to be created to make some of the necessary arrangements. Teacher centers are examples of such structures. Teacher centers often go beyond informal memoranda of agreement to establish a formal legal entity, whose board of directors is empowered to hire staff, expend funds, etc. As indicated in the final chapter, teacher centers include some of the best examples of collaboration in school improvement.

## COMMUNITY INVOLVEMENT

The tactics necessary to deal with the administrative issues relating to community involvement need special attention. While community groups are not considered to be one of the primary partners in our model, we want to emphasize their importance for the local school. Each professional partner should establish mechanisms to form liaisons with community groups. These groups may represent tax payers, parents, or special interest groups, but they are all important sources for human and material resources.

Arthur F. Wileden[5] has studied this situation carefully and has developed several hypotheses that are related to the responsibilities of citizens of a local community to the educational system. He believes that the people in the community have the responsibility for keeping informed about their community and how they can best relate to the world around them. This is primarily an educative process. Consequently, educators have a responsibility to provide some of this information for the community.

Wileden believes that the people in each local community are responsible for the destiny of that community and must be involved in setting goals and priorities that guide local government, education, and social agencies. In turn, the schools and churches can help establish formats and arenas for these kinds of interactions.

Wileden points out the necessity for the community to determine how these goals and priorities are implemented. This involves a study/discussion/decision-making process. This process is particularly important for the schools in the community.

Finally, the people are responsible for seeing that their ideas are put into action. The schools should be open for advice in this regard; but we believe once the goals have been set using community involvement, professional educators must be given the responsibility of implementing the goals of the community in the manner the professionals consider most effective.

Perhaps the cycle could be described as follows: The people of the local community elect school board members who hire professional educators who in turn attempt to carry out the goals of the community. In this process we are recommending that professional groups form partnerships to maximize the resources available for each school. Each of these partnership groups should receive input from their constituents as the partnership focuses on the local school.

As a result, partnerships designed to improve educational practice in elementary and secondary schools play a significant role. The community is represented through these partners who, as professionals, implement the policies in the most effective manner possible. If the community loses faith in the school, then the cycle starts over through the democratic process of school board elections. School boards have an opportunity to make necessary adjustments and complete the cycle. This sequence can be described as a cycle-collaborative process. As noted by Denemark and Yff:

> Partnership does not imply identity of competencies and perspectives, but it does imply equality of opportunity and responsibility in contributing one's competencies and perspectives. The basic premise of a joint relationship is that educational problems cannot be attacked effectively by the isolated efforts of any one group. A truly effective attack obtains when it incorporates the different competencies of community, school and university people and their different orientations toward curricular, instructional and teacher education problems.[6]

In the preface to this report, Denemark states a most important rationale for the pooling of resources in a partnership effort designed to improve the educational needs of society. He states:

> Such a partnership demands new sensitivities, new commitments, new responses from each of the partners—schools, colleges and universities, communities, organized professionals, and governmental agencies. Each must approach this shared concern with willingness to admit possible earlier lapses and openness to a joint search for new ways of meeting the educational challenge confronting our nation.[7]

From a practical point of view, the local administration must decide what specific procedures will be used to maximize citizen input in this cyclical-collaborative process. There are several ways that have proven successful in various communities. One of the most effective is the formation of citizens' advisory groups. These groups function best if they are school-based and serve to transmit information from the school to the community and provide feedback for the school from the community.

However, increased citizen participation may have a negative impact on the school unless some controls and guidelines are established. Each building administration must develop its own guidelines which are specific to their situation. However, we do advise the following general items for consideration:

1. Do not expect the formal Parent Teachers Association to perform this function. The PTA is an important group and has its own objectives which can be coordinated with the citizens' advisory groups, but neither of these groups should supplant each other.

2. A basic charter must be prepared for each group that is formed.
3. This charter contains such items as by-laws, administrative guidelines, operational procedures, and legal as well as moral limitations. Included in these statements should be a description of the formal relationship with the local school board.
4. The charter must have approval from the school district board of education.
5. The charter should include a proviso which states that the group can never meet without the presence of the local school principal or the principal's designate.
6. In addition, an effective charter will include the following specifics:
   a. statement of purpose
   b. provisions for meeting times and places
   c. description of the procedures for conducting meetings such as Robert's Rules or some similar guidelines for decision making
   d. provisions for some means for the group to replace itself—usually on a rotating basis with provisions for term length which guarantees a balance between new members and carry-over members (these provisions should also include a method of disbanding when the group is no longer effective)
   e. a system for evaluating the group's effectiveness
   f. methods and means of publishing the minutes or results of the meetings
   g. the recommendation that matters of specific personnel problems be avoided
   h. meetings should be open to the public
   i. student representation is strongly urged.

As mentioned previously, each school must work out the details applicable to its situation but "work" is the key. Forming advisory groups as well as the total process of community involvement is a sensitive administrative issue which takes a great deal of time and effort to ensure efficacy.

The emphasis in this section of the chapter has been on community involvement. Emerging from our discussion has been the belief that all who are involved—who will be affected in any way—should be significantly involved in the change effort. As far as the community is concerned, this means that parents, leaders from business, industry, and labor, governmental agency personnel, and others should be informed and provided opportunities to participate in the partnership approach to school improvement. To ignore these resources is to ignore an important potential for a successful change effort.

## ENDNOTES

1. Tony Petrella and Peter Block, "Managing with Teams," in *The Dallas Connection*, ed. Robert A. Luke, Jr. (Washington, D.C.: National Training and Development Service, 1974), p. 88.

2. Paul R. Mico, "The Collaborative Model," in *First Tango in Boston*, ed. Robert A. Luke, Jr. (Washington, D.C., National Training and Development Service, 1973), pp. 10–11.

3. John H. Coleman, Jr. and William D. Cushnie, "Organizing Neighborhood Task Forces," in *First Tango in Boston*, pp. 22 and 25.

4. Petrella and Block, "Managing with Teams," p. 95.

5. Arthur F. Wileden, "The Professional Leader," in *Leadership and Social Change*, ed. William R. Lassey and Richard R. Fernandez (La Jolla, Calif.: University Associates, Inc., 1976), p. 246.

6. George W. Denemark and Joost Yff, *Obligation for Reform: Final Report of the Higher Education Task Force on Improvement and Reform in American Education* (Washington, D.C., American Association of Colleges for Teacher Education, 1974), p. 13.

7. Ibid., p. 8.

# Chapter 18

# Developing Knowledge Resources

Another tactical problem in school improvement is how to locate and make use of knowledge related to local school problems. In fact, one popular way to conceptualize the process of planned educational change is to think of it as a process of knowledge transfer. On the one hand, there are knowledge producers, who create theoretical and applied knowledge; on the other, there are knowledge users who put theory and knowledge into practice. From this "communications" point of view, the way to improve education is to improve knowledge production and utilization (KPU). Havelock's Linkage Model is such a communications view, in which strong linkages between knowledge producers and knowledge users are recommended both to improve knowledge production (by relating it to user problems) and knowledge use (by making relevant knowledge more available to users). In recent years this knowledge production and utilization view has been widely employed in the formulation of federal educational policy.

In this chapter, the KPU process in education will be reviewed with special emphasis on the problem of knowledge utilization in the process of school improvement. First, the Research, Development, and Dissemination (RD&D) Model of KPU will be discussed and its limitations noted. Next, an alternative view, the Configurational Perspective, will be described. Finally, recommendations will be made for making effective use of knowledge resources in the school improvement process.

## RESEARCH, DEVELOPMENT, AND DIFFUSION MODEL OF KPU

The systematic development of knowledge to solve a problem or to create a new product has been a widespread practice in large industrial firms and in the military. Many large firms employ a special staff to conduct basic and applied research that leads to new or improved products. Heavy spending on research and development (R&D) is characteristic of such private industries as electronics, communications, drug manufacturing, automobiles, and chemicals. The military establishment is an even bigger spender for R&D, much of it on contract to universities or private businesses. For example, the aerospace industry incorporates large amounts of basic and applied research in government contracts to develop new aircraft or missiles. The same is true of other industries that develop new technologies for the military. The space program is often used as a prototypic example of systematic R&D, combining a vast array of theoretical and applied research with the development of production and management systems necessary to accomplish the remarkable goal of space travel. During the period from 1950 to 1970 many educational policy makers adopted the view that systematic R&D, as it was practiced in industry and the military, could provide major improvements in American school practices.

Glaser,[1] for example, noted the importance of scientific knowledge about learning as a basis for educational practice, emphasizing that scientific theories are rarely available for practical use without extensive work in translation and development. He cited a parallel between the invention of a new method of teaching arithmetic and the development of the transistor.

First, theoretical research explores basic phenomena that may be related to a practical problem. In the case of the transistor, the research may be on the nature of conductivity; in the case of arithmetic, the research may be on the processes of learning. Second, fundamental development research is conducted to discover the basic variables involved and their relationships (for example, the basic qualities of semi-conductor materials or the variables in learning arithmetic). Third, specific development builds on previous inquiries to produce a working model, whether a transistor or an arithmetic program. Fourth, the working model undergoes further design and testing, being modified to function efficiently in a variety of field conditions. Finally, after the product has been fully developed, information about the new product must be disseminated to users.

The final step in the R&D process, dissemination (or diffusion), has a special significance in education. After new educational products are developed, substantial problems exist in getting educators to know about and adopt the new products. Thus it has been common in discussing educational innovations to talk about research, development, and diffusion (RD&D).

Havelock, in his summary of strategic orientations to educational innovation, characterized the RD&D Model as based on five assumptions.[2] First, the development and application of an innovation is assumed to take place in an orderly sequence that includes research, development, and packaging prior to a mass dissemination procedure. Second, the management of this sequence requires extensive planning over a long time period. Third, a division and coordination of labor is necessary among elements in the RD&D system. Fourth, a rational consumer is assumed who will adopt an innovation on the basis of a mass dissemination program. Fifth, high initial development costs are balanced by the long-term benefits that come from an efficient, high quality innovation that can be widely used by a mass audience.

The RD&D model became an important ingredient in federal education policy during the 1960s. Previously, the federal government had played little part in educational research and development. Even after the establishment of the U.S. Office of Education in 1867, the primary role of the federal government had been as a social bookkeeper. USOE kept records on the functioning of the state and local education agencies and published appropriate statistical summaries. Only after 1954, beginning with the Cooperative Research Act, did the federal government begin to support other research projects, which at first were primarily contracts with individual researchers in colleges, universities, and state education agencies. Then, the acceleration of the Cold War extended federal participation in education, including educational research and development. Beginning in 1958, the National Defense Education Act (NDEA) was passed with provisions to support research and development on language learning and educational media. At about the same time, the National Science Foundation received funds to design and disseminate new curricula in mathematics and science.

During the 1960s, federal commitments to educational R&D mushroomed. The Vocational Education Act of 1963 established nine federally funded R&D centers devoted to the creation of new knowledge. Other R&D centers were soon established in the field of education for the handicapped. These led to plans to establish twenty-one R&D centers—ten with their own content emphasis and eleven focused on high priority government problems. Also, twenty regional laboratories were established to develop products and to relate product development directly to work in schools. The laboratories and centers were accompanied by over one-hundred graduate training programs for R&D workers and by the establishment of the ERIC system, a storage and retrieval system for educational information and the results of educational research. A variety of ERIC clearinghouses were established in different content areas to assist in the accumulation and dissemination of knowledge about education.

The expansion of the federal role in educational research and development exemplified a "unified-system" view of educational knowledge production and utilization (KPU), as indicated in Figure 18–1. Either by contract with existing institutions or by direct subsidy, the federal government sought to

| Stages | Institutions |
|---|---|
| Research | |
| 1. Exploratory Research—basic, theoretical studies | Colleges, universities, R&D centers |
| 2. Fundamental Development—applied research | |
| Development | |
| 3. Specific Development—pilot model | Regional educational laboratories |
| 4. Design and Proving—field model | |
| Diffusion | |
| 5. Dissemination—production, packaging, distribution agencies | USOE, ERIC, Publishers |
| 6. Adoption | State and local education agencies |

FIGURE 18–1.   Unified-System View of Educational Knowledge Production and Utilization (KPU)

strengthen educational KPU in each of its stages: research, development, and diffusion. Colleges and universities plus R&D centers (sometimes attached to universities) were to conduct exploratory research and fundamental development activities. Regional education laboratories were to engage in specific development, design, and proving of new educational materials and practices. Dissemination of the products was to be conducted by the laboratories plus ERIC, publishing firms, and state education agencies. Finally, adoption of new products would be facilitated by state and local education agencies.

Reviewing these developments, Guba and Clark characterized the development of this unified-system view of educational KPU as the culmination of a twenty-year history of federal involvement in education R&D.[3] Its good points, according to Guba and Clark, were that it remedied deficiencies in the first federal efforts, which had focused only on educational research to the exclusion of development and diffusion. Also, the unified-system policy provided a better balance between the research efforts of individual scientists and programmatic research directed at national needs. On the other hand, the unified-system view of education KPU was sharply criticized by Guba and Clark for its lack of realism. The facts are that educational R&D in America is not an orderly, sequential process with various institutions playing specialized roles. Instead, educational R&D is better described as a "community" rather than a sequential "system." Guba and Clark, who called their own description "a configurational perspective," argued that the unified-system view, being unrealistic, had actually contributed to the disappointments with federal efforts to improve schools by establishing unreachable goals and by ignoring the individual goals of members in the educational KPU community.

## CONFIGURATIONAL PERSPECTIVE OF EDUCATIONAL KPU

The major point of the configurational perspective is that educational KPU is not a unified system, but a complex set of diverse organizations more or less engaged in research, development, and/or diffusion. These institutions are not related to one another in any formal organizational sense, nor does each specialize exclusively in one aspect of the KPU process. Furthermore, the idea that educational innovation flows in a sequential process beginning with pure research and ending with implementation is itself a gross oversimplification.

Based on their analysis, Guba and Clark described the KPU community as having two prominent characteristics. First, the total population of individuals and agencies is very large and diverse. However, members of the community do not group themselves primarily on the basis of their KPU functions. Thus, a large city school may be more like an education laboratory in its KPU activities than a small rural school district. Second, members of the KPU community do not share a common view of KPU goals or strategies. Their roles in KPU are overlapping, but they function independently in many respects. For example, schools within a single school district or within a state may behave quite differently with respect to knowledge production and utilization activities.

Clark and Guba summarized as follows:

Thus, the KPU community is described, in the configurational view, as highly decentralized, consisting of a number of more or less independent and co-equal members, who may from time to time find it helpful to form temporary alliances but who, in the main, retain their independence, shun authority and activity relationships, and engage in as many different kinds of KPU activities as seem to be needed and feasible for them to maintain their self-sufficiency.[4]

We believe that this "messy" view of educational knowledge production and utilization accurately describes the current situation. Although the unified-system view may be a useful guide in developing more systematic approaches to educational improvement, nevertheless, it can be quite misleading if one takes it as a description of reality. Unfortunately, many who are involved in educational improvement have acted as if the unified-system view were a recipe for how to change schools. This can be a serious mistake because the reality of school improvement is radically different from the process used to put a man on the moon.

## KNOWLEDGE RESOURCES IN SCHOOL IMPROVEMENT

If the configurational perspective is accurate, what are the implications for knowledge utilization in the school improvement process? They are implicit in the Partnership Model, a central theme of which is the improvement of knowledge use in local school improvement. The model recognizes the great diversity and complexity of the educational system, focusing upon the local school-building organization as a unique unit for knowledge use. Two important processes are recommended for strengthening knowledge utilization by the local school. First, an "inner" process of knowledge production and utilization is recommended. This is a process of action research in which the local school organization seeks knowledge about its own needs, aspirations, and current status. This "local knowledge" is used to set goals and develop action plans for self-renewal. Later, as action plans are implemented, knowledge about "how things are going" is gathered and used in a continuous process.

Second, an "outer" process of knowledge use is also recommended for strengthening local schools. Based on local problems and an assessment of need, a search is made for outside knowledge resources to help the school solve its problems and meet its needs. Here, linkage is important. Because of the many sources of information and the complex influences on the local school, a flexible pattern of search is desirable. Thus, in the Partnership Model linkages are provided to teachers' organizations, colleges, the school district administration, the state education agency, and parents. Each of these organizations, in turn, draws upon many sources of useful information.

The secret to success in school improvement is to bring together these two knowledge processes, both inner and outer, so that school problems are carefully defined and so that outside resources are used to solve the problems that have been identified. This is a primary function of the partnership.

The "inner" and "outer" processes of knowledge production and use are illustrated in Figure 18–2 from each of the four strategy options. One example of how "inner" processes might be strengthened is found in Havelock's focus on the steps in the problem-solving process of the user. Another is Schmuck's emphasis upon communication and problem-solving skills within the school organization. A third example is Goodlad's encouragement of DDAE—dialogue, decision making, action, and evaluation—within the local school. A final example of "inner" processes is the stress in the Change Agent Study Model upon a local implementation process to encourage mutual adaptation of the school organization and a new program or practice.

The "outer" processes are illustrated by Havelock's change agent linkage of the local school to outside knowledge resources, by Schmuck's concepts of consultation and OD intervention, and by Goodlad's League of Cooperating Schools. In the Change Agent Study Model, the "outer" process is illustrated by support for change provided by the school district and the state education agency.

Another perspective on local knowledge production and utilization processes is provided in Figure 18–3, which gives examples of KPU activities in relation to the Partnership Model. During the formation of a partnership, knowledge production and utilization structures are automatically being developed as roles of researcher, trainer, and facilitator are identified and assigned. The organizational diagnosis is an example of action research in which outside expertise helps the organization to produce knowledge about itself. The knowledge from the diagnosis is utilized in making the discrepancy analysis, where goals are set for school improvement. Members of the partnership group then

| Strategy Option | Inner Processes | Outer Processes |
| --- | --- | --- |
| Havelock | Problem-solving process of user | External Linkage to knowledge producers via change agent |
| Schmuck | Communication and problem-solving skills in school organization | Consultation OD intervention |
| Goodlad | Dialogue Decision making Action Evaluation | Support of League members League office staff |
| Change Agent Study | On-line planning On-going training Mutual adaptation | Support of school district and state agency |

FIGURE 18–2.  Examples of "Inner" and "Outer" Processes of Knowledge Production and Utilization

| Stage | KPU Activity |
|---|---|
| Form partnership | Establish KPU structures |
| Organizational diagnosis | Acquire knowledge of school organization |
| Initiation | Discrepancy analysis<br>Identify and evaluate alternatives<br>Adopt action plan |
| Implementation | Process evaluation<br>Product evaluation<br>Staff training |
| Integration | Continue evaluation<br>Revise diagnosis |

FIGURE 18-3. Knowledge Production and Utilization Activities in the Partnership Model

provide important links to external knowledge sources to identify and evaluate possible courses of action. This knowledge is used by the school organization to develop an action plan.

In the implementation stage, knowledge is again produced through action research. In this case, the knowledge consists of evaluation results, which can be used to adjust the change process. Another important activity during this stage is staff training in which external knowledge is acquired and used by staff members as they adapt new practices and procedures to the local school.

During the integration stage, evaluation and feedback activities continue. This leads naturally into a revised organizational diagnosis and a new cycle of school improvement.

## ENDNOTES

1. Robert Glaser, "Learning," *Encyclopedia of Educational Research, 4th ed.*, ed. Robert L. Ebel (New York: The MacMillan Company, 1969), pp. 706-733.
2. Ronald Havelock, *The Change Agent's Guide to Innovation in Education* (Englewood Cliffs, N.J.: Educational Technology Publications, 1973), p. 161.
3. Egon G. Guba and David L. Clark, "The Configurational Perspective: A New View of Educational Knowledge Production and Utilization," *Educational Researcher* (April 1975): 6-9.
4. Ibid., p. 9.

# Chapter 19

# Training and Staff Development

The need to strengthen training and staff development is among the most pressing problems in school improvement. College and university training programs are often impractical, and in-service training days in schools are frequently a waste of time.

No easy solution to the problem of staff training and development has been found. In fact, current educational conditions appear to make training problems more difficult. For one thing, schools have fewer opportunities to recruit new personnel with desired skills; changes depend almost entirely on retraining existing staff. At the same time, resources to provide retraining are scarce, and the needs for change continue to multiply. Nevertheless, recent experience in educational change efforts makes one thing clear. Success in school improvement depends on the availability to school personnel of training opportunities specifically related to changes being introduced. Therefore, ways *must* be found to supply the needed training. The Partnership Model provides a mechanism to meet this need.

Those trying to provide training and staff development activities for school improvement must operate within the context of established patterns of pre-service and in-service training. These patterns include certification and accreditation mechanisms that have to be taken into account in selecting tactics for staff training and development.

## PRE-SERVICE EDUCATION

The most realistic approach to pre-service programs for the preparation of school personnel is to view them as readiness activities. In other words, through pre-service training the individual is helped to develop entry-level competencies for a specific educational assignment. It is assumed that prospective elementary and secondary teachers or individuals studying to become specialists and administrators at the graduate level will complete a degree program with sufficient knowledge, skills, and understandings to cope with most of the problems they will face during their initial year in the profession.

Such pre-service programs usually consist of a prescribed number of credit hours to be taken from the areas of general studies, subject-area specialties, and professional education (which includes clinical studies). These experiences are determined by the faculty of the college/university, with little participation by other members of the educational community. Although the graduates of pre-service programs are probably better prepared than a few years ago, nevertheless school practitioners are rarely encouraged to help determine the content of the pre-service educational programs. This is one concrete step that can be taken by a partnership to strengthen pre-service programs in relation to local needs. Pre-service programs should, however, be considered as only one element in a comprehensive design that includes both initial *and* continuing education of school personnel; that is, objectives should be established for what is expected throughout the stages of professional development. For example, what competencies should a classroom teacher of twenty years be expected to demonstrate when compared with a classroom teacher of ten years? While the development of such a design is a difficult task, it is only within such a design that the training needs of individuals and schools can be matched to training resources. Bush has emphasized the uniqueness of individual teachers and their need for personalized training programs in the following manner:

> In any in-service training program, we must consider the needs of each teacher, taking into account his unique qualities. We must consider the differences in teaching ability, noting that some teachers perform better in certain areas than in others, and that certain approaches may be more appropriate for certain outcomes than for others. The problem is not finding the best method to be used by all teachers on all pupils, but taking these variations into account and obtaining the proper matching of method with teacher with pupil with regard to the particular purposes we wish to accomplish.[1]

Two major advantages of this comprehensive continuous educational development approach to the pre- and in-service training of school personnel become immediately evident. First, it emphasizes the need for all elements of the education profession to collaborate in planning, since considerations such as salaries, certification, and evaluation policies and procedures are involved as well as the training program itself. Second, the comprehensive model should include staff development programs for faculty members in colleges or departments of education, thus eliminating the status problems associated with elementary and secondary classroom teachers as being the only members of the profession in need of retraining.

In the final analysis, the pre-service preparation of educational personnel must become an important first stage of the continuous educational development model for the profession. This initial stage must be clearly defined by the partners and lead to a commitment to life-long learning.

## IN-SERVICE EDUCATION

No single expectation of the profession has received more criticism than that of in-service education. This is true despite the fact that the vast majority of school personnel feel the need for continuous professional development activities.

The Phi Delta Kappa Commission on Professional Renewal studied the negative feelings held by many members of the profession toward in-service education and professional renewal in an attempt to determine what steps could be taken to enhance the perceptions of school personnel toward these programs. A summary of the commission's findings is cited:

> The effectiveness of local IS/PR (In-service/Professional Renewal) can be dramatically improved we believe, through creative and cooperative attention to (1) selection of real needs and attainable objectives, (2) balancing of personal and organizational benefits as well as individualized and collective offerings, (3) cooperative determination of topic feasibility, (4) commitment on the part of those to be affected by IS/PR, (5) skillful and imaginative planning and programming necessary to make the experience rewarding, (6) proficient implementation of the planning, and (7) purposeful evaluation of its effects.[2]

A crucial recommendation of the commission was to focus on local needs as opposed to those that are system-wide or state-wide. This is consistent with the Partnership Model, which calls for the program to be located in the local school building, directed by the principal and staff of that building, and organized to meet educational needs identified by the staff and clientele of that school. This approach creates a climate of ownership essential to any school improvement effort. Change efforts based on these basic principles improve communication within the school, enhance teacher attitudes toward continuous educational development, develop ownership in the instructional program of the school, and foster improved relationships between administrators and staff. Two critical elements omitted from the commission's report were (1) the need for an acceptable schedule of incentives or compensation for teachers, and (2) the utilization of state education department and university resources. In the Partnership Model, these elements are also essential in a successful school improvement effort.

The concept of continuous professional development for school personnel beginning with the pre-service program and ending at the age of retirement is a radical concept. If accepted, it would require a comprehensive approach to the life-long learning of professionals in education. Roles and functions for school personnel at each level of development would need to be identified and clearly stated for each subgroup (teacher, counselor, supervisor, principal, etc.) within the profession. New types of certificates, salary schedules, and role expectations for the experienced teacher and administrator might be required. Although a single partnership committee might not bring about such changes, nevertheless such a group might make significant changes in a particular local area.

Individuals selected to provide instruction for school personnel should remember that they are teaching adults rather than college undergraduates. Knowles,[3] in his book, *The Modern Practice of Adult Education,* describes the differences inherent in teaching adults as opposed to younger learners, using the term *andragogy* to describe the principles of assisting adults to learn. An excellent summary of these andragogical principles has been provided by Ingalls.[4] As indicated in Figure 19–1, teachers of adults must recognize that the best adult learning is self-directed, experiential, related to social or occupational roles, and problem-centered.

| Characteristics of Adult Learners | Implications of Adult Learners | Implications for Facilitators or Teachers of Adults |
|---|---|---|
| 1. Self-concept: The adult learner sees himself as capable of self-direction and desires others to see him the same way. In fact, one definition of maturity is the capacity to be self-directing. | 1. A climate of openness and respect is helpful in identifying what the learners want and need to learn.<br><br>Adults enjoy planning and carrying out their own learning exercises.<br><br>Adults need to be involved in evaluating their own progress toward self-chosen goals. | 1. Facilitators recognize adults as self-directing and treat them accordingly.<br><br>The facilitator is a learning reference for adult learners rather than a traditional instructor; facilitators are, therefore, encouraged to "tell it like it is" and stress "how I do it" rather than tell participants what they should do.<br><br>The facilitator avoids talking down to adult learners, who are usually experienced decision makers and self-starters. The facilitator instead tries to meet the learners' needs. |
| 2. Experience: Adults bring a lifetime of experience to the learning situation. Youths tend to regard experience as something that has happened to them, while to an adult, his experience is him. The adult defines who he is in terms of his experience. | 2. Less use is made of transmittal techniques; more of experiential techniques.<br><br>Discovery of how to learn from experience is key to self-actualization.<br><br>Mistakes are opportunities for learning.<br><br>To reject adult experience is to reject the adult. | 2. As the adult is his experience, failure to utilize the experience of the adult learner is equivalent to rejecting him as a person. |
| 3. Readiness to learn: Adult developmental tasks increasingly move toward social and occupational role competence and away from the more physical developmental tasks of childhood. | 3. Adults need opportunities to identify the competency requirements of their occupational and social roles.<br><br>Adult readiness to learn and teachable moments peak at those points where a learning opportunity is coordinated with a recognition of the need to know.<br><br>Adults can best identify their own readiness to learn and teachable moments. | 3. Learning occurs through helping adults with the gaps in their knowledge. No questions are "stupid"; all questions are "opportunities" for learning. |

| 4. A problem-centered time perspective: Youth thinks of education as the accumulation of knowledge for use in the future. Adults tend to think of learning as a way to be more effective in problem solving today. | 4. Adult education needs to be problem-centered rather than theoretically oriented.<br><br>Formal curriculum development is less valuable than finding out what the learners need to learn.<br><br>Adults need the opportunity to apply new learning quickly. | 4. The primary emphasis in adult learning is on learners learning rather than on teachers teaching.<br><br>Involvement in such things as problems to be solved, case histories, and critical incidents generally offer greater learning opportunity for adults than "talking to" them or using other one-way transmittal techniques. |

FIGURE 19-1.    Principles of Adult Learning    John D. Engalls, *Human Energy: The Critical Factor for Individuals and Organizations* (Reading, Mass.: Addison-Wesley Publishing Company, 1976), pp. 144–145. Reprinted with permission.

Wagner has identified ten characteristics of successful in-service workshops in terms of what teachers like in training programs. These "likes" are in general agreement with the andragogical learning principles advanced by Knowles for the adult learner. The ten suggestions are:

1. Teachers like meetings in which they can be actively involved. Just as students do not want to be passive, most teachers prefer Dewey's "learning by doing."
2. Teachers like to watch other teachers demonstrate various techniques in their teaching field. Demonstration teaching can serve as a model that teachers can take back to their classrooms.
3. Teachers like practical information—almost step-by-step recipes—on how others approach certain learning tasks. Too often, in-service programs are theoretical and highly abstract.
4. Teachers like meetings that are short and to the point. The introduction of guests at a meeting is often ego-filling for those introduced, but cuts into valuable in-service time.
5. Teachers like an in-depth treatment of one concept that can be completed in one meeting rather than a generalized treatment that attempts to solve every teacher's problems in one session.
6. Teachers like well-organized meetings.
7. Teachers like variety in in-service programs. If the same topics are covered every time, attendance may drop off.
8. Teachers like some incentive for attending in-service meetings; released time, salary increments, advancement points on rating scale.
9. Teachers like inspirational speakers occasionally. Such speakers can often give a staff the necessary drive to start or complete a school year.

10. Teachers like to visit other schools to observe other teachers in situations similar to their own. These visits, even when observing poor teachers, are highly educational.[5]

Training or staff development activities for school personnel desiring to change the school's structure or instructional program may take many different forms depending upon the objectives to be achieved. Workshops, seminars, classes, independent study, structured discussion, and on-site visits to schools in which the desired change has been successfully implemented are but a few of the options possible. In each of these options, however, a follow-through system should be planned in order to evaluate the effectiveness of the training program, provide reinforcement for participants, and correct misunderstandings acquired during the training period.

A factor that complicates the training process for school personnel is that of college credit. In many school systems, salary levels are based, in part, on the number of graduate credits earned by the teacher and administrator. Thus, school personnel are forced to enroll in graduate level courses at a local or nearby institution of higher education. The results are typically disappointing in that the in-service teacher feels that the course content and teaching styles did not meet his or her needs. While this criticism appears widespread, it should be recognized that most courses offered by institutions of higher education were not developed for in-service school personnel, but rather individuals training to enter the profession as an administrator, supervisor, or counselor. This inherent conflict will probably continue until the type of collaborative partnership described in this book becomes a reality.


## CERTIFICATION

The process of certification as it relates to training and staff development projects is both a blessing and a curse. The concept that every individual working with children or youth in the school must be certified is a blessing in that it provides a guarantee to the community that these individuals have been judged by state officials to be competent. The judgment of competence is usually based on evidence that certain specified courses have been completed in an approved institution of higher education. While alternative methods of establishing evidence of competence have been advanced (for example, competency-based teacher education), the traditional, credit-counting approach, plus an institutional recommendation, remains the most common practice.

The curse of certification in the change process arises when it becomes necessary to shift school personnel from one assignment to another. Teacher A, for example, may be fully certified in mathematics but as a result of personal study, attending workshops, training laboratories, etc., has developed skills, understandings, and attitudes needed in another subject area to facilitate the change effort planned for the school. In most states, this individual could not be certified to assume a teaching or administrative position outside of mathematics. Such changes are becoming increasingly necessary as enrollments decline. Even though most states have developed special certificates for such emergency situations, the fact remains that even these require a minimum number of specified graduate credits for initial issuance.

Thus, certification may be viewed as a factor that either facilitates or inhibits the change process in a local school. While this situation appears to present a dilemma for the school, the Partnership Model advanced in this text could work to alleviate the problem. Since teachers, administrators, and representatives from the State Department of Education and a nearby institution of higher education are working together in this model in a continuous change process designed to improve the school, needs could be anticipated and training provided to insure needed certification for key participants in the change effort. This ability to anticipate and make provisions for meeting emerging needs is one of the strongest arguments for the Partnership Model. The following assertions concerning certification were advanced by the *Bicentennial Commission on Education for the Profession of Teaching of the American Association of Colleges for Teacher Education.* We strongly endorse them.

1. *Certification is not a life-long license. Permanent certification is an anachronism.* Because every professional must develop continual renewal through a program of life-long learning, it is incongruous for a profession to certify people for life. No one design for periodic recertifications will be sufficient for all states and institutions. What is important, however, is that the profession of teaching commit itself to the concept of continual recertification by using as many means as possible to insure that educators remain up-to-date, effective practitioners.
2. *The granting of certification should be a shared, professional process.* Certification is not the sole responsibility of state departments, professional teacher groups, higher education institutions, or local communities. It is the responsibility of all these groups, a relationship that requires collaboration, feedback, and mutual assistance.
3. *The state must be the source for formal certification; the profession must develop, recommend, and monitor a professional educator's continuing education.* This process will exemplify the collaborative process because it combines a legally recognized source and a professional group to insure the life-long learning of the educator.
4. *Certification implies a "safety-to-the-client" concern.* Much certification procedure and rationale speak to what candidates have learned and what candidates have experienced. Certification must emphasize the advantages and benefits for potential clients. The profession must become more consumer-oriented and less practitioner protective.[6]

These assertions are extremely compatible with the Partnership Model, including the need for appropriate community involvement in all school improvement efforts.

## ACCREDITATION

Certification is to the individual school practitioner what accreditation is to the total school as an institution. Thus, while certification seeks to identify an individual as qualified (in terms of training and experience) to perform certain functions competently, accreditation provides the same "safety-to-the-client" guarantee for the entire school. The factors usually considered in the accreditation process for a school include: budget (per pupil expenditures, etc.); quality of faculty (degrees, certificates, etc.); faculty load (teacher-pupil ratio, etc.); evaluation procedures for faculty and instructional program; scope and sequence of school curriculum; special services and programs for students, including exceptional students; size and quality of school library; conditions and availability of space; teacher-administrator relationships and operational procedures; home-school relationships; grading practices; and others.

Advocates of accreditation see self-improvement of the institution as a major result of the process. In reality, however, the accreditation process is primarily concerned with quality control within the context of the goals adopted by a particular school or institution. Thus, while the school may attempt to use accreditation standards to acquire additional faculty, library holdings, etc., questions of change or improvement are usually secondary in the accreditation process.

Responsibility for formulating and administering accreditation standards rests primarily with State Departments of Education. A major problem in the accreditation process, especially at the state and regional level, is the conflict which arises because the accrediting agencies may ignore the practitioner's input. This same problem has permeated state-level certification processes as well. The fundamental principle being invoked by the organized teaching profession (NEA and AFT) is simply that it should play the major role in determining the content of teacher preparation programs, who enters the profession, and the institutions and schools that should be accredited, to the exclusion of other institutions such as higher education. While this debate within the profession is interesting from a philosophic position, the outcome will probably have little positive influence on the quality of the instructional program or structure of an individual institution or local school. In fact, this movement on the part of the organized profession may well have an adverse effect on the quality of the school. By rejecting the contributions of faculty members from higher education, the knowledge base for improving the instructional process will be drastically reduced and programs will suffer accordingly.

Today, due to declining enrollments in teacher education, many institutions of higher education are seeking new clients. Off-campus sites are being developed in great numbers. Some of these sites may be thousands of miles from the main campus. In one such program, for example, faculty members from an institution are flown from a college of education in the Midwest to the east coast to teach graduate level guidance courses. Since the program on the main campus is accredited, the off-campus program is also advertised as being accredited. Officials from accrediting agencies at the state, regional, and national levels, however, are beginning to question this practice. In many cases, the quality of these off-campus programs simply is not as high as the same programs offered on the main campus. Reasons for the decline in quality are (1) many of the more experienced members of the program faculty refuse to travel to the off-campus site, (2) the amount of student-faculty time for advising and discussion is usually severely limited, (3) the availability of library reference and audiovisual materials is less than the resources available to the on-campus student.

Many of the off-campus programs described have been developed to provide training for in-service school personnel. While the intent on the part of the institution of higher education may be good, the quality of the services rendered is usually inferior when compared with the on-campus program. In fact, there have been cases in which an institution of higher education merely sells its credits to a local school district or state. In these cases, courses are developed and taught by local school personnel under the banner of the sponsoring institution, which is paid a set amount for each student enrolled. This practice of "selling credits" is not widespread, but violates all accrediting guidelines and must be eliminated.

Our conclusion is that training and staff development for in-service school personnel is an essential element in any attempt to change the local school—its structure and/or programs. Change demands that new missions, goals, and objectives be established for the instructional program. In meeting these new purposes, teachers and administrators need to develop new competencies or refine old ones. While some school personnel believe that they can provide their own in-service training, we believe that colleges of education, state departments of education, and other outside resources are also required to provide what is needed.

The staff development program may take differing forms in terms of length and time of day. One rule-of-thumb to follow is that, wherever possible, the training program should be taken to the site of the local school rather than expecting school personnel to return to campus for all courses, workshops, etc. Another generally accepted rule is that, whenever possible, training programs should be conducted during the regular school day rather than in the evening hours or on weekends. In many cases, where laws permit, experienced student teachers, practicum students, or interns can cover the classrooms while teachers are attending staff development programs.

Certification and accreditation, while posing some problems for the school attempting to change, are really blessings in disguise. The major focus of certification is to guarantee clients that teachers or administrators have met the minimum requirements for their professional role. Accreditation, on the other hand, guarantees clients that the school or institution as a whole has met a minimum standard of quality established by professionals in the field.

Many questions relating to both certification and accreditation are being asked today, both inside and outside the profession. Clients appear to be demanding greater assurance that the quality of both practitioner and institution is above reproach and capable of delivering advertised services. Within the profession, there exists much confusion over the governance and control of the certification and accreditation process. While a total profession approach is most logical, individual segments of the profession continue to battle for power.

## ENDNOTES

1. Robert N. Bush, "Curriculum-Proof Teachers: Who Does What to Whom," in Louis J. Rubin (ed.) *Improving In-Service Education Proposals and Procedures for Change,* ed. Louis J. Rubin (Boston: Allyn & Bacon, Inc., 1971, pp. 45–56.
2. James C. King; Paul C. Hayes; and Isadore Newman. "Some Requirements for Successful In-service Education," *Phi Delta Kappan* (May 1977): 687.
3. Malcolm S. Knowles, *The Modern Practice of Adult Education: Andragogy vs. Pedagogy* (New York: Associated Press, 1970).
4. John D. Engalls, *Human Energy: The Critical Factor for Individuals and Organizations* (Reading, Mass.: Addison-Wesley Publishing Company, 1976), pp. 144–145.
5. Hilmar Wagner, "What Teachers Like," *NASSP Spotlight* (April 1975), p. 1.
6. Robert B. Howsam; Dean Corrigan; George W. Denemark; and Robert Nash. *Educating a Profession: Report of the Bicentennial Commission for the Profession of Teaching of the American Association of Colleges for Teacher Education* (Washington, D.C.: American Association of Colleges for Teacher Education, 1976), pp. 115–116.

# Chapter 20

# Evaluation Tactics

Few educators argue against evaluation as a desirable part of school management, especially in efforts to improve current practices. However, many educators are becoming increasingly cynical about the usefulness of evaluation to the school administrator.

First, resources available to conduct evaluations are usually minimal. In the busy, ongoing life of a school, the time and energy needed to evaluate school policies and practices are usually absent. In special projects, evaluation funds are often token amounts limited by the desire to place maximum emphasis upon the delivery of services to students.

Second, the quality of evaluations of school programs and practices is often poor. When evaluation resources are scarce, the evaluation effort is low and the results may be equivocal. Also, because the technology available for evaluating complicated educational programs and practices is still weak, even with high effort, convincing answers to the most important evaluation questions may still be missing.

A third reason for cynicism about evaluation is that results of evaluation, even when they seem clear, are often ignored. Programs or practices that have received positive evaluations may, nevertheless, be dropped for a variety of reasons. Such educational decisions usually involve complex choices in which several alternatives are weighed against a number of criteria. Results of evaluations are only one ingredient. Too often, educational decision makers appear to disregard formal evaluation results in favor of casual personal impressions, the advice of professional acquaintances, or political considerations.

As a result, many educators treat formal evaluation as peripheral to the business of operating schools. Evaluation is conducted as "window dressing," expected or mandated by a higher authority. Many go through the motions of evaluation, but evaluation may not seem vital to the "real" activities and decisions of schools.

Despite problems and limitations with existing evaluation procedures, we believe that evaluation is one of the central activities in school improvement. Perhaps one reason why schools have found it so difficult to change for the better is that evaluation procedures are weak and the results are little used.

A significant result of the federal government's participation in school improvement is an increased emphasis on evaluation of school programs and practices. Mandated evaluation in federal programs has produced much practical wisdom about school evaluation and many lessons about the role of evaluation in educational change. In the Partnership Model the emphasis is placed on *realistic* and *useful* evaluation. Evaluation procedures must be carefully designed to serve the decision-making process in local school improvement projects. The information gathered is to be used at the key decision points in the school improvement process.

## INITIATION

As has been stressed throughout this book, school improvement projects are most likely to be successful when they meet local needs or solve local problems. Thus, during the initiation stage of school improvement the focus of evaluation is on assessing local needs, diagnosing local problems, and identifying discrepancies between local goals and current status. Then, alternative proposals for action need to be evaluated in terms of the promise each holds for meeting the needs identified. The organizational diagnosis process explained in Chapter 10 is used to initiate a specific improvement project.

**Discrepancy Analysis.**   Any number of useful systems exist for need analysis and problem identification. All of them, either explicitly or implicitly, involve a comparison of what ought to be with what is. Often, they begin with a school philosophy translated into goals and objectives, which in turn become the criteria for judging strengths and weaknesses of existing school programs and practices. Some are extensive, as in state and regional accreditation manuals. Others may be simple and home-made. For the school improvement strategy suggested here, we recommend that the choice of a needs assessment procedure be a local matter. This is one task for which the partnership group is particularly suited. The following are suggested criteria for the choice:

1. The procedure clearly identifies aspects of the school program in which improvement is needed.
2. The opinions and judgments of all those affected are obtained (school officials, teachers, other employees, parents, students).
3. The procedure identifies needs and goals in a priority order to assist in the development of action plans.
4. The procedure is not overly burdensome to those who must conduct the procedure nor to those who contribute data.
5. Above all, the results should provide data convincing to those responsible for decision making.
6. There is a general belief among participants that the evaluation process will, in fact, make a difference.

**Evaluating Alternative Plans of Action.**   Another crucial task in initiating a successful school improvement project is selecting a promising plan of action to meet identified needs. Many failures in school improvement occur at just this point. The temptation is to jump on the nearest bandwagon, to try something that has worked in another place, or to accept any suggestion for which outside funding is available. If anything has been learned about successful school improvement, it is that new practices will fail if they do not fit a local situation and if they do not genuinely meet a local need. Thus, we recommend that the partnership group take responsibility for identifying appropriate alternative plans of action and to see that each is evaluated according to criteria such as these:

1. Is the proposed plan of action sound in its conception? Is the idea or theory connected with the plan of action well-developed and consistent with the views of the local school and community?
2. Has the suggested plan of action been successfully followed in other settings? What practical advantages and disadvantages have been experienced?
3. How well does each suggested plan of action fit the local circumstances? Can it gain the support from the people involved? How difficult will it be to adapt local practices to the new course of action?
4. Is the suggested alternative better than existing practice? If the course of action is adopted, what are the costs? Are these costs worth the benefits?

The partnership group is in a particularly good position to perform evaluation functions during the initiation phase of school improvement. It has links to all the parties with a stake in school improvement. Thus, one can get the perspectives on needs and problems, as well as on alternative plans of action, from the school administration, from the teachers, from the state education agency, and from a local higher education institution. Each member of the partnership leader group has access to the people who will be involved in decisions or will be affected by them (including parents and students). Also, members of the partnership group are linked to important resources that can contribute to identifying alternatives and evaluating suggested courses of action. School personnel can visit sites where proposed programs are being used. State Department of Education personnel can locate alternatives and examples of their use. College/university educators can help evaluate the theoretical base, the formal evaluation results, and the requirements for training. Thus, during the initiation stage the partnership group exemplifies the values of collaboration through its ability to evaluate from a variety of perspectives and to bring to bear on local problems a variety of resources. The result should improve chances for success in the organization development of a school.

**Establishing a Program Plan.**   In the stage of initiation the cooperating agencies need to establish a leadership group with equal representation from each of the participating constituencies. It is important that these representatives be individuals who have the authority to make policy decisions for the various agencies involved. Once the group has been organized, the initial task of devising a working plan and an evaluation design should be undertaken. This step will guide the activities scheduled for a specified period of time. If followed, the evaluation plan enables partners to work together to solve a common problem in a systematic fashion. See Appendices C and D.

For example, suppose the leadership group of an imaginary partnership school had the following members:

There will be product needs and process needs. One process need in a collaborative project will be that of establishing partner parity. Before assessing program needs, the partners must assess "where they are" in terms of shared decision making or partner parity. To do this, each representative could complete an attitude questionnaire indicating personal perceptions about the degree to which partner parity has been achieved in the past between the collaborative groups.

| | |
|---|---|
| College of Education: | Director of Reading Studies Center<br>Language Arts Instructor |
| Department of<br>Public Instruction: | Supervisor of Reading<br>Supervisor of English Language Arts |
| Local District: | District Supervisor of Reading Language Arts<br>Elementary Principal of Marwood School |
| Teacher's Union: | Elementary Team Leader of 4th grade Language Arts at Marwood School<br>Building Union Representative at Marwood School |

Figure 20–1 illustrates the area of need overlap that the four groups have to discover.

A number of attitude questionnaires can be used to assess willingness to participate in shared governance. A number of different questionnaires have been included in the appendices of this book, all of which focus on the assessment of group process.

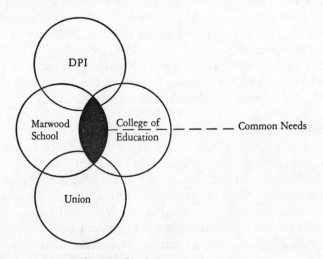

**FIGURE 20-1.   Overlapping Needs of Partners**

Since partner parity is a difficult concept in governance, special efforts are needed to measure whether or not the partnership is achieving its stated goals. One such attempt is described below.

Joseph Caruso[1] performed a content analysis of the literature dealing with organizational theory, political theory, cooperation in teacher education, the governance of teacher education, and the etymology of the term *parity*. He identified twenty-three variables of parity. (Figure 20–2). These were given to a panel of judges who rated the variables on their importance to the decision-making processes of a teacher education consortia. A Parity Profile Questionnaire, consisting of 146 questions were given to members of eleven different consortia yielding mean scores on each of the variables. These means were then plotted for each variable, producing a graphic profile for each group. The profile is useful because it describes the consortium members' present "state of parity," which can be used to assess what changes need to be made in the structure as procedures of the consortium. Caruso states that it can also be used to measure the extent to which state-mandated collaboration achieves parity.

| *Ethos Variables* | |
| --- | --- |
| Mutual trust | The confidence, faith, and reliance consortium members have in each other |
| Mutual respect | The attention, concern, and consideration members possess towards each other as human beings who have unique qualities, competencies, and expertise |
| Feeling of equality | Members' perception or feeling of themselves as being on "an equal footing" with other members |
| Values parity | The worth and importance that consortium members place on the parity notion |
| Openness | The prevailing atmosphere as it encourages members to genuinely express their views, feelings, concerns, and ideas which may be conflicting with other members in a listening, understanding, receptive climate |
| Commitment to change | The determination of a group to change the structure and strategy of the governing system, as well as program content and design of teacher education |
| Potency | The significance and meaning a consortium has for its members |
| Interdependence | (1) Individual and institutional autonomy within a consortium, <br> (2) the mutual dependence each individual and agency has on each other, and <br> (3) the establishment by a consortium of its own identity |
| *Organization Variables* | |
| Shared goals | Consortium members' perception of the presence of common superordinate goals |
| Shared leadership | Consortium members' assumption of the responsibilities of the functions of leadership |

| | |
|---|---|
| Shared communication | (1) The adequacy of information flow through a communications linkage network<br>(2) The comprehension of what is being said or written by consortium members<br>(3) The amount of interaction and communication among members |
| Collaborative strategy | The adoption by the organization of a strategy which encourages members to work together, to cooperate with each other, to achieve common goals |
| Clarity of role | Members' comprehension, recognition, and perception of the behavioral expectations that other group members have for their office |
| Shared responsibility | The responsibility felt by each member of a consortium's policy board for achieving its goals |
| Needs/rewards | The satisfying of individual and group needs by a consortium through compensation and positive reinforcement |
| *Power Structure Variables* | |
| Resource utilization | A consortium's identification and use of its resources to benefit members and to achieve organization goals |
| Reciprocity | (1) The presence of a group expectation which requires members to help each other,<br>(2) The exchange and trade of resources among individuals, agencies, and institutions within a consortium to benefit each other and achieve organizational goals |
| Influences decisions | (1) The belief by consortium board members that they influence decisions (change or modify the attitudes and/or behavior of other members or of the organization itself so as to affect decisions) in various phases of program development<br>(2) The belief that other board representatives influence decisions in various phases of program development |
| Appeals and reviews decisions | The belief by consortium representatives that they can reexamine, question, or modify decisions which have been made by the policy board |
| Equal suffrage | A constitutional guarantee of equal voting rights among elected representatives who comprise a consortium's policy-making body |
| Equal representation | The presence of a guarantee of equal numerical representation from each category of membership on a consortium's policy-making board by its Constitution |
| Authorization | The belief by consortium representatives that they have authority (rightful vested power) to act for the groups they represent on a policy-making board |
| Accountability | A feeling of obligation by consortium board representatives to give account to their clients |

**FIGURE 20-2.   Dimensions of Parity**   Joseph J. Caruso, "Parity in Designing, Conducting and Evaluating Teacher Education Programs: A Conceptual Definition," unpublished paper, date unknown, Wheelock College, Boston, 02215 (ED 100 807). Reprinted with permission.

Once the leadership group has come to an agreement on the needs as they exist in relation to governance procedures, the group can focus on the problem which prompted the partnership to form. For instance, let's say that this partnership was organized at the request of the Marwood School because students were performing below the national mean in reading at all grade levels. The group could formulate a list of what they perceived to be the problems relating to students' poor performance. These needs could then be translated into attitude survey statements which would be sent to a sample of individuals in each of the four cooperating groups. The data received from this questionnaire should be compiled in order to answer the next questions, which take us to the implementation step.

## IMPLEMENTATION

Evaluation also plays a critical role in the school improvement process during the implementation of action plans. In fact, a central thesis of this book is that on-going evaluation, including structured feedback to those involved, is a powerful variable in making desirable changes. Furthermore, we know that successful changes require a process of mutual adaptation, in which the school as an organization and a proposed new program or practice are both changing. There is a continuous need to monitor new programs and practices, to spot problems and needed adjustments, and to make arrangements for whatever adjustments and adaptations are required.

The partnership group can play an important role in this formative evaluation process. First, in making plans for changes in programs and practices the partnership group can make sure that needed provisions are included for on-going evaluation, feedback, and corrective action. Second, the partnership group can conduct its own evaluations of an on-going program of school improvement. Because it represents different elements in the educational system, the partnership group has the unique perspective on "how things are going." Especially because significant changes involve the total school community, this perspective is essential.

Naturally, formative evaluation procedures will vary greatly depending upon the local circumstances and the types of changes being introduced. Some general recommendations can be made.

1. Is implementation taking place as planned? A number of managerial systems (for example, PERT) are available to specify objectives, actions, persons responsible, resources needed, and a timetable for actions. Such a preliminary plan needs to be monitored regularly to find out whether or not implementation is going forward as planned. Often, preliminary plans need to be modified time and again as unexpected circumstances arise. The partnership group might be particularly helpful in this regard, recommending needed changes in the plan.

2. How are people reacting to the changes? Much useful information can be gained from monitoring opinions of the school administration, teaching

staff, pupils, and parents. Even if such monitoring is modest in scope, it can provide important information to guide the implementation process In particular, difficulties can be spotted early and corrected.

3. What results are apparent? Too often, results are evaluated only after a project is finished. Although a final evaluation may be useful, it cannot substitute for an on-going assessment of whether the plan seems to be producing the results desired. This is in keeping with the action research model mentioned earlier. Even if the evidence of results is meager, it is important. Here again, the partnership group may be in the best position to judge whether or not preliminary results are in line with original objectives. This, of course, is the most important basis for "mid-course corrections."

A variety of sources speaks to product evaluation problems in schools.[2] These would be very important during the implementation step. It is obviously important to collect data on student achievement, for example, if curricular changes were part of the OD procedures. There are fewer examples to draw upon in process evaluation, but one will be explained here because it concerns an important process issue, morale, and because it is easy to explain and administer. This form of morale study also coincides with our other preference for organizational diagnosis—that of being locally generated. The following is a description of how a morale study that should prove to be of high practical value during the implementation period can be conducted.

The basic consideration about morale is to determine the degree of negative and positive attitudes that employees or clients have about their organization. This can be accomplished with an action research model first by devising a list of topics that are of mutual concern to the local school. This list could be collected by talking to a few people. It might include broad areas such as salary, security, happiness, working conditions, loyalty, etc. Second, those topics are converted into unfinished sentence stems, which are then placed on an instrument which all of the employees or clients are asked to complete anonymously. All of this procedure is best designed by a local committee. Some sample sentence stems follow:

- My principal is _____.
- This school is best described as _____.
- The (name of school) school is a _____ place to teach.
- The parents in this school ought to _____.
- Most of our students _____.
- The district office supports _____ more than _____.
- I would describe the administration of this building as _____.
- "_____" is the way I would express my thoughts about the new curriculum.

Participants respond to the sentence stems by completing the sentence. This is a form of projective testing. The next step is to appoint a committee to evaluate the completed sentences as to their degree of positive or negative con-notations. A five-point rating scale is suggested (5, very positive; 4, positive; 3, neutral; 2, negative; and 1, very negative). Each item (from all respondents) on the morale form is totaled and then averaged (mean score) so that there is a quantitative value for each concept represented by a sentence stem. This provides a morale index, indicating, for example, that, "This school is best de-scribed as (4.2 positive)." These data can be summarized and made public. In keeping with the action research model, some adjustments or interventions can be made to improve the morale factors. The study is repeated as many times as thought necessary in order to maintain a reading on the morale during the im-plementation stage.

## INTEGRATION

Another type of information is required to make decisions about the continua-tion of the changes that have been introduced. In our developmental view of school improvement we have emphasized the evolutionary nature of changes, such that some elements of a change may be continued, sometimes in a differ-ent form, while other proposed changes are discarded. Whenever possible, these decisions should be based on a cost/benefit analysis that returns to the needs assessment data. Thus, another evaluation function of the partnership group can be to arrange cost/benefit information to guide decisions about the evolution of a school improvement process. Furthermore, the partnership school may believe that it has the responsibility to disseminate the results of its project to interested parties through newsletters, journals, or convention papers.

One of the evaluation considerations during the integration step concerns standardized testing. Many states have accountability programs that in one way or another test students in the basic skills. These achievement scores are used in a variety of ways and in general cause a high degree of controversy. There are some inherent problems with all kinds of standardized tests, but surely some good comes from the various accountability programs. If there is a state law pre-scribing certain tests, schools will have to comply whether one believes in the standardized approach or not. Of course, many school districts have used stan-dardized tests for years for various reasons.

The partnership school, particularly during the integration step, *must not accept the standard accountability measures as the only source of evaluation. Each partnership school must base its evaluation on its own individual school goals.* Tests can be helpful, but schools must not assume that evaluation has been "taken care of" just because there has been a large testing program.

The reasons for this are that most accountability tests are not specific in either content inclusion or general subjects tested; the results of the testing may take a long time to receive; they are generally framed in a context of compari-son with other schools and other districts which may or may not have a bearing on the partnership school; they may not provide satisfactory explanations to parents regarding individual achievement; they tend to be psychologically threatening to teachers, administrators, and students alike; and they may not coincide with the management-by-objectives program for local organizational goals and purposes.

Consequently, we recommend the following during the integration steps:

1. The task force or leadership group should be in the position to make decisions or recommendations for decisions that are based on a comprehensive picture of evaluation.
2. Standardized accountability tests should be used with prudence, and only as one aspect of a larger evaluation program.
3. Both product and process evaluations should be established, implemented, and publicized.
4. At least 5 percent of the time, effort, and energy should be devoted to evaluation programs.
5. Evaluation must relate to the goals of the organization as established in the OD process.
6. The partnership parity should be reviewed as an on-going process.
7. The partnership team should be involved in the evaluation as a team—evaluation is not something a university professor does after everyone else has done their work.

## EVALUATING PARTNERSHIPS

A final aspect of evaluation that is important to our Partnership Model of School Improvement is the continuing evaluation of the partnership itself. From time to time, therefore, it is suggested that the partners make a deliberate assessment of the collaboration process to identify problems for solution. One way to implement this idea would be to conduct an OD intervention within the partnership task force or group itself. For example, the leadership group could look for ways and means to improve its own effectiveness. One specific activity that is usually helpful is to plan a weekend self-renewal workshop. These are most successful when an outside facilitator can be employed to help the group with its process, relationships, effectiveness, complaints, resentments, or other social-psychological impediments that might be discussed. Often groups that work together get stale and establish normative behavior that is not always effective. A retreat for "regrouping" can be most beneficial.

## ENDNOTES

1. Joseph J. Caruso, "Parity in Designing, Conducting and Evaluating Teacher Education Programs: A Conceptual Definition," unpublished paper, date unknown, Wheelock College, Boston, 02215 (Microfiche ED 100 807).
2. James R. Sanders and Donald J. Cunningham, "A Structure for Formative Evaluation in Product Development," *Review of Educational Research* 43 (1973): 217.

# Chapter 21

# Examples of
# Collaboration in School
# Improvement

Probably no existing school demonstrates the Partnership Model exactly. On the other hand, there are many situations in which elements of the Partnership Model are operating. There are examples of schools working successfully with OD, examples of partnership and collaborative ventures, examples of change efforts focused on a single school, examples of successful linkages with colleges or State Departments of Education, and examples of schools that are reacting well to problems of economic constraints or enrollment declines. In this final chapter, a number of such examples are described. In each case, elements of the Partnership Model may be noted and the strengths and weaknesses of each collaboration recognized.

## TEACHER CORPS

The Teacher Corps originated in 1965 as one among many programs designed to bring about "The Great Society." Patterned after the Peace Corps, the Teacher Corps was originally conceived as an attempt to recruit promising graduates of liberal arts colleges to teaching in inner-city schools.

The primary purpose of the Teacher Corps was to improve the quality of education for "disadvantaged" young people; that is, those from low-income families. Although focused on the training of new teachers, the Corps has throughout its history been designed as a force for improvement in local schools and in teacher training institutions. Not only have participants been specifically trained as change agents, but also each Teacher Corps program was to be an attempt at local school improvement.

From the beginning, the Teacher Corps has utilized a decentralized approach. A constant theme has been the formation of partnerships among local school personnel, college educators, and representatives of the local community. Each project was to include these three groups on a steering committee, which was responsible for overall program and policy decisions, and a school community council, which was responsible for supporting, directing, and coordinating teacher training. The functions of these groups included a concern for general improvements in the local school made possible by involvement in the Teacher Corps program. In fact, according to William L. Smith, Director of

Teacher Corps, the major purpose of the Corps was "to demonstrate better ways to function" and to be "a means for creating a comprehensive approach to installing improvement, change, and reforms."[1]

The Teacher Corps, therefore, represents an important body of practical experience in collaboration to improve local schools. Over the course of its history hundreds of such collaborations have been supported. The experience has not always been peaceful and rewarding. For example, young interns, eager to reform the public schools, were sometimes tossed unceremoniously from classrooms by teachers unwilling to give up responsibility and control. Colleges and universities often proved inflexible in tailoring requirements to the needs as viewed by local communities and schools.

Looking back on the first ten years of Teacher Corps, Hite and Drummond summarized the Teacher Corps experiences with collaboration. One painful lesson was that collaboration always involved some group or person who was asked to give up power or control over some aspect of the educational process. This was rarely accomplished without difficulty. Another lesson was that parity could operate as a principle in setting goals and broad policies, but did not succeed on the operational level where partners differed in expertise. According to Hite and Drummond, the ingredients for successful collaboration, based on the Teacher Corps experience, appeared to be these:

1. Administrative leaders must see the value of inter-organizational collaboration and give their support to joint efforts.
2. The attitudes of the rank and file in the organizations must favor collaboration.
3. Both intra- and inter-organizational communication mechanisms must have been established.
4. Organizations and institutions must have a history of cooperative action and a broad participation in goal setting.
5. The organizations and institutions must consider themselves competent in the potential areas of collaboration.
6. The organizations and institutions must have resources for helping personnel learn new roles or new ways of working.
7. Tangible, short-range benefits must be seen as probable results of collaboration.
8. The organizations and institutions involved must be clear about their own missions and objectives.
9. The organizations and institutions must be free of legal, political, and financial constraints which prohibit collaboration.
10. The organizations or institutions involved must be within reasonable geographic proximity.

Collaboration is not easy, nor is it beautiful. Different organizations with different goals, administrative arrangements, and norms find collaboration anxiety-producing, time-consuming, and in the short run inefficient. Often, collaboration requires change in the ways people work with others both within and outside their organizations or

> institutions. If we knew of any other way to achieve the goals of Teacher Corps, we would recommend it, but collaboration is the only way we know that works.[2]

And work it does. The record of the Teacher Corps includes a long list of successful collaborations. A number of program themes stand out. First, the Teacher Corps is responsible for the development of multicultural programs in many schools. In these programs the emphasis is on respect for cultural diversity and recognition of strengths in ethnic identity, such as language, history, and values. School programs are improved by drawing on such strengths. Second, individualized instruction has been a common successful theme in Teacher Corps projects. Emphasis on individual diagnosis and prescription as a basis for teaching and learning is especially important to support children who have fallen behind in basic learning skills. Third, an emphasis on competency-based teacher education has been a theme of Teacher Corps. In this case, school improvement results from a careful specification of teacher behaviors that are needed to make local school improvements. This specification of teacher training objectives in the light of local school improvement goals is a major contribution of the Teacher Corps model. Fourth, the use of community resources in the educational process is a strong theme of Teacher Corps programs. The fact that parents and community representatives participate in decisions about local school programs has helped to make this concept functional. Community members functioning as staff have also made significant contributions to school-community relations.

During the 1970s the Teacher Corps shifted its emphasis to in-service teacher training in order to meet the changing conditions in American education. In reassessing the direction of Teacher Corps programs, its director, William Smith, emphasized two conclusions from the Teacher Corps experience.

> First, change is a slow process. Diffusion of change from one institution to another is a function of the acceptance and credibility of both the practices and products developed, and of the institutions involved. Therefore, an institution must have a time span long enough for it to develop and share the documentation of these practices, processes, and products. Training, dealing with the critical problems faced by interns, teachers, and pupils in poverty schools, must focus on the schools and the staffs as they exist. The school itself is the smallest unit of change. In addition, there must be at least five years after the planning year to insure continuity of purpose and to provide the time needed to develop and orchestrate the basic or modified designs generated from the complex endeavor of bringing about change.

> The second conclusion is that schools are social systems—formal organizations. Therefore, systems theory and organizational behavior theory must be used in the conceptualization of pre-service and in-service training. The basic assumption is that many good and talented teachers feel unable to work effectively because they believe the hierarchical structure of administrators and supervisors, and the environmental field force known as "community,"

have placed unwarranted constraints upon them. A sense of alienation and a sense of powerlessness have to be overcome. If schools are to be changed for the better, as organizations and as social systems, all with a role or an investment in the education of kids must be involved in the change process, in roles of equality to whatever extent possible. Hence, the issue of parity, which is defined as deliberate, mutual collaborative planning and decision making on the part of those giving as well as those receiving services. To operationalize the parity concept is of major importance for both the university and the local education agency, as well as for society today. They are having problems doing it.[3]

One gains from the Teacher Corps experience an appreciation for the fact that some of the most difficult educational problems in American schools have been faced, and progress made, through the collaborative process recommended in this book. The process is difficult and often painful, but the process is necessary if improvements are to be made. Furthermore, a focus on the local school organization as the primary target for change obtains strong support from the Teacher Corps experience.

## TEACHER CENTERS

Other examples of the Partnership Model for School Improvement can be found among the many teacher centers established in recent years. The growth of teacher centers has been so striking that it may qualify as a national movement. Based on a field survey conducted in 1973–1974, Schmieder and Yarger[4] estimated the existence of 4,500 teacher center programs in America. Since then, the federal government established a National Teacher Center Program with federal funds to support such centers.

A striking feature of the teacher center movement is the great diversity among teacher centers. Many place the emphasis on pre-service teacher education with cooperative arrangements between local schools and colleges for the purpose of providing student teaching experiences. Many Teacher Corps projects were of this type. Other teacher centers stress in-service education of teachers, often with an emphasis on teachers sharing ideas with each other. Often the inspiration for this type of teacher center comes from British teacher centers that support open classroom models.

Teacher centers have many governance patterns. Sometimes, teacher centers are controlled by school district administration or by the teaching staff; in other cases, they are governed by colleges or by partnerships. The National Teacher Center Program emphasizes governance of teacher centers by local education agencies with heavy participation by members of the teaching staff. Teacher centers also vary in emphasis on student and parent involvement.

The common elements among the variety of teacher centers appear to be the following:

1. Dissatisfaction with existing mechanisms for school improvement and teacher education have led to the creation of teacher centers. Special dissatisfaction is expressed with existing in-service programs arranged by local or state education agencies and by colleges and universities.
2. The goal of teacher centers is to improve the quality of educational programs through teacher education, now especially through in-service education.
3. Greater participation by teachers, and sometimes parents and students, is assumed to be a major step towards strenthening programs of school improvement and staff development.
4. A formal organization, or at least a physical location, is needed to strengthen linkages among teachers, between teachers and administrators, between school personnel and college personnel, and between school personnel and community representatives. Such an enterprise needs special recognition and support, including budgetary support for the necessary planning, implementing, and evaluating activities.

One useful view of teacher centers was provided by Devaney and Thorn in a personalized national survey of teacher centers. Their survey grew from a special interest in centers that stress informal sharing among teachers about open education. The authors identified and interviewed personnel from over forty such centers. They summarized as follows:

A generalized statement of the premise shared by teachers' centers we interviewed is: teachers must be more than technicians, must continue to be learners. Long-lasting improvements in education will come through in-service programs that identify individual starting points for learning in each teacher; build on teachers' motivation to take more, not less, responsibility for curriculum and instruction decisions in the school and the classroom; and welcome teachers to participate in a design of professional development programs.[5]

Devaney and Thorn found that teacher centers in their study had grown from a desire by classroom teachers to find practical solutions to everyday problems. Teachers in these centers shared a common belief about children that was different from much conventional practice. These teachers sought mutual support and help from others who were similarly inclined and who believed in a new professionalism among teachers. The latter theme is particularly significant. Teacher centers must be viewed as a part of a growing sense of professionalism among teachers which accompanies a growing strength of the organized teaching profession. This is a major fact of life in school improvement which is reflected in the growth of teacher centers.

Another perspective on teacher centers is provided in the movement toward competency-based teacher education. As illustrated in the Teacher Corps, collaboration among school personnel, community members, and college officials is a common element in teacher training programs that emphasize the development of teaching competencies. In many states, competency-based teacher education has been a vehicle for improving teacher certification processes and in the accreditation of teacher education programs. In some cases, California, Oregon, and Minnesota for example, new state-wide commissions on teacher certification and licensing with teacher majorities pushed these developments. In a number of states legislative mandates for competency-based teacher education were passed. In such cases, New York, Florida, and Pennsylvania for example, the design of teacher education programs required collaboration among college and school personnel and sometimes community representatives. Thus, state officials have become much involved in the establishment and maintenance of partnerships related to both pre- and in-service teacher education programs.

A practical outcome of these developments has been the creation of teacher centers, jointly governed by local school officials and college educators, for the purpose of developing cooperative teacher education programs. In some cases, these developments are the occasions for power struggles over the control of teacher education. The teacher organizations wish to increase their power over teacher education, especially in-service teacher education. School administrators, as representatives of the local school boards, have their own authority at stake, as do colleges and universities. Despite the wrangling, the development of teacher centers around cooperative teacher training programs is a major step forward in collaboration. Teachers must be granted opportunities to chart their own destiny; local school administrators must make decisions about staff development and school renewal; and the resources of higher education are unique and valuable aspects of the American educational system. If higher education has not served school improvement in local cases, then changes should be made, but the resources themselves must not be dismissed. Teachers by themselves, or in their local school organizations, do not have the links to knowledge and training resources necessary to bring about significant change.

A persuasive model for teacher centers in which higher education can play a central role has been provided in *Obligation for Reform*,[6] the report of a special task force commissioned by the United States Office of Education. The report stresses the need to commit resources in higher education to the task of improving American schools. Furthermore, the vehicle recommended for this commitment is the formation of teacher centers (called "Personnel Development Centers" in the report). The Personnel Development Centers were to be the organizational mechanism for forming partnerships in teacher education that would become key elements in educational reform. Specific recommendations were made for establishing such centers, including cooperative governance and funding of the centers. Through collaboration, goals for school improvement could be identified and training resources brought to bear on their achievement.

An example of one such teacher center that involves collaboration between a university, a city school district, a teachers' association, and a local community is the Syracuse Urban Teacher Center.[7] Growing out of a Teacher Corps Project, the Syracuse Center was established by joint action of Syracuse University and the Syracuse City School District. However, its governing board includes representatives from the teachers association and the community. The focus of the center is the development of pre- and in-service teacher education which is undertaken by the Program Development Committee, which is also a collaborative group.

## CHANGE PROGRAM FOR IGE

An outstanding example of a partnership strategy for school improvement is the/I/D/E/A/Change Program for Individually Guided Education (IGE). As the educational affiliate of the Charles F. Kettering Foundation, /I/D/E/A/ (Institute for Development of Educational Activities, Inc.) has as its primary purpose the identification and implementation of promising innovations in elementary and secondary schooling. During recent years a major program of the Institute has been the Change Program for IGE. The Change Program utilizes a nation-wide network of "Intermediate Agencies" and "Facilitators" to assist groups of local schools to utilize the concepts of Individually Guided Education.

Building on the work of Herbert J. Klausmeier at the Wisconsin Research and Development Center for Cognitive Learning, concepts of IGE emphasize the need for personalized learning programs for each student. Guidelines for re-creating a local school to provide such personalized learning include suggestions for school organization, administration, curriculum, and instruction. Thus, Individually Guided Education is not just a new method of teaching and learning, but a plan for making each local school a self-improving unit.

The components of IGE, as developed by Klausmeier and his colleagues, include the following:[8]

1. *Multiunit organization.* To facilitate an individualized approach to learning, IGE schools are organized into multi-age units. Each unit contains 100–150 students from several age groups taught by an instructional team. The team is composed of a unit leader, several staff teachers, and aides. Unit leaders serve with parent representatives and specialized instructional personnel on an instructional improvement committee chaired by the principal. Thus, unit leaders share responsibility for decisions with the principal.
2. *Individual programming.* Instructional programming is individualized. Educational objectives are specified not just in terms of the school or grade level, but in terms of each individual pupil. Individual learning programs are established and pursued with the help of the teaching team. The student is aided in developing a sense of personal responsibility and confidence in his or her own learning ability.
3. *Evaluation for decision making.* Careful evaluation of student progress is another important component of IGE. Continuous measurement of stu-

dent performance in comparison to personalized learning objectives is recommended as a basis for subsequent instructional programming.

4. *Curriculum materials.*   The success of IGE depends upon the availability of curriculum materials that lend themselves to individualized programming and to continuous evaluation of student performance.

5. *Community relations.*   Emphasis is given to parent and community input both at the school district level and at the level of the local school building.

6. *Supportive environment.*   External support is needed not just from the school district but also from the state education agency and from teacher education institutions. State and regional organizations of schools interested in IGE also provide support.

7. *Research and development.*   The IGE model emphasizes continuing research and development to evaluate IGE and how it is operating in a given school.

Since 1972, the Change Program of IGE has departed somewhat from the Wisconsin model. Giving heavy emphasis to John Goodlad's strategies for school improvement, the /I/D/E/A/ Change Program has stressed the development of Leagues of Cooperating Schools, whose purpose is to support processes of self-examination, decision making, action, and evaluation in each local member school. In-service training of school staff members provides the skills needed in the self-renewal process. Leadership in each League of Cooperating Schools is provided by an Intermediate Agency, such as a college, university, or State Department of Education.

As summarized in /I/D/E/A/'s *Guide to an Improvement Program for Schools,*[9] the assumptions of the Change Program for IGE include the following:

1. The individual school is a strategic unit of educational change.
2. The culture of the school is central both to understanding and effecting educational improvement.
3. Given existing social and educational constraints, most individual schools are not strong enough to overcome the inertia against change built into the typical school district.
4. Each school needs a process by which it can deal effectively with its own problems and effect its own change.
5. Some screening, legitimizing, and communicating of ideas beyond what individual schools might do informally must be built into the new social system.
6. Individuals asked to take risks are more willing to do so when some elements of success are already built into the structure.

Working from these assumptions, the /I/D/E/A/ staff developed the Change Program for IGE in a series of steps. First, a set of thirty-five desirable outcomes of the change program were specified. These items, which are given in Figure 21-1, specify two conditions that must be present before a school implements the IGE program (items 1 and 2). The others (items 3–35) describe goals toward which IGE schools should strive. These outcomes become the yardstick by which the success of the change program is measured.

Next, a few development sites were identified to refine the change strategies. Emphasis was given to the individual school as a focus for change. On the basis of the experience in development sites, training materials and change strategies were revised and incorporated into new training materials. These training materials included illustrations of successful practices that had emerged during the pilot development. A variety of films, filmstrips, and books was then created to carry the IGE message.

With training materials and change methods in hand, the IGE program then identified a variety of intermediate agencies to work with school districts. By 1978, over 200 such intermediate agencies had worked with /I/D/E/A/, including 69 school districts, 67 universities, 12 archdioceses and 16 State Departments of Education. These intermediate agencies became a home for "facilitators" who were specially trained to carry the change program to individual schools. From 1971 through 1977 almost 1,000 workshops were conducted for facilitators. The training content includes small group techniques, methods for individualizing student learning, and directions for facilitating the adoption of IGE by a local school. Included in the training are recommendations to establish leagues of cooperating schools in which a number of local schools, each interested in adopting IGE, can create a forum for the exchange of ideas and for mutual support.

The /I/D/E/A/ Change Program for IGE has gained impressively widespread acceptance. By 1977, over 1,700 elementary and secondary schools had been involved and over 34,000 teachers had participated in the program. In addition, there were 182 leagues with two or more participating schools. This is

**FIGURE 21-1.**

---

1. All staff members have had an opportunity to examine their own goals and the IGE outcomes before a decision is made to participate in the program.

*2. The school district has approved the school staff's decision to implement the /I/D/E/A/ Change Program for Individually Guided Education.

*3. The entire school is organized into Learning Communities with each Learning Community composed of students, teachers, aides and a Learning Community Leader.

*4. Each Learning Community contains a cross section of staff.

*5. Learning Community members have an effective working relationship as evidenced by responding to one another's needs, trusting one another's motives and abilities and using techniques of open communication.

6. Each Learning Community is composed of approximately equal numbers of two or more student age groups.

*7. Each student has an advisor whom he or she views as a warm supportive person concerned with enhancing the student's self concept; the advisor shares accountability with the student for the student's learning program.

8. Personalized in-service programs are developed and implemented by each Learning Community staff as a whole as well as by individual teachers.

9. The Learning Community maintains open communication with parents and the community at large.

(Continued)

*10. Sufficient time is provided for Learning Community staff members to meet.

*11. Learning Community members select broad educational goals to be emphasized by the Learning Community.

12. Role specialization and a division of labor among teachers are characteristics of the Learning Community activities of planning, implementing and assessing.

*13. Each student learning program is based on specified learning objectives.

14. A variety of learning activities using different media and modes is used when building learning programs.

*15. Both student and teacher consider the following when a student's learning activities are selected:

—Peer relationships          —Interest in subject areas
—Achievement                 —Self-concept
—Learning styles

*16. Students pursue their learning programs within their own Learning Communities except on those occasions when their unique learning needs can only be met in another setting using special human or physical resources.

*17. Learning Community members make decisions regarding the arrangements of time, facilities, materials, staff, and students within the Learning Community.

18. The staff and students use special resources from the local community in learning programs.

*19. A variety of data sources is used when learning is assessed by teachers and students, with students becoming increasingly more responsible for self-assessment.

20. Each student (individually, with other students, with staff members, and with his or her parents) plans and evaluates his or her own progress toward educational goals.

*21. Teachers and students have a systematic method of gathering and using information about each student which affects his or her learning.

*22. The Program Improvement Council formulates school-wide policies and operational procedures and resolves problems referred to it involving two or more Learning Communities.

23. The Program Improvement Council coordinates school-wide in-service programs for the total staff.

24. The school is a member of a League of schools implementing IGE processes and participating in an interchange of personnel to identify and alleviate problems within the League schools.

25. The school as a member of a League of IGE schools stimulates an interchange of solutions to existing educational problems plus serving as a source of ideas for new development.

26. The Learning Community analyzes and improves its operations as a functioning group.

*27. Learning program plans for the Learning Community and for individual students are constructively critiqued by members of the Learning Community.

*28. The Program Improvement Council analyzes and improves its operations as a functioning group.

29. Each student can state learning objectives for the learning activities in which he or she is engaged.

30. Each student accepts increasing responsibility for selecting his or her learning objectives.

31. Each student accepts increasing responsibility for selecting or developing learning activities for specific learning objectives.

32. Each student demonstrates increasing responsibility for pursuing his or her learning program.

33. The Program Improvement Council assures continuity of educational goals and learning objectives throughout the school and assures that they are consistent with the broad goals of the school system.

34. Students are involved in decision making regarding school-wide activities and policies.

35. Teacher performance in the learning environment is observed and constructively critiqued by members of the Learning Community using both formal and informal methods.

---

*Items with high implementation ratings in follow-up studies.

**FIGURE 21-1.    Desired Outcomes of the Change Program of IGE**  Jon S. Paden, *Reflections for the Future*, /I/D/E/A/, 1978, pp. 23–26. Reprinted with permission.

a remarkable achievement, giving ample testimony to the power of the change strategy employed.

Follow-up studies of IGE schools have shown a consistent pattern of change toward the objectives of the program. Schools differ in the rate at which they reach objectives and in which objectives they reach first. It appears that different schools select clusters of objectives for emphasis. Overall, as indicated by the asterisks in Figure 21–1, a number of IGE outcomes are commonly implemented. These include the adoption of the multi-unit organization, moves toward individualized student learning, and the successful performance of a Program Improvement Council to make decisions about school programs. There is substantial evidence that IGE schools made genuine progress toward program goals.[10]

## EDUCATIONAL FIELD AGENTS

From time to time, recommendations are made to create for public elementary and secondary schools something like the agricultural field agents of the Cooperative Extension Service. Such agricultural field agents have a long and distinguished record of service to farm producers, especially in linking them to university-based agricultural research. Cooperative Extension Agents, who are characterized by a problem-solving orientation and a philosophy of service, strive to meet the needs of clients by providing information directly or by arranging consultations, meetings, short courses, etc., where farmers can learn about recent developments in agriculture knowledge.

An inspiring account of the agricultural extension philosophy in action is the story of Norman Borlaug, winner of the Nobel Prize and father of the "Green Revolution," who saved millions in developing countries from starvation through the development and dissemination of improved agriculture methods.[11]

Before one adopts the practices of agricultural field agents, the differences between educational institutions and the agricultural enterprise must be understood. First, schools are government bureaucracies, operating as local monopolies, while agriculture is a profit-making, private enterprise. The incentives for change are very different in the two areas.

Second, because the goals of schools are difficult to specify and measure, it is extremely difficult to demonstrate "increased yield" from new methods in education as is done in agriculture. Therefore, educational demonstration projects often fail to provide clear proof of success.

Third, the agriculture experiment stations and the cooperative extension services are maintained by long-term federal subsidies for research and dissemination. Nothing comparable has been available for education. Also, educational agencies at the state and local levels have been unable to afford large investments in research and dissemination. The success of agricultural field agents depends, to a great extent, on their position within a larger research and dissemination enterprise.

Nevertheless, the agricultural field agent model has been an excellent source of practical suggestions for those trying to improve schools. Two examples will be presented: (1) the Pilot State Dissemination Program, which became the inspiration for expanded information services in a variety of state education agencies; and (2) the Del Mod System, one of two state-wide efforts by the National Science Foundation to improve the coordination of curriculum dissemination efforts.

**Pilot State Dissemination Program.**    A particularly intriguing study of educational field agents was conducted by Sieber and others in their evaluation of the Pilot State Dissemination Program.[12] Under the sponsorship of the U.S. Office of Education, this program explored the use of educational extension agents to help local school personnel use knowledge being generated in Regional Educational Laboratories and R&D Centers, as well as information contained in the ERIC system. Pilot projects were funded in three states—Oregon, South Carolina, and Utah. In each state, field agents worked with clients in local schools to identify needs or problems. Identified needs were referred to a retrieval staff located in the State Department of Education. The retrieval staff performed necessary information searches and delivered results to the client in as short a time as possible. Field agents then assisted clients in interpreting and using the information; in some cases, they even helped with the implementation of new ideas. The field agent also tried to improve the flow of information within local schools and between the local schools and the state agency. Overall, the program bore a strong family resemblance to the county agent system in agriculture.

Despite the fact that field agents had little power and formal authority, Sieber found that the pilot programs produced concrete reforms in administrative and classroom practice. This happened even in areas which were regarded as educationally backward and in small, rural schools, which are usually resistant to change.

Sieber characterized the successful role of these field agents as "undercover change-agents in the guise of information specialists." Evidently, the field agent's role as a neutral outsider, anxious to help local personnel, placed him or her in an excellent position to foster educational change.

An interesting aspect of Sieber's study was the use of field observations to document the work of field agents. In consequence, his recommendations have an authoritative, practical ring. With respect to the organization of such state-wide information services, Sieber recommended that they be carefully insulated from the regulatory functions of the state education agency. For example, he recommended that field agents be housed in intermediate agencies, such as county districts. Sieber also found that information retrieval services needed constant monitoring on the basis of client satisfaction and that "self-renewal structures" at the school-building level facilitated the use of field agent services.

With respect to the field agents themselves, a graphic description of desirable personality traits was given.

> . . . an individual hired as a field agent should be non-authoritarian, patient with clients who have trouble articulating their needs or using information, able to tolerate delay and ultimate frustration in obtaining results, have a low need for ego-aggrandizement, and enjoy performing a variety of activities and meeting a wide range of people without a sense of becoming "hassled." When the situation demands, he should be able to exercise leadership. Further, he should be capable of thinking and speaking clearly with a minimum of jargon and aura of expertise. Curiosity about educational developments and national trends should be a part of his professional make-up; but he must be able to resist the temptation to become a "missionary" for any particular practice. Above all, he should be adaptable to different situations and individuals, adopting a personal or impersonal manner as the situation dictates. Finally, he should be orderly and able to maintain record and report systems.[13]

Subsequently, Colin Mick and others[14] utilized the results of the Pilot State Dissemination Project in recommendations for training personnel for state dissemination systems. Much emphasis was placed on the informal contacts needed by field agents to establish trust and credibility with local school personnel. Training for field agents in the social organization of schools, including communication and decision-making channels, was recommended so that field agents might devise appropriate strategies for a particular local setting. As a staff member of the state education agency, the educational field agent's primary role was to provide linkage between local information users and the retrieval personnel of the state's educational extension service. However, considerable flexibility was included in the role description to allow field agents to play a variety of change agent roles in local schools.

These recommendations became the basis for expanding information retrieval services in state education agencies in the mid-1970s through the State Dissemination Capacity Building Program of the National Institute of Education. The concept of the educational field agent fits precisely the role envisioned for a state education agency representative on a local partnership committee as recommended in this book.

**Del Mod: A State-Wide System for School Improvement.**     Another illustration of an educational field agent program is provided by the Del Mod System, a state-wide project to improve science and mathematics education in the elementary and secondary schools of Delaware. Two of the authors played important roles in the system, which functioned from 1970–1976 with substantial grants from the DuPont Company and the National Science Foundation. The system was designed as a collaboration between the institutions of higher education and the public schools of Delaware to identify and pursue state-wide goals for improving science and mathematics education through a coordinated set of teacher training activities. A central feature of the system was a state-wide network of curriculum resource centers and educational field agents.

The Del Mod System grew out of disappointments with efforts during the 1960s to implement new science and mathematics curriculum materials. The former reliance upon in-service courses and summer institutes, in which individual teachers were trained in college settings, had certain weaknesses. In particular, better coordination was desired between various training efforts within a geographic region and between training objectives and the plans of schools for bringing about curriculum change. Thus, the principal objectives of the Del Mod System were to coordinate all elements of science and mathematics education in Delaware in a state-wide plan for improving the quality of science teaching in the schools of state.

The governing board for the Del Mod System consisted of the presidents of the institutions of higher education, the state superintendent of public instruction, and a representative of the governor's office. A director, responsible to this governing board, worked with a group of component coordinators (one from each cooperating institution) and a staff of field agents to develop and conduct a comprehensive program of school improvement. A central feature of the program was the establishment of curriculum resource centers throughout the state. Field agents worked directly with school personnel, linking them to curriculum materials and knowledge about science and mathematics teaching that were housed in the resource centers. Activities within the system were guided by a set of state-wide priorities for the improvement of science and mathematics education. It was intended that all science and mathematics education activities in the state would be affected by such a systematic, collaborative approach.

As judged by its clients and teams of outside evaluators, the most successful aspect of the Del Mod System was the combination of resource centers and educational field agents. Like the field agents in the Pilot State Dissemination Project, Del Mod agents adopted a philosophy of service to local teachers. Field agents, recruited from among master teachers with advanced graduate training in science or mathematics education, were able to gain the confidence of classroom teachers and building administrators. Not only did they provide information, but also they acted as change agents to stimulate interest in new patterns of teaching, to provide support and encouragement for innovative efforts, and to provide specific training needed to implement newer curriculum procedures. The fact that field agents did not directly represent either the local school administration, the universities, or the State Department of Education appeared to be a crucial factor in their help, for teacher-defined needs was a central aspect of the field agent strategy.

Another characteristic of successful field agent work was the autonomy and flexibility granted to each agent. Field agents were encouraged to adopt a style of operation suited to their own personalities and to the situations in local schools. Thus, each agent functioned in a somewhat different fashion. Differences in style were noted especially between rural, suburban, and urban agents.

Although the field agent program was successful, when special funding ended, so did the field agent program. Original hopes to continue the Del Mod System were confounded by the growing economic problems of education in the state. The special expense and effort required to maintain the system proved too great a cost. Neither the colleges, the university, the Department of Public Instruction, nor any coalition of institutions came forward to perpetuate the system.

The Del Mod System also provided a dramatic example of the problems and prospects for state-wide collaboration in school improvement. Institutional autonomy was a constant problem, and the system operated more as a political system than as an engineering system, as designed. As hard economic times arrived, it became apparent that the collaborating institutions were also competitors for state educational dollars. Also, each institution gave low priority to the linkage function that was the basis for the educational field agent program.

Two other shortcomings of the Del Mod Project are apparent in retrospect. First, the absence of the organized teaching profession from the system became a growing problem, especially because of the pressures placed on teachers by their organizations to limit "extra work" without extra pay. Second, insufficient attention was given to the strength of local school-building organizations. The field agent strategy emphasized support for the individual teacher without systematic attention to organization development. The emphasis in the Partnership Model on involving teacher organizations and organization development is, in part, an outcome of the author's experience in the Del Mod Project.[15]

## NATIONAL DIFFUSION NETWORK

Another example of federal efforts to disseminate the results of educational research and development is the National Diffusion Network.[16] Beginning in 1974, the network was a major attempt to improve the process by which local development successes were identified, communicated to other local schools, and adopted to the new local settings.

The Network grew from efforts of educators trying to improve the dissemination of successful Title III Projects. Title III of the Elementary and Secondary Education Act (ESEA) of 1965 had supported an enormous number of local demonstration projects through State Title III organizations. State leaders and federal officials concerned with Title III were at that time developing a system for validating local successes and disseminating results to other local schools. A particular concern was to improve the flow of information across state lines. One of the authors was deeply involved in the process as Chairman of the National Association of State Advisory Council Chairmen, Title III.

A key element in the National Diffusion Network is the Joint Dissemination Review Panel (JDRP), which includes representatives from the U.S. Office of Education and the National Institute of Education. The Review Panel judges reports of local demonstration projects, including those funded under the several federal programs supporting local change (especially ESEA Title I, III, VII, and Right to Read). Each project is carefully scrutinized for evidence of successful impact on students and for its potential for use in other sites. If approved, each program becomes eligible for dissemination through the Network.

A limited number (due to lack of funds) of projects have been chosen as Developer/Demonstrator Projects. These receive special funds to pay for orientations, in-service training, materials, and other costs arising from attempts to help other schools adopt the validated practices. This special support strengthens a local project's ability to describe its success story to other potential users.

Another unique feature of the Network is the state facilitator. State facilitators, many of whom operate from a local school district base or from consortia, provide human links between validated programs and local schools seeking assistance. State facilitators use a variety of methods to promote adoption and implementation of programs approved by the JDRP. They use mass mailings, educational fairs, and personal contact to make local educators aware of exemplary programs. They may arrange for educators to visit Developer/Demonstrator Programs or bring Developer/Demonstrators to the local site.

State facilitators make use of a special catalog, *Educational Programs That Work,*[17] which contains a summary description of approved projects. Also, a number of Project Information Packages have been developed under federal sponsorship to explain details of selected projects to interested users. A number of these packages have been evaluated in terms of their ability to assist local school personnel in implementing the approved programs. Another useful resource for state facilitators is the *Catalogue of NIE Education Products,*[18] which describes a wide variety of materials developed under federal sponsorship.

The early results of the National Diffusion Network were extremely positive. Evaluations indicated that the people involved were almost universally positive about the program, and the Network showed great promise as an effective and inexpensive way to promote successful practices.

Certain features of the National Dissemination Network deserve special comment. First, the use of a national panel to review and validate successful local efforts has proven to be of high value. By 1978, over 300 local successes had been documented. Not only do each of these projects provide examples of exemplary educational practices, but collectively they also document the fact that local school improvement projects can be successful. In view of the many disappointing attempts at educational improvement, these projects are truly "lighthouses" that can show the way to improvements in American education.

Second, the experience of the Developer/Demonstrator Program has reemphasized the importance of interpersonal contact between developer and implementor. Successful replications also show the importance of local needs assessment and a firm local commitment. Furthermore, they highlight the importance of in-service training for both teachers and administrators, including visits by personnel to demonstrator sites. Community support is another important factor.

Third, the experience of state facilitators is consistent with lessons learned from educational field agent programs. State facilitators have discovered the importance of informal local contacts and separation from the regulatory flavor of state education agencies. Success involves a philosophy of service to local needs, especially the timely provision of needed information to assist local units in solving problems.

Finally, the Network illustrates a cost-effective approach to in-service training. Local schools can obtain needed ideas, materials, and expertise at bargain basement prices. No expensive internal development process is needed and no expensive external consultants are required.

The National Diffusion Network illustrates a vital role that can be played by state and federal education agencies to assist local schools in self-improvement. Furthermore, the experience in the Network affirms the principles of the Partnership Model, in which the local school site is the focus for improvement. Procedures that put local schools in touch with counterparts who have implemented successful changes is a vital contribution. Providing resources during implementation of new practices is another important ingredient in success. The Partnership Model provides for these factors by suggesting that a representative from the state education agency be a link between local school problems and federal resources for local change. The state facilitator in the National Diffusion Network is just such a person.

## CONCORD HIGH SCHOOL: A CASE STUDY

In the decade before the Age of Slowdown there were numerous examples of individual schools that were transformed into innovative, dynamic organizations through concentrated change efforts. It seems appropriate to report on at least one of these as an example of extensive school improvement practices that were successful: Concord High School of Wilmington, Delaware.[19] One of the authors served as principal of the high school in the early seventies; and a brief account of the events from that experience illustrates features of many of the principles of this book.

Concord High School was a suburban high school of about 1,400 students located in an upper middle-class community. A high percentage of the students attended college upon graduation. The school is now part of the New Castle County School District as a result of a court-ordered desegregation plan. Consequently the original, innovative identity of the school is somewhat submerged in the new school district with different students (some bussed), teachers (some transfers), and administrators (now all different).

The process that gave Concord the reputation as one of the most unique and innovative high schools on the East coast took five years. At the end of the five years, the school had implemented many of the then available new concepts such as team teaching; continuous progress curriculum; independent study; flexible scheduling (including unscheduled "free time" for students); an elaborate instructional materials center with satellite academic centers scattered throughout the building; an active student cabinet with powers and authority unheralded in the area (for example, students were active in screening new teachers); innovative counseling and guidance programs; and many others.

While the school itself was new, the school district in which the school was located was typically conservative. Consequently, changes that occurred were scrutinized very carefully by the school board, parents, teachers' association, students, and district office supervisors.

The strategies that contributed to this successful change process coincide with many of the important elements that have been discussed in this book. They are summarized below.

**The Single School As a Target for Change.**    There were no attempts to change other schools in the district along the same lines. The superintendent professed an administrative policy of school-building autonomy and the principal was viewed as the manager of the organization. The principal's responsibilities were seen as those that followed the local school-building goals and objectives. Small amounts of extra funds were made available to Concord for these change efforts and limited federal grants were awarded; but all of these were targeted for Concord High School only. In other words, a great effort was applied to a small unit organization—Concord High School.

**Goals, Objectives, and Long-Term Planning.**    A great deal of time and energy was spent on articulating the goals and objectives of the building. The principal was explicit as to the philosophic direction in which he wanted the staff to develop the program. The goals appeared in writing, and were expressed in public meetings and school meetings with faculty and students. An indication of this is the fact that many people in the Concord community woud speak of the "Concord Philosophy." This is very important. Many innovative schools are controversial, as was Concord, but at least the goals need to be reasonably clear. All of these goals were part of a five-year plan that was implemented. At the end of that time period, the principal left to take a position as an assistant superintendent in another district.

**Involvement.**    While the principal was the obvious initiator and change agent for this project, students and teachers were heavily involved in goal setting, selection of methods, and evaluation of each program. This involvement process was a good example of the adaptation theory expounded upon by the Rand Study. There were numerous committees that were involved in important decisions; and much program authority was delegated to teaching teams. As an example of this delegated authority, there was a time in which each department devised their own grading system and sent reports to parents at different times. During the first five years of this hectic and controversial project, the school building had less teacher turn-over than any building in the district. This must be viewed as some indication of the level of involvement and "ownership" that is so crucial in successful change projects.

**The Variables in School Improvement.**    There was continual awareness of the variables of the organization that played a part in changing that organization. Goals of both the *organization* and *individuals* were discussed and frequently adjusted. The *structure,* which was drastically different from any other high school in the area, was constantly analyzed; but most important, the *process* was dealt with on a continual basis. Meetings, sensitivity sessions, liaison committees, personal chats with the principal, an active school newspaper which aired comments from teachers and students about the process, and other procedures were evident. Process was deemed important by the principal, and recognition of this variable of the organization was invaluable to the entire staff.

**Knowledge Utilization.**   Extensive efforts were made to secure and utilize the latest available information on educational research and innovative practices. Teachers were sent to conferences, consultants were hired to bring new ideas to the school, visitations were made to other schools, and teachers' mailboxes were constantly posted with the latest journal articles. The staff had access to the current knowledge production that applied to their local goals.

**Change Agent Leadership.**   Many of the change strategies (Havelock, in particular) speak to the importance of a charismatic change agent. There were several people who served as change agents from time to time, but the principal was certainly a dominant figure as the central facilitator in the change process. Other consultants were hired; the district office staff were utilized; and the State Office of Education sent representatives. There were also ample "change agent types" in the building in the role of teachers. All of these indicate that leadership was available in several forms.

**District Office Support.**   The district office was supportive. Its help to the school was primarily as a public relations effort. In other words, the superintendent and his staff, were "loyal" to the Concord efforts. Positive statements appeared in press releases, local newsletters, public meetings, and in private conversations. There were times when the Concord program frightened the district office staff, but that concern was never made public. Concord would not have existed in its present form without district office support. That is not to say there were not controls from the district office, because there were many debates that took place between the Concord administration and the district office, but overt support was expressed to the public.

**Readiness to Change.**   Although it is difficult to assess the reasons for readiness behavior, many of the Concord teachers were accepting of change itself and this smoothed the road for others who tended to be more doubtful.

**Organization Development.**   While the staff was somewhat ignorant of the OD concept, the ingredients of action research, total school involvement, careful evaluation procedures, goal-setting procedures, and action planning were present.

The school staff was practicing OD without being aware of it, and perhaps increased awareness would have been helpful in later years when the school began to settle into a more complacent state.

**Partnership.**   While certain efforts were made to form linkages with outside resources and involve the community at large in the process, no real partnerships were formed. This deficiency was instrumental in the school's reverting to a more conservative and traditional posture once the principal-change agent left. In one way of speaking, the *integration phase* was not complete because there were no sustaining partnerships with colleges of education or the department of instruction or the local or state teachers' organization. Student teachers came to the school unprepared for the unique environment. The teachers' association began to question the job descriptions and assignments of professional staff because many roles (differentiated staffing) were different from the established procedures of other schools in the district. No one was preparing for or even reinforcing either the philosophy or the training necessary to maintain a self-renewing, dynamic school. The parents and taxpayers began to bring pressure to bear against some of the new procedures because they were not involved deeply enough in the initial stages of the changes.

In summary, the story of Concord High School serves as an example of a successful attempt to change and improve traditional educational practices. There were many schools that have gone through similar histories. Generally, this change process has been spearheaded by an industrious principal. However, when the principal leaves or the emerging problem is temporarily solved, there is a tendency for the organization to slip into complacency. This is usually due to the lack of any one important component. In the case of Concord High School, it was the lack of any longstanding partnership contracts.

## ENDNOTES

1. William L. Smith, "Facing the Next Ten Years," *Journal of Teacher Education* 26, No. 2 (1975): 151.
2. F. Herbert Hite and William H. Drummond, "The Teacher Corps and Collaboration," *Journal of Teacher Education* 26, No. 2 (1975): 134.
3. Smith, "Facing the Next Ten Years," p. 152.
4. Allen A. Schmieder and Sam J. Yarger, *Teaching Centers: Toward the State of the Scene* (ERIC Clearinghouse on Teacher Education, November, 1974).
5. Kathleen Devaney and Lorraine Thorn, *Exploring Teachers' Centers* (San Francisco: Far West Laboratory for Educational Research and Development, May, 1975), p. 7.
6. George W. Denemark and Joost Yff, *Obligation for Reform: The Final Report of the Higher Education Task Force on Improvement and Reform in American Education* (Washington, D.C.: The American Association of Colleges for Teacher Education, January, 1974).
7. Robert L. Evans and Allan Kilgore, "The Syracuse University Teaching Center: A Model for Preservice/Inservice Development," *Phi Delta Kappan* 59 (April 1978): 539–541.
8. See Herbert J. Kausmeier, "Individually Guided Education: 1966–1980," *Journal of Teacher Education* 27, No. 3 (1976): 199–205.
9. */I/D/E/A/'s Guide to an Improvement Program for Schools* (Dayton, Ohio: Institute for Development of Educational Activities, Inc., no date).

10. Jon S. Paden, *Reflections for the Future* (Dayton, Ohio: The Institute for Development of Educational Activities, Inc., 1978).

11. Lennard Bickel, *Facing Starvation: Norman Borlaug and the Fight Against Hunger* (New York: Readers Digest Press, 1974).

12. Sam D. Sieber et al., *The Use of Educational Knowledge: Evaluation of the Pilot State Dissemination Program. Vol. 1: Goals, Operations and Training. Final Report* (New York: Columbia University Bureau of Applied Social Research, September, 1972), ED 065 739.

13. Ibid., p. 588.

14. Colin Mick et al., *Development of Training Resources for Educational Extension Services Personnel. Vol. 1. Final Report* (Stanford, Calif.: Stanford University Institute for Communication Research, April, 1973).

15. Daniel C. Neale, *Del Mod: A State-wide System for School Improvement,* (Newark: College of Education, University of Delaware, September, 1977), ED 150 684.

16. Shirley Boes Neill, "The National Diffusion Network: A Success Story Ending?" *Phi Delta Kappan* 57 (May 1976): 598–601.

17. U.S. Office of Education, *Educational Programs that Work,* vol. VI (San Francisco: Far West Laboratory for Educational Research and Development, Fall, 1979).

18. National Institute of Education, *Catalog of NIE Education Products* (Washington, D.C.: U.S. Government Printing Office, 1975).

19. A more complete description is provided in William J. Bailey, *Managing Self-Renewal in Secondary Education* (Englewood Cliffs, N.J.: Educational Technology Publications, 1975).

## SUMMARY OF PART IV

A variety of tactics for local school improvement has been presented. First the change agent roles of initiator, researcher, trainer, and facilitator were discussed in relation to the stages of school improvement. Suggestions were made for assigning change agent roles and for hiring outside consultants, if needed.

Second, group dynamics topics were discussed as a background for making local partnerships succeed. Collaboration in change requires careful attention to group process and to conflict resolution.

Third, successful partnerships require clear understandings about shared governance. Furthermore, problems of finance, personnel, and community involvement must be solved in order for partnerships to be successful.

Next, the use of knowledge resources in local school improvement was discussed. Although a "unified-systems" view of educational research, development, and diffusion may be a desirable goal, it does not represent current reality. Therefore, local schools need to be linked in a flexible way to a variety of knowledge sources.

Training and staff development must take account of current realities in teacher education, certification, and accreditation. Members of partnership groups must work hard to see that training opportunities meet local needs.

Finally, special attention must be given to evaluation procedures at each stage in the school improvement process. Special steps are recommended to evaluate the partnership itself.

Examples of successful collaboration in local school improvement are widespread. Several examples were presented to illustrate aspects of the Partnership Model in practice. Collaboration in local school improvement, while difficult, can succeed.

## PART IV DISCUSSION QUESTIONS

1.  A successful change effort moves through the stages of initiation, implementation, and integration. What are the roles of the researcher, trainer, and facilitator in each of these stages?

2.  Successful group process requires that participants pay attention to both the task and maintenance functions of the group. In a partnership effort, how might the skills associated with these functions be learned and implemented?

3.  Team building involves the establishment of mutual trust and agreement relative to goals, strategies, and operational procedures between the partners in a successful partnership effort. What steps can be taken to eliminate the climate of isolation and distance that exists between teachers, administrators, representatives of higher education, and state departments of education in order to implement the Partnership Model advanced in this text?

4.  The governance issues in the Partnership Model advanced in this text demand that roles, functions, and responsibilities for each partner be described in detail. Develop a Memorandum of Agreement (MOA) setting forth the specific elements of an MOA that you consider essential to a successful partnership effort.

5.  A major principle of adult learning (androgogy) is that to negate the learner's experiences is to negate the learner as a person. In in-service training programs, how would the implementation of this principle alter the content and instructional strategies of the activities and experiences planned for school personnel?

6.  For each example presented in Chapter 21, identify elements of the Partnership Model that are present and those that are missing. How well does each example fit current conditions in education? Suggest modifications to make the example timely.

7.  Select an example from Chapter 21 and consider its usefulness in your own local school situation. Suggest modifications to make the example fit the local conditions.

## SUGGESTED READINGS

Bailey, William J. *Managing Self-Renewal in Secondary Education*. Englewood Cliffs, N.J.: Englewood Technology Publications, 1975.

Bentzen, Mary M. *Changing Schools: The Magic Feather Principle*. New York: McGraw-Hill Book Company, 1974.

Bishop, Leslee J. *Staff Development and Instructional Improvement: Plans and Procedures*. Boston: Allyn and Bacon, Inc., 1976.

Devaney, Kathleen and Thorn, Lorraine. *Exploring Teachers' Centers*. San Francisco: Far West Laboratory for Educational Research and Development, 1975.

Likert, Rensis and Likert, Jane G. *New Ways of Managing Conflict*. New York: McGraw-Hill Book Company, 1976.

Mann, Dale, ed. *Making Change Happen?* New York: Teachers College Press, Columbia University, 1978.

Park, Jeanne S. *Education in Action: 50 Ideas that Work.* Washington, D.C.: U.S. Government Printing Office, 1978.

Roberts, Arthur D., ed. *Educational Innovation: Alternatives in Curriculum and Instruction.* Boston: Allyn and Bacon, Inc., 1975.

Rubin, Louis, ed. *The Future of Education: Perspectives on Tomorrow's Schooling.* Boston, Allyn and Bacon, Inc., 1975.

Saxe, Richard W. *School-Community Interaction.* Berkeley, Calif.: McCutchan Publishing Corporation, 1975.

Tallmadge, G. Kasten. *The Joint Dissemination Review Panel Ideabook.* Washington, D.C.: U.S. Government Printing Office, 1977.

United States Office of Education. *Educational Programs that Work,* Volume VI, 1979.

# Sample Forms for Action Research

### ORGANIZATION DEVELOPMENT
### EVALUATION

_____
(Date)

1. Considering the sessions in general, please rate your personal satisfaction:

_____

    displeased            satisfied           very pleased

2. Compared to the other kinds of professional activities in which you normally engage, such as task-oriented and information meetings, how do you contrast experiences:

_____

   do not prefer       some preferences      very much prefer

3. On the scale below, rate the sessions as to their beneficial effects on your personal growth:

_____

    not helpful      somewhat beneficial      very helpful

4. On the scale below, rate your evaluation of the value of these exercises to the progress of the school as a whole:

_____

very little influence       some influence      great deal of impact

### Questions
(Continue on back if you wish)

1. How can the facilitator improve the sessions?

2. How helpful was the research information?

3. Which training activities did you like the most? Why?

4. Shall we continue with these OD activities? If so, please comment on time and frequency.

5. Are you interested in more sessions with these consultants?

## SUMMARY OF WORKSHOP EXPERIENCES

Name_____

1. How do you feel about the workshop in general? (please check one)

   |_____|_____|_____|_____|_____

   very          somewhat     neutral     somewhat     very
   dissatisfied  dissatisfied             satisfied    satisfied

   COMMENTS:

2. How do you feel about the trainer's ability in increasing your sensitivity to the needs of others?

   |_____|_____|_____|_____|_____

   very        somewhat     neutral     somewhat     very
   ineffective ineffective              effective    effective

   COMMENTS:

3. What are the possibilities of transferring these workshop experiences towards establishing improved communications with your students?

   |_____|_____|_____|_____|_____

   very       somewhat     neutral     somewhat     very
   unlikely   unlikely                 likely       likely

   COMMENTS:

OTHER GENERAL COMMENTS:

## DAILY-MEETING REACTION SHEET

Date_____

Place_____

Time_____

1. How did you feel about today's meetings? (check)

   |_____|_____|_____|_____|_____|

   very               somewhat          neither           somewhat          very
   dissatisfied       dissatisfied      satisfied         satisfied         satisfied
                                        nor
                                        dissatisfied

2. Please comment on why you felt this way.



3. Were there times when you wished to speak but did not?

   |_____|_____|_____|_____|_____|

   never          a few times     fairly often     very            almost all
                                                    often           the time

4. What did the facilitator do that *helped* you to take part in the meetings?



5. What did the facilitator do that *hindered* you from taking part in the meeting?



6. How could our next meetings be improved?

## SMALL GROUP EVALUATION FORM

Session: _____

Session leader: _____

Session recorder: _____

Number of participants: _____

I. Recommendations discussed: _____

_____

_____

II. Major concerns of discussions: _____

_____

III. Strategies for bringing about action: _____

_____

IV. Suggestions to aid the discussion leaders: _____

_____

_____

_____

V. Evaluation of the discussion leader: _____

_____

_____

_____

_____

Productivity of group:
1. Very Productive    ◯
2. Productive    ◯
3. "So so"    ◯
4. Not too productive    ◯
5. Not productive at all    ◯

245

# Prepared OD Instruments

## ANNOTATED BIBLIOGRAPHY

Harrison, Roger. "Diagnosing Organization Ideology." Development Research Associates, Homestead Farm, Mountain Bower, Wilshire, England.

Looks at organizations from four orientations: power, role, task, or self. Brief and easy to administer.

Harrison, Roger and Oshry, Barry. "Organization Behavior Describer Survey (OBDS)." 1976 *Annual Handbook for Group Facilitators*. La Jolla, Calif.: University Associates, 1976.

Interpersonal behavior index investigating rational-technical competence, verbal dominance, consideration, and emotional expressiveness. Useful for management development. Twenty-five items, somewhat complex.

Hersey, Paul and Blanchard, Ken. "Leader Effectiveness and Adaptability Description (LEAD)." Athens, Ohio: Center for Leadership Studies, Ohio University.

A leadership style instrument with a sophistication of the task/relationship grid work. Brief, but somewhat complex analysis.

Kehoe, D.T. and Reddin, W.J. "Organization Health Survey." Organizational Tests, Ltd. Box 324, Fredericton, NB Canada.

Measures organization in productivity, structure, communication, conflict, participation, and creativity. Brief and easily scored.

Likert, Rensis. "Organization Climate," *The Human Organization*. New York: McGraw-Hill, 1967.

Climate typology systems. Authoritarian, paternalistic, consultative, and participative. Brief, easily scored.

Litwin, George and Stringer, Robert, Jr. "Organizational Climate Questionnaire." *Motivation & Organizational Climate*. Cambridge: Harvard University Press, Harvard University, 1968. Also, Harvard Business School, Soldiers Field, Boston.

Scales relate to structure, responsibility, reward, risk, warmth, support, standards, conflict, and identity. Brief test, easily scored.

Schutz, William. "Educational Values." 577 College Avenue, Palo Alto, Calif.: Consulting Psychologists Press, Inc.

Measures interpersonal relationships and educational values. Can be used with community. Medium length, fairly complex.

Stern, George. "Organizational Climate Index." Syracuse, New York: Psychological Research Center, Syracuse University.

Thirty characteristics inventory from true/false statements. Long and complex scoring and analysis.

# Program Development Planning Guide

## PART I: OVERALL PLAN

1. *Baseline Data*

   Program development has as its foundation a clear definition of an existing situation. This establishes the areas to be improved and provides the information needed to begin determining goals and selecting a process. The collection of baseline data is often referred to as needs assessment because the description of a current situation generally yields a profile which points out areas of need. In the context of innovative programs, a need is defined as the existence of a difference between the current status and the desired outcome.

   1.1 *Describe the procedure used to assess the present situation.*

      Since the entire program development process evolves from the baseline data, it is important to ascertain that the data is accurate. In describing the assessment procedures employed, include such information as: the instruments used to collect the data, the validity and reliability of the instruments, how the data was analyzed, the criteria used to identify needs, and the recentness of the information.

   1.2 *Indicate the human and material resources contributing to the assessment.*

      Effective utilization of resources is vital to all phases of program development. It is an important beginning step to carefully identify all potential resources, both human and material, that can contribute to the project. In identifying resources, include not only those in the schools but also those in the community and elsewhere. In this section of the application indicate which of these resources contributed to the design and implementation of the assessment. Keep in mind that there is a definite relationship between commitment to the baseline data and the eventual success of the project. Before people will enthusiastically build upon the data, they must first accept the data; they are more likely to accept them if they were involved in preparing them.

   1.3 *Itemize in behavioral terms the results of the assessment.*

      Having established and carried out a carefully documented process of assessment, you are ready to prepare descriptive statements of the existing situation. These may be the same statements developed at the preliminary stage, but in most cases they will now be more complete.

These should be presented in behavioral terms. Since the focus of education is on people, things are only important to the extent that they have an affect on people. The organizational pattern of a school, for example, is only a meaningful descriptor if it is ultimately related to student learning. It is acknowledged, however, that certain kinds of programs do not readily lend themselves to conversion. It would be difficult, for example, to discuss program budgeting in terms of student learning; however, it is still possible to use some behavioral indicators of other kinds (e.g., the voters have defeated the line-item budget for five consecutive years). The written statements should be expressed in precise terms that are clearly capable of being compared. To say, "Students are doing poorly in math," does not define the situation precisely enough to allow for a comparison with another group at another time. To say, "Sixty percent of the middle school students scored below grade level on the Iowa Test of Basic Skills," does provide for comparative measurement.

2. *Goals*

Once the existing situation has been clearly defined, attention should be given to describing the desired behavioral characteristics that are sought. These constitute the major objectives of the program. They predict in measurable terms both the nature and scope of the improvement that will be made by the constituent population.

2.1 *Describe how the goals were determined.*

Based on the needs assessment, certain growth directions were indicated. Describe the procedures that were used to arrive at the goals and performance expectations. Tell what criteria were used in selecting the goals, and discuss the relationship between these goals and the philosophy and objectives of the school district.

2.2 *Indicate who was involved in defining the goals.*

Earlier in the development process you identified your potential resources, such as students, teachers, parents, community representatives, libraries, agencies, organizations, industries, etc. Tell which of these resources contributed to this phase of the development.

2.3 *Itemize in behavioral terms the new situation which will result.*

Using clear and simple language and defining specifically any terms with ambiguous meaning, describe the situation that you plan to create by the end of the project. These statements should be directly correlated to the needs assessment previously reported. They should be presented in priority order in case temporal or financial limitations later require modifications in program goals. Each goal is considered a major objective and should contain three elements: identification of constituent population (e.g., students, teachers, etc.); nature of the new behavior (e.g., will read, will remain in school, etc.); and minimum level of performance (e.g., ninth-grade level on the Tests of Academic Progress, an increase of 40 percent, etc.). Essentially you are describing what it is that your target population will be able to do or to produce in order to demonstrate their knowledge, skills, preferences, or beliefs. Just as in the section on the existing situation, precise and measurable statements are required. To say that the dropout rate "will improve" does not provide you with an accurate target. To say, "Ninety percent of all minority group students entering ninth grade will remain in school and graduate," does provide a measurable projection. Keep in mind when completing this section that you will later be asked to list detailed intermediate objectives for each of these goals.

3. *Research*

Now that you have described where you are and where you want to go, you are ready to begin work on a plan to accomplish the change. This plan should be based upon sound theoretical and experimental research in education. A strong theoretical base for evaluating your problem will permit you to see its relationship to the fundamental questions of education. Such questions include those of learning theory and systems organization.

Second, good discussions of theoretical questions will help you discover experiments that were designed to solve problems similar to yours. Examining the strategies and evaluations of these experiments will give you alternative approaches to solving your problem. With this background you should be able to put together a plan which will build upon proven experimental designs. This may mean adopting proven designs in part or wholly, adapting them or rejecting them as inapplicable, and designing your own. These decisions will be made according to the data listed earlier in this application. This approach will help you avoid needless duplication and permit you to achieve a higher level of success.

The questions in this section are the guideposts for this examination of theoretical and experimental research. As a result of this process you should be able to devise a plan that will contribute to experimental research in education.

3.1 *Describe the theoretical question(s) which your problem raises.*

Whose discussions of these questions are the most helpful to you in analyzing your problem? For example, if your problem is the failure and apathy of a significant portion of the students in your district, you will want, at least, to consult the best discussions of learning theory and motivation theory. This will give you the important ideas about the way people learn. With this information you can begin to examine the learning situation in your district to identify its strengths and weaknesses.

3.2 *Describe the best experimental research on problems similar to yours.*

What are the best types of experiments that have been designed to solve problems (or their components) that are similar to yours? Have these experiments been successful? Why or why not?

To continue the example started in 3.1, if you want to overcome student failure and have identified the major fault(s) of the leaning situation in your school district, you should now examine several types of experiments that have been carried out to correct such faults. These experiments might be in diverse areas such as behavior modification techniques used by teachers, curriculum design, class or classroom organization, parent involvement in the classroom, etc.

3.3 *Give the alternatives that were considered.*

Which experiments (3.2) or modifications of them offer viable alternative strategies to solve your problem? What is the basis for your selection? If you reject these experiments to design original ones, explain the reasons for this decision.

3.4 *Describe how the final plan was selected.*

What criteria did you use to select a final plan from among the alternatives identified in 3.3? If your plan has original components, what criteria were used for their design? Who was involved in selecting the final plan?

3.5 *Describe what you believe will be your contribution to experimental research.*

Now that you have examined the theoretical and experimental research on your problem and have selected a final plan, how do you anticipate that your project will contribute to this body of research?

4. *Strategies*

Your overall plan should be a projection of your activities for the length of time that you expect Title III funding to last. This plan will show the major *strategies* you expect to use to accomplish the *goals* outlined in question 2.

4.1 *Strategy overview and timeline*

Briefly describe the major strategies you have decided to implement during each projected year of the project. For example:

1. *year one*, strategies might include curriculum development for grades 3 and 4, and in-service training for administrators and third- and fourth-grade teachers;

2. *year two* might include, field testing of the program in grades 3 and 4, development of curriculum for grades 5 and 6 and training of fifth- and sixth-grade teachers.

4.2 *Major strategy description.*

For each major strategy (i.e., curriculum development, in-service training, development of a master plan, development of an accountability model), describe the characteristics of that strategy, including techniques to be used, people to be involved, format of the final product, etc. For example, a major strategy of curriculum development might be described in this way:

*Curriculum Development*–the new 3–6 curriculum will be based on performance objectives. The objectives will be selected by a committee of three teachers, one administrator, and the project director from available lists of objectives; additional objectives will be developed to meet local needs. Assessment instruments will be identified or developed by project staff and consultants and keyed to objectives. At least two alternative student activities will be developed for accomplishing each objective. Objectives, assessment tools, and activities will be arranged in sequential order under major headings. For each heading a separate booklet will be produced. The booklets will be used by the teachers in guiding each student's learning.

5. *Evaluation Design*

Evaluation is a process in which information is collected and analyzed so that the degree of success and the relative value of a particular practice can be determined. Since the purpose of Title III is to demonstrate the value of an innovation, a sound evaluation of the program is critical. The most important part of any educational process is its effectiveness, sometimes referred to as products or output. The anticipated effectiveness was specified in the statement of *goals* (question 12) wherein changes in behavior were projected. Evaluation measures the extent to which the changes came about and verifies the conditions under which they occurred. As a result of that measurement and verification, decisions can be made about the value of the changes.

In this section you are asked to give an overall evaluation design to measure the goals. In a later section you will be asked to give the individual evaluation designs for the specific goals of the plan for the first year.

5.1 *Describe the resources used to develop an evaluation design.*

Of all the resources available to your project, indicate which contributed to this aspect of your program development.

5.2 *List the indicators that will be used to measure each of the changes projected in question 2.3.*

Before beginning a program it is important to consider exactly what data will provide evidence of success. In trying to assess student motivation, for example, indicators might include such things as changes in the dropout rate, rate of participation in cocurricular activities, responses to a questionnaire, etc.

5.3 *Describe the measurement techniques to be used.*

After you have determined precisely what it is you want to measure, decide what instruments will provide the necessary measurement. Instruments might include such things as anecdotal reports, checklists, opinions of outside experts, standardized tests, rating scales, questionnaires, pre-test and post-test research designs, etc.

5.4 *Explain how the data will be collected.*

Indicate in this section who will be responsible for evaluation arrangements and who will administer the instruments. Describe any special conditions of the measurement, and explain the evaluation schedule.

5.5 *Explain how data will be analyzed.*

Discuss the types of comparisons and correlations that will be made, including provisions to account for any external factors which might affect the results.

## PART II: SPECIFIC PLAN FOR THE FIRST YEAR OF THE PROJECT

6. *Plan for each goal.*

Now that you have established your baseline data, identified your goals, and developed your major strategies based on the total projected life of your project under Title III support, you are ready to develop in detail your first year plan. For each goal previously identified (question 2), you will need to give the information requested in 8.1 to 8.11. Each goal and the supporting material will become a separate section of your application. While each goal is based on the total project period (one, two, or three years), the material for 8.1 to 8.11 is to be based on the *first year* of the project.

6.1 *Take each goal previously stated and restate that goal in terms of your accomplishment projections for the first year.*

*For example:*

*three-year goal*—The dropout rate will be reduced by 75 percent.

*first-year goal*—The dropout rate will be reduced by 15 percent.

In some cases no part of the overall goal will be accomplished during the first year, because efforts are being directed at changing behaviors of people other than those of the *prime* target group. For example, the attitudes of teachers may be the focus during the first year. In this case the dropout rate might not be reduced during year one but you expect this change in behavior to bring about a large decrease in year two. If this is the case in your project you would insert a zero in the first year goal statement in front of the percent sign.

6.2 *Itemize all of the small elements or groups of people that must change in order to accomplish the first year projections for each goal.*

6.3 *Describe the nature of the change each must make.*

Once you have determined everything that must change, explain how each must change. In completing this section of the application you will, in effect, be preparing intermediate objectives for each of your major goals. Accordingly, these statements should also be expressed in behavioral terms. For example, "Teachers will indicate a willingness to work personally with students with problems rather than referring them to the office to the extent that referrals will decrease by 25 percent." "Guidance counselors will spend 50 percent more time with potential dropouts." All of these intermediate objectives should form such a complete composite that if they are all successful, the major objective will be achieved.

6.4 *Describe all the things that must be considered in effecting each of these changes or groups of changes.*

In developing effective strategies nothing can be taken for granted. Potential problems and resistance must be anticipated and provided for. All linkages in social and psychological systems must be thoroughly explored. For example, if counselors spend twice as much time with potential dropouts, will there be serious negative effects on other parts of the program? How will teachers feel about handling a greater portion of their own discipline problems? What effect will their attitude have? Will this offset the advantage of having them more personally involved with these students? These are the kinds of questions that must be explored in depth before a strategy can be finalized for it is in this realm of subtleties where success is often determined.

6.5 *Itemize and describe the sets of activities that you plan to carry out to bring about each change or group of changes.*

Only after you have thought through all of these considerations are you ready to select the activities which will most effectively bring about the desired change. Activities are actually process objectives in that they are measurable statements describing a projected situation; however, instead of projecting a behavior, they are projecting a process. For example "Two teacher aides will be assigned to each special education class." "Learning activity packages will be developed for ten social studies units." Activities should be directly correlated with each intermediate objective or group of intermediate objectives stated in section 8.3.

6.6 *Indicate what people will constitute the target group(s), how many of them, and for what period of time.*

For each of the activities or groups of activities described in section 8.5, tell who the activity will be directed toward (e.g., first and second graders, social studies teachers, etc.); how many of that group will be directly involved through direct participation; and the time dimensions of that participation (e.g., four hours a day for six weeks in the summer, one day a week during the school year, etc.)

6.7 *Describe the resources used to develop the evaluation design.*

6.8 *List the indicators that will be used to measure each of the changes projected in question 8.3.*

6.9 *Describe the measurement techniques to be used.*

6.10 *Explain how the data will be collected.*

6.11 *Explain how the data will be analyzed.*

7. *Illustrate your complete project implementation plan by showing the interrelationships of all events and activities, including time estimates. Define network entries with a detailed activity listing.*

You have now determined the goals of your program, the activities that will meet those goals, and the personnel who will carry out the activities. There is need for a basic time schedule showing manpower considerations and showing which events and activities are interdependent and which can proceed concurrently. The Program Evaluation and Review Technique (PERT) illustrates these relationships and is also a valuable management tool for monitoring the progress of a program after it is operational. Districts with complex projects may wish to have their PERT professionally done; however, the Department of Education and its intermediate units do offer some PERT training sessions. The following is an overview of the technique.

PERT is essentially an activity network. The beginning and end of each activity is called an event. Activities are represented by lines; events are represented by circles, each of which is numbered. For example:

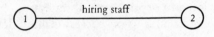

Event 1 is the beginning of hiring staff; event 2 is the conclusion of hiring staff; the straight line represents the activity itself, hiring staff.

The estimated time (TE) for each event is written above it:

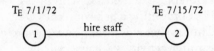

The manpower needed for each activity is written below it in a simple formula in which .2 equals one person for one day. Therefore,

0.4 = 1 person for 2 days (or 2 people for 1 day)
0.6 = 1 person for 3 days (or 3 people for 1 day)
0.8 = 1 person for 4 days (or 4 for 1 day; 2 for 2 days)
1.0 = 1 person for 1 week (or equivalent)
1.2 = 1 person for 1 week + 1 day or 6 days
2.0 = 1 person for 2 weeks (or equivalent)

To show that hiring staff is expected to take one person two weeks, 2.0 is written below the activity line:

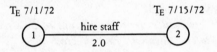

If several different activities begin at the same time, several lines may emit from the same event number:

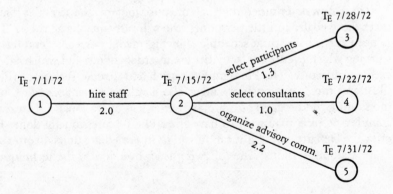

If several activities end at the same time, the lines may join at a common event number;

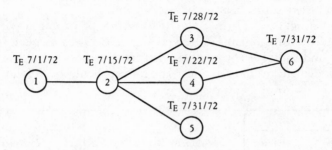

Events with different times may not share a common number. Separate activities must have separate lines.

If an activity does not take any time, it is called a dummy activity and is represented by a dotted line:

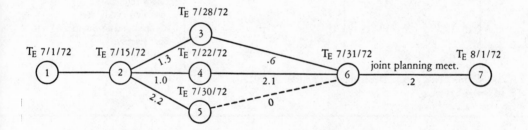

In the above example no real activity is taking place between events 5 and 6, but event 6 cannot proceed until 3, 4 and 5 are completed; therefore, the dotted line shows that a relationship exists between the events but no additional time is required.

When the basic PERT is finished, the activity lines which represent the longest time intervals between events should be darkened:

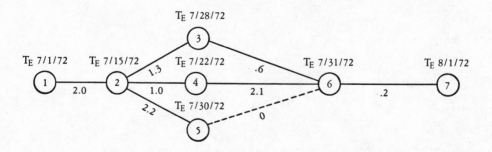

This is called the critical path. Because the critical path marks the activities which take the longest time, it tells you which events cannot fall behind schedule without affecting the completion date of the project. Using the preceding example, events 3 and 4 could conceivably take a few extra days without holding up the progress of 5, 6, etc.; but if 5 is late, it will delay the beginning of event 6 and every subsequent event.

After completing the PERT chart, the final task is to prepare an activity dictionary listing. This listing identifies each activity on the network plan. It includes beginning and ending event numbers, activity descriptions, and a brief listing of the key elements of the activities. The format should be as follows:

| Event Numbers | | Activity Description | Explanation |
|---|---|---|---|
| Beginning | Ending | | |
| 1 | 2 | Hire staff | Prepare announcement of openings<br>Publicize in district<br>Advertise positions: newspapers, colleges, etc.<br>Check references<br>Interview candidates<br>Recommend to Board<br>Board action<br>Notify applicants |

State of New Jersey, Department of Education, 1972.

# How to Evaluate
# Education Programs

## HOW TO COLLECT EVALUATION INFORMATION

You can collect evaluation information in many different ways. If you need information to find out whether an innovative elementary school reading center has actually improved student reading ability, for example, you would probably ask this question: *How much have students' reading skills improved?*

To provide a credible answer to the question, you could use any of the following information collection techniques:

- Give parents a rating scale to assess their children's reading performance.
- Send questionnaries to teachers to get their opinion about student reading performance.
- Interview students to ask their opinion about student reading performance.
- Observe students as they read and rate their reading ability.
- Have students keep a diary of their progress.
- Give students a nationally normed achievement test that assesses reading performance.
- Have students take a teacher-developed test.
- Review student records for achievement test scores, report card grades, and teachers' comments.

This list illustrates six alternative techniques an evaluator might use to answer the question about improved reading skills. They are interviews, questionnaires, rating scales, standard observations, record reviews, and achievement tests.

To choose the best technique for answering a particular question, you should consider four factors. First, the method should be agreeable to your client and colleagues. If you want to use questionnaires, but the district's staff prefers interviews, you must decide just how serious the consequences of imposing your own choice might be.

Second, the information collection techniques should be technically sound and the data collected from them should be reliable, valid, and targeted to the evaluation questions. Third, the information collection techniques should provide the best data the evaluation budget can afford, which means that you will have to decide such things as whether to buy or develop your own measures,

Reprinted with permission of Capitol Publications, Inc.

and whether to use more than one technique for each evaluation question. Fourth, you must be sure that the methods you choose will allow enough time for gathering and analyzing the data.

### Should You Use Paper and Pencil Tests of Ability?

Paper and pencil tests are among the most commonly used measurement techniques in education.

*Achievement tests* measure competency in a given subject. They can be developed by the program or evaluation staff or you can buy them from publishers. Achievement tests can be used to measure a student's knowledge of basic English usage or a class's ability to solve quadratic equations.

The advantages of achievement tests are that they can be administered to large groups at relatively low cost and that carefully developed and validated tests are available in many subject areas.

One disadvantage is that achievement tests must be properly validated to provide accurate information, and this can be a costly procedure. Another is that having high scores on a test of factual knowledge doesn't always mean that the student can apply that knowledge.

*Aptitude tests* are measures of potential. The most common measure of aptitude is an IQ test. Aptitude tests have the same advantages and disadvantages as achievement tests.

### What About Paper and Pencil Self-Report Measures?

Paper and pencil self-report measures ask people to tell about their attitudes, beliefs, feelings, and perceptions. Questionnaires, rating and ranking scales, the Semantic Differential, the Q-sort, and diaries are among the techniques most frequently used in evaluating education programs.

*Questionnaires* are self-administered survey forms that consist of a set of questions. Answers to questionnaire items can require free responses (short answers) or they can be structured into "forced" choices (multiple choice items). Questionnaires are frequently used in large scale evaluations to obtain participants' reactions and opinions. They are less expensive to construct than most measures, but the kind of information you can get from them is limited, and people don't always answer the questions truthfully. Don't forget that you will have to follow up on those who don't respond, and that's an expensive undertaking.

*Rating scales* can be used for self assessment or for appraisals of other people, groups, events, or products. Student attentiveness, for example, can be rated on a five-point scale from 1 for not very attentive to 5 for very attentive. Rating scales are particularly useful when you need to reduce judgmental data to a manageable form. They are relatively easy to complete and they produce objectified data.

Unfortunately, they are subject to many types of bias—some raters are lenient and others are not, and sometimes raters let their personal feelings influence their ratings (a halo effect). Further, the amount of information you can obtain from rating scales is limited because the rating categories are never perfect.

*Ranking scales* involve putting a set of items into a hierarchy according to some value or preference. Asking a teacher to rank four textbooks from one to four according to their reading difficulty is an example. Like rating scales, ranking scales are easy to complete and produce objectified data. But remember that rank ordering a long list of items is no fun and it takes a lot of time. Ranking scales sometimes ask people to make distinctions among things where they can't really see any difference.

*Semantic Differential* is used to measure attitudes by relying on the indirect meanings of words.

For example, students might be asked to rate their country using a series of seven point scales like the following:

### United States

| | | | | | | | |
|---|---|---|---|---|---|---|---|
| Good | ___ | ___ | ___ | ___ | ___ | ___ | ___ | Bad |
| Passive | ___ | ___ | ___ | ___ | ___ | ___ | ___ | Active |
| Small | ___ | ___ | ___ | ___ | ___ | ___ | ___ | Large |
| Democratic | ___ | ___ | ___ | ___ | ___ | ___ | ___ | Undemocratic |
| Rich | ___ | ___ | ___ | ___ | ___ | ___ | ___ | Poor |

The Semantic Differential is relatively easy to complete, it produces objectified data, and respondents usually find it harder to choose "socially acceptable" answers than when they use an ordinary rating scale. However, the Differential can be difficult to score.

*The Q-sort* requires individuals to place a series of items or statements into rating categories so that some minimum number of items is assigned to each category. For example, teachers could be asked to rate ten textbooks as "above average" or "below average" so that at least two texts are assigned to each category (the remaining texts can be rated either way).

Q-sorts produce objectified data and they force respondents to establish priorities among items that are being compared in an evaluation. But the Q-sort requires people to make very difficult distinctions, the directions are often hard to follow, and the resulting data can require complex analysis methods.

*Diary techniques* ask people to keep daily or weekly accounts of specific behaviors, attitudes, thoughts, or events. The *critical incident* technique asks people to record only those things that are particularly important, unique, useful, or revelatory. For example, you could ask students to keep a daily diary of the amount of time spent in free reading, or to record the names of any books they liked or disliked.

Diaries and critical incidents permit people to describe unique situations in their own words, but people sometimes forget to maintain them and they are often difficult to score and interpret.

### Why Not Try Observations?

Another information collection technique frequently used in evaluations is an eye witness account of individual behavior or program activities. You could use observations, for example, to find out which visual aids teachers are using. The information collected by observers can be reported by checklists, rating scales, field notes, and summary reports.

*Standard observations* require careful planning so that the information obtained is accurate. Observations can give information collectors first-hand information about a program, and they are often the only feasible and economical way to gather certain kinds of information. But it is costly to train observers, and several may be needed to get reliable results. Another drawback is that people who know they are being observed may not behave normally.

*Time sampling observations* involve repeated observations of a given situation. For example, observers may note how many students and which ones ask direct and indirect questions during ten consecutive five-minute intervals.

Time sampling allows first hand observations of a program, and the many observations make it possible to identify unusual events that you might otherwise think were routine occurrences. When all the observations are made one after the other, however, they are likely to depict only one particular situation and not the program as a whole.

### Are Interviews Feasible?

An interview is an information collection technique in which one person talks to another or to a group. Interviews can be completely unstructured and spontaneous, or you can decide ahead of time the kinds of questions to ask. If you use multiple choice questions, even the response categories are predetermined.

*Face-to-face interviews* might be used, for example, to find out why participants dropped out of a program, and might consist of three basic questions with a series of two or more in-depth questions for each basic question asked. The best thing about the face-to-face interview is that it permits you to probe sensitive subjects like attitudes or values. But these interviews are usually time consuming and expensive, and you will have to give interviewers special training.

*Telephone interviews* also permit in-depth probing of sensitive issues and are less costly than face-to-face interviews. They are still expensive when compared to questionnaires, however, You should also remember that not everyone has a telephone, and some people are reluctant to reveal their feelings or give personal information over the phone.

### Are Performance Tests the Answer?

*Performance tests* require people to complete a task or make something, and then you assess the quality of the performance or product. One example of a performance test is when you have someone type a letter and then you count the number of words typed correctly in a set amount of time. Another example is when a group of experts observe a teacher instructing a class and then use a rating scale to indicate their appraisal of the teacher's ability.

The major advantage of performance testing is that it relies on tasks that are close to "real world" activities. It is often very time consuming and expensive, however, because performance tests generally have to be administered individually and they sometimes require the use of special equipment.

### Would Record Reviews Be Enough?

*Record reviews* mean that you collect evaluation information by going through program related documents. In a program where older pupils tutor younger ones, for example, you might review attendance records to see if either the tutors or the children they taught came to school more regularly after the program began.

Record reviews are "unobtrusive" in the sense that they do not interfere with the activities of the program being evaluated. They can also be relatively inexpensive because no new data collection is required. One problem is that program documents may be disorganized or unavailable.

| Information Collection Alternatives | | Advantages | Disadvantages |
|---|---|---|---|
| Paper and Pencil Tests of Ability | Achievement Tests  Aptitude Tests | Can be administered to large groups at relatively low costs  Many published, standardized tests are available | Expensive to develop and validate  High scores do not necessarily imply that the tested knowledge can be applied |
| Paper and Pencil Self-Report Measures | Questionnaires | Can be administered to large groups at relatively low costs | Can be difficult to obtain sensitive information  Respondents may not always be truthful  Must follow-up to obtain adequate numbers of respondents |
| | Rating Scales | Easy to complete  Produces objectified data  Reduces judgmental data into a manageable form | Responses may be biased because some raters are lenient and others are strict  Amount of information obtainable is circumscribed by the rating categories  Halo effect |

(Continued)

| Information Collection Alternatives | | Advantages | Disadvantages |
|---|---|---|---|
| | Ranking Scales | Easy to complete<br><br>Produces objectified data | Difficult to rank a long list of items<br><br>Distinctions are called for that are not perceived |
| | Semantic Differentials | Easy to complete<br><br>Produces objectified data<br><br>More difficult to give "socially acceptable" responses | Difficult to score |
| | Q-Sorts | Produces objectified data<br><br>Forces respondents to establish priorities among items | Distinctions are called for that are not perceived<br><br>Directions can be too elaborate<br><br>Can require complex data analysis methods |
| | Diaries and Critical Incidents | Permits people to describe unique situations in their own words | People don't maintain them<br><br>Difficult to score and interpret |
| Observations | Standard Observations | Can observe events at first hand | Observers can change the environment<br><br>Inter- and intra-observer reliability can be difficult to obtain |
| | Time Sampling Observations | Can observe events at first hand<br><br>More opportunities to observe | Observers can change the environment<br><br>Inter- and intra-observer reliability can be difficult to obtain |
| Interviews | Face-to-face Interviews | Permits indepth probing<br><br>Sensitive issues can be discussed | Costly<br><br>Inter- and intra-rater reliability can be difficult to obtain |
| | Telephone Interviews | Permits indepth probing<br><br>Sensitive issues can be discussed<br><br>Less costly than face-to-face interviews | Costly<br><br>Some people may not have telephones<br><br>More difficult to probe or discuss sensitive issues |

| Information Collection Alternatives | | Advantages | Disadvantages |
|---|---|---|---|
| Performance Tests | | Close to real world situations | Costly<br>Generally must be administered individually<br>Can require special equipment or apparatus |
| Record Review | | Unobtrusive<br>Can be inexpensive<br>No new data collection required | Documents may be disorganized or unavailable |

# Consortium Policies
# and Procedures

## NORTHWEST PROFESSIONAL DEVELOPMENT
## CONSORTIUM POLICY PROCEDURES AND BY-LAWS

### ARTICLE 1—NAME OF THE CONSORTIUM

**Section 1.** Northwest Professional Development Consortium

### ARTICLE 2—PURPOSE OF THE CONSORTIUM

**Section 1.** The Consortium will establish and implement programs leading to recommendation of candidates to the State Superintendent of Public Instruction for (a) preparatory, (b), initial, and (c) continuing certification as specified in the *Guidelines and Standards for the Development and Approval of Programs of Preparation Leading to Certification of School Professional Personnel* (July 9, 1971).

**Section 2.** The Consortium will also establish and implement programs for the inservice education of educators

### ARTICLE 3—MEMBERSHIP

**Section 1.** Membership in the Consortium will consist of the Arlington School District #16, the Arlington Education Association, and Western Washington State College.

**Section 2.** Membership in the Consortium will be open to other interested school districts, professional associations, and universities/colleges that request admission in writing to the Consortium's Policy Board. The Policy Board will approve applications for admission.

a. Established Consortium policies and by-laws will pertain to all members admitted to the Consortium.

Roy A. Edelfelt, ed., *Inservice Education* (Bellingham, Washington: Western Washington State College, 1977), pp. 119–126.

b. A school district and its respective professional association may seek admission to the Consortium only if both apply jointly.

c. Any member group may withdraw from the Consortium by notifying the Policy Board of that intent in writing. Such withdrawal may occur at any time unless an obligation assumed by the member has not been fulfilled. In such a case, withdrawal will follow completion of the obligation.

d. The withdrawal of a school district or its respective professional association will automatically effect the withdrawal of the other group.

## ARTICLE 4—GOVERNANCE AND MANAGEMENT

**Section 1.** The chief administrators or their surrogates of the school districts, professional associations, and the unit for teacher education of the College or University(s) will serve on the Policy Board. Each member of the Policy Board will be responsible for appropriate consultation with officers or councils of their respective memberships on all matters requiring formal action by the Policy Board.

**Section 2.** Advisory Committees and Task Forces. The Policy Board will appoint advisory committees and task forces to carry out the purposes as described in Article 2.

**Section 3.** Policy and Program Approval. Policies and program approvals may not be formally adopted by the Policy Board at the same meeting they are initially proposed.

**Section 4.** Management. All management responsibilities and roles will conform to the procedures outlined under the provision for consortium management established within the 1971 *Guidelines*.

**Section 5.** Voting Procedures. All Policy Board decisions will require a unanimous vote by the Policy Board.

## ARTICLE 5—AMENDMENTS TO THE CONSORTIUM POLICIES AND BY-LAWS

**Section 1.** Amendments to and revisions of these policies and by-laws may be made by a unanimous vote of the Consortium Policy Board.

## PRELIMINARY DRAFT OF CONTRACT USED BY
## WESTERN WASHINGTON STATE COLLEGE TEACHER CORPS
## TEACHER-DESIGNED INSERVICE EDUCATION PROJECT

Title: _____

Need addressed: _____

_____

Teacher: _____

School: _____

Abstract: _____

_____

_____

_____

_____

_____

_____

_____

_____

_____

Compensation:

Course _____    Credits _____    Grade _____

Enrollment period:    Fall _____    Winter _____    Spring _____

Other_____

|  | | Proposal | Interim Report | Final Report |
|---|---|---|---|---|
| Approvals: | | | | |
| Team Leader | _____ | _____ | _____ | _____ |
| Clinical Professor | _____ | _____ | _____ | _____ |
| School Administrator | _____ | _____ | _____ | _____ |

## PERSONNEL REQUIREMENTS

| | | Proposal Preparation | Proposal Review* | Planning** | Implementation** | Evaluation |
|---|---|---|---|---|---|---|
| Investigating Teacher's Time | *Planning* | | | | | |
| | *Classroom Released* | | | | | |
| | *Additional* | | | | | |
| Other Teachers' Time | *Planning* | | | | | |
| | *Classroom Released* | | | | | |
| | *Additional* | | | | | |
| Administrator's Time | | | | | | |
| Clinical Professor | | | | | | |
| Team Leader | | | | | | |
| Graduate Intern | | | | | | |
| Instructional Aide | | | | | | |
| Clerical Aide | | | | | | |
| Consultant | | | | | | |

*These figures will be supplied by the individuals reviewing the proposal.
**These figures should be estimated by the individual preparing the proposal and amended by the proposal review group.

CONTRACT (continued)

## MATERIAL REQUIREMENTS

| | Proposal Preparation | Proposal Review* | Planning* | Implementation** | Evaluation** |
|---|---|---|---|---|---|
| General Supplies | | | | | |
| Special Supplies | | | | | |
| New Materials | | | | | |
| Rentals | | | | | |
| Transportation | | | | | |
| Telephone | | | | | |
| Per Diem | | | | | |
| Miscellaneous | | | | | |

Note: When the cost of an item is not known, the item should be listed on another sheet and the space in the table marked with a check (✓).

*These figures will be supplied by the individuals reviewing the proposal.

**These figures should be estimated by the individual preparing the proposal and amended by the proposal review group.

## ANTICIPATED BENEFITS AND LIABILITIES

|  | Benefits | Evidence | Liabilities |
|---|---|---|---|
| Students |  |  |  |
| School Building |  |  |  |
| Teacher |  |  |  |
| Others |  |  |  |

# SCHOOL IMPROVEMENT BIBLIOGRAPHY

Abramowitz, Susan, and Rosenfeld, Stuart, eds. *Declining Enrollment: The Challenge of the Coming Decade*. Washington, D.C.: National Institute of Education, 1978.

Adams, John D., ed. *New Technologies in Organization Development*. La Jolla, California: University Associates, Inc., 1975.

Alderfer, Clayton P., and Brown, L. Dave. *Learning from Changing: Organizational Diagnosis and Development*. Beverly Hills, California: Sage Publications, 1975.

Argyris, Chris. *Management and Organizational Development*. New York: McGraw-Hill Book Company, 1971.

Averch, Harvey A.; Carroll, Stephen J.; Donaldson, Theodore S.; Kiesling, Herbert J.; and Pincus, John. *How Effective is Schooling? A Critical Review and Synthesis of Research Findings*. Santa Monica, California: The Rand Corporation, 1972.

Bailey, William J. *Managing Self-Renewal in Secondary Education*. Englewood Cliffs, New Jersey: Educational Technology Publications, 1975.

Baldridge, J. Victor, and Deal, Terrence E. *Managing Change in Educational Organizations*. Berkeley, California: McCutchan Publishing Corporation, 1975.

Beckhard, Richard, and Harris, Reuben T. *Organizational Transitions: Managing Complex Change*. Reading, Massachusetts: Addison-Wesley Publishing Company, 1977.

Bell, Terrel H. *A Performance Accountability System for School Administrators*. West Nyack, New York: Parker Publishing Company, Inc., 1974.

Bennis, Warren G. *Beyond Bureaucracy: Essays on the Development and Evolution of Human Organization*. New York: McGraw-Hill Book Company, 1966.

Bennis, Warren G. *Changing Organizations*. New York: McGraw-Hill Book Company, 1966.

Bennis, Warren G. *Organization Development: Its Nature, Origins, and Prospects*. Reading, Massachusetts: Addison-Wesley Publishing Company, 1969.

Bennis, Warren G.; Benne, Kenneth D.; and Chin, Robert, eds. *The Planning of Change: Readings in the Applied Behavioral Sciences*. 3rd ed. New York: Holt, Rinehart and Winston, 1976.

Bentzen, Mary M., ed. *Changing Schools: The Magic Feather Principle*. New York: McGraw-Hill Book Company, 1974.

Berman, Paul, and McLaughlin, Milbrey. *Federal Programs Supporting Educational Change.* Volume 1: *A Model of Educational Change.* Santa Monica, California: The Rand Corporation, 1975.

Berman, Paul, and McLaughlin, Milbrey. *Federal Programs Supporting Educational Change.* Volume 4: *The Findings in Review.* Santa Monica, California: The Rand Corporation, 1975.

Berman, Paul, and McLaughlin, Milbrey. *Federal Programs Supporting Educational Change.* Volume 8: *Implementing and Sustaining Innovations.* Santa Monica, California: The Rand Corporation, 1978.

Berman, Paul, and Pauly, Edward W. *Federal Programs Supporting Educational Change.* Volume 2: *Factors Affecting Change Agent Projects.* Santa Monica, California: The Rand Corporation, 1975.

Bishop, Leslee J. *Staff Development and Instructional Improvement: Plans and Procedures.* Boston: Allyn and Bacon, Inc., 1976.

Brickell, Henry M. *Organizing New York State for Educational Change.* Albany: New York State Department of Education, 1961.

Bronfenbrenner, Urie. *A Report on Longitudinal Evaluations of Preschool Programs.* Volume II: *Is Early Intervention Effective?* Washington, D.C.: Department of Health, Education, and Welfare, 1974.

Burke, W. Warner, ed. *New Technologies in Organization Development: 1.* La Jolla, California: University Associates, Inc., 1975.

Bushnell, David C., and Rappaport, Donald, eds. *Planned Change in Education: A Systems Approach.* New York: Harcourt Brace Jovanovich, Inc., 1971.

Carlson, Richard O.; Gallaher, A.; Miles, M. B.; Pellegrin, R. J.; and Rogers, E. M. *Change Process in the Public Schools.* Eugene, Oregon: University of Oregon Press, 1965.

Carson, Robert B., ed. *Change and Innovation.* Calgary, Alberta, Canada: Department of Educational Administration, University of Calgary 1968.

Cohen, Arthur M., and Smith, R. Douglas. *The Critical Incident in Growth Groups: A Manual for Group Leaders.* La Jolla, California: University Associates, Inc., 1976.

Cohen, Arthur M., and Smith, R. Douglas. *The Critical Incident in Growth Groups: Theory and Technique.* La Jolla, California: University Associates, Inc., 1976.

Cremin, Lawrence A. *Traditions of American Education.* New York: Basic Books, Inc., Publishers, 1977.

Cunningham, Luvern L.; Hack, Walter G.; and Nystrand, Raphael O., eds. *Educational Administration: The Developing Decades.* Berkeley, California: McCutchan Publishing Corporation, 1977.

Cunningham, Luvern L., and Nystrand, Raphael O. *Citizen Participation in School Affairs.* Washington, D.C.: The Urban Coalition, 1969.

Davies, Don. *Citizen Participation in Education: Annotated Bibliography.* New Haven, Connecticut: Institute for Responsive Education, 1974.

Denemark, George W., and Yff, Joost. *Obligation for Reform: Final Report of the Higher Education Task Force on Improvement and Reform in American Education.* Washington, D.C.: American Association of Colleges for Teacher Education, 1974.

Devaney, Kathleen, and Thorn, Lorraine. *Exploring Teachers' Centers.* San Francisco: Far West Laboratory for Educational Research and Development, May, 1975.

Donleavy, Mary Rita, and Pugh, Clementine A. "Multi-Ethnic Collaboration To Combat Racism in Educational Settings." *The Journal of Applied Behavioral Science* 13 (1977): 369–372.

Donley, Marshall O., Jr. *Power to the Teacher.* Bloomington, Indiana: Indiana University Press, 1976.

Eidell, Terry L., and Kitchel, Joanne M., eds. *Knowledge Production and Utilization in Educational Administration.* Eugene, Oregon: University Council for Educational Administration, University of Oregon, 1968.

English, Fenwick W. *School Organization and Management.* Worthington, Ohio: Charles A. Jones Publishing Company, 1975.

Ford Foundation. *A Foundation Goes to School: The Ford Foundation Comprehensive School Improvement Program, 1960–1970.* New York: The Foundation, 1972.

Fox, Thomas G., Jr., ed. *Federal Role in School Reform from Sociological and Educational Perspectives.* Madison, Wisconsin: School of Education, University of Wisconsin-Madison, 1974.

Franklin, Jerome L. *Organization Development: An Annotated Bibliography.* Ann Arbor, Michigan: Institute for Social Research, University of Michigan, 1973.

French, Wendell L., and Bell, Cecil H., Jr. *Organization Development.* Englewood Cliffs, New Jersey: Prentice-Hall, Inc., 1978.

Friedmann, John. *Retracking America—A Theory of Transactive Planning.* Garden City, New York: Anchor Press/Doubleday, 1973.

Fullan, Michael, and Pomfret, Alan. "Research on Curriculum and Instruction Implementation." *Review of Educational Research* 47 (1977): 335–397.

Gardner, Neely, D. *Group Leadership.* Washington, D.C.: National Training and Development Service Press, 1974.

Gellerman, Saul W. *The Management of Human Resources.* Hinsdale, Illinois: The Dryden Press, 1976.

Gideonse, Hendrik D. *Educational Research and Development in the United States.* National Center for Educational Research and Development. Washington, D.C.: U.S. Government Printing Office, 1970.

Goodlad, John I. *The Dynamics of Educational Change: Toward Responsive Schools.* New York: McGraw-Hill Book Company, 1975.

Goodlad, John I., and Klein, M. Frances. *Looking Behind the Classroom Door.* Worthington, Ohio: Charles A. Jones Publishing Company, 1974.

Greenwood, Peter W.; Mann, Dale; and McLaughlin, Milbrey. *Federal Programs Supporting Educational Change.* Volume 3: *The Process of Change.* Santa Monica, California: The Rand Corporation, 1975.

Gross, Neal; Giaquinta, Joseph; and Bernstein, Marilyn. *Implementing Organizational Innovations.* New York: Basic Books, Inc., 1971.

Guba, Egon G., and Clark, David L. "The Configurational Perspective: A New View of Educational Knowledge Production and Utilization." *Educational Researcher* 4 (April 1975): 6–8.

Haberman, Martin, and Stinnett, T. M. *Teacher Education and the New Profession of Teaching.* Berkeley, California: McCutchan Publishing Corporation, 1973.

Hage, Jerald, and Aiken, Michael. *Social Change in Complex Organizations.* New York: Random House, Inc., 1970.

Hansen, John H., ed. *Governance by Consortium.* Syracuse, New York: Syracuse University School of Education, 1974.

Havelock, Ronald G. *Bibliography on Knowledge Utilization and Dissemination.* Ann Arbor: Center for Research on the Utilization of Scientific Knowledge, University of Michigan, 1968.

Havelock, Ronald G. *The Change Agent's Guide to Innovation in Education.* Englewood Cliffs, New Jersey: Educational Technology Publications, 1973.

Havelock, Ronald G.; Guskin, Alan E.; Frohman, M.; Havelock, Mary C.; Hill, M.; and Huber, Janet. *Planning for Innovation Through Dissemination and Utilization of Knowledge.* Ann Arbor: Center for Research on Utilization of Scientific Knowledge, University of Michigan, 1969.

Havelock, Ronald G.; Havelock, Mary C.; and Markowitz, Elizabeth A. *Educational Innovation in the United States.* Volume 1: *The National Survey: The Substance and the Process.* Ann Arbor, Michigan: Institute of Social Research, Center for Research on Utilization of Scientific Knowledge, University of Michigan, 1973.

Havelock, Ronald G., et al. *Educational Innovation in the United States.* Volume 2: *Five Case Studies of Educational Innovation at the School District Level.* Ann Arbor, Michigan: Institute of Social Research, Center for Research on Utilization of Scientific Knowledge, University of Michigan, 1974.

Herriott, Robert E., and Gross, Neal. *The Dynamics of Planned Educational Change.* Berkeley, California: McCutchan Publishing Corporation, 1979.

Herriott, Robert E., et al. *A Multidisciplinary Study of Planned Educational Change.* Cambridge, Massachusetts: Abt Associates, Inc., 1975.

Hicks, Herbert, and Gullett, C. Ray. *Organizations: Theory and Behavior.* New York: McGraw-Hill Book Company, 1975.

Howard, Eugene, and Brainard, Edward. *How School Administrators Make Things Happen.* West Nyack, New York: Parker Publishing Co., Inc., 1975.

Howsam, Robert B.; Corrigan, Dean C.; Denemark, George W.; and Nash, Robert J. *Educating a Profession.* Washington, D.C.: American Association of Colleges for Teacher Education, 1976.

Huse, Edgar F. *Organization Development and Change.* St. Paul: West Publishing Co., 1975.

Iannaccone, Laurence, and Cistone, Peter J. *The Politics of Education.* Eugene, Oregon: Eric Clearinghouse on Educational Management, University of Oregon, 1974.

Ingalls, John D. *Human Energy: The Critical Factor for Individuals and Organizations.* Philippines: Addison-Wesley Publishing Co., Inc., 1976.

Jones, Garth N. *Planned Organizational Change: A Study in Change Dynamics.* New York: Frederick A. Praeger Publishers, 1969.

Kaufman, Roger A. *Educational System Planning.* Englewood Cliffs, New Jersey: Prentice-Hall, Inc., 1972.

Lassey, William R., and Fernandez, Richard R., eds. *Leadership and Social Change.* 2nd ed. La Jolla, California: University Associates, Inc., 1976.

Leonard, George B. *The Transformation: A Guide to the Inevitable Changes in Humankind.* New York: Delacorte Press, 1972.

Levinson, Harry. *Organizational Diagnosis.* Cambridge, Massachusetts: Harvard University Press, 1972.

Likert, Rensis, and Likert, Jane G. *New Ways of Managing Conflict.* New York: McGraw-Hill Book Company, 1976.

Lippitt, Ronald; Watson, Jeanne; and Westley, Bruce. *The Dynamics of Planned Change.* New York: Harcourt, Brace, and Company, Inc., 1958.

Lortie, Dan D. *Schoolteacher.* Chicago: The University of Chicago Press, 1975.

Luke, Robert A., Jr. *First Tango in Boston: A Seminar on Organizational Change and Development.* Washington, D.C.: National Training and Development Service Press, 1973.

Luke, Robert A., Jr., ed. *The Dallas Connection: A National Focus on Creating Responsive Organizations.* Washington, D.C.: National Training and Development Service Press, 1974.

Luthans, Fred, and Kreitner, Robert. *Organizational Behavior Modification.* Glenview, Illinois: Scott, Foresman and Company, 1975.

Maguire, Louis M.; Temkin, Sanford; and Cummings, C. Peter. *An Annotated Bibliography on Administering for Change.* Philadelphia: Research for Better Schools, Inc., 1971.

Maier, Norman R. F.; Solem, Allen R.; and Maier, Ayesha A. *The Role-Play Technique: A Handbook for Management and Leadership Practice.* La Jolla, California: University Associates, Inc., 1975.

Mann, Dale, ed. *Making Change Happen?* New York: Teachers College Press, Columbia University, 1978.

Mann, Floyd C., and Neff, Franklin W. *Managing Major Change in Organizations.* Ann Arbor, Michigan: Foundation for Research on Human Behavior, 1961.

Miles, Matthew B., ed. *Innovation in Education.* New York: Bureau of Publications, Teachers College, Columbia, 1964.

Morphet, Edgar L., and Ryan, Charles O., eds. *Planning and Effecting Needed Changes in Education.* New York: Citation Press, 1967.

National Institute of Education. *Catalog of NIE Education Products.* Volume 1. Washington, D.C.: U.S. Government Printing Office, 1975.

National Institute of Education. *Catalog of NIE Education Products.* Volume 2. Washington, D.C.: U.S. Government Printing Office, 1975.

National Institute of Education. *The Status of Education Research and Development in the United States: Databook.* Washington, D.C.: U.S. Government Printing Office, 1976.

Owens, Robert G. *Organizational Behavior in Schools.* Englewood Cliffs, New Jersey: Prentice-Hall, Inc., 1970.

Owens, Robert G., and Steinhoff, Carl R. *Administering Change in Schools.* Englewood Cliffs, New Jersey: Prentice-Hall, Inc., 1976.

Park, Jeanne S. *Education in Action: 50 Ideas that Work.* Washington, D.C.: U.S. Government Printing Office, 1978.

Pfeiffer, J. William, and Jones, John E., eds. *The 1976 Annual Handbook for Group Facilitators.* La Jolla, California: University Associates, Inc., 1976.

Pincus, John. "Incentives for Innovation in the Public Schools." *Review of Educational Research* 44 (1974): 113–144.

Reischauer, Edwin O. *Toward the 21st Century: Education for a Changing World.* New York: Vintage Books, Random House, Inc., 1974.

Roberts, Arthur D. *Educational Innovation: Alternatives in Curriculum and Instruction.* Boston: Allyn and Bacon, Inc., 1975.

Rogers, Everett M. *Diffusion of Innovations.* Glencoe, New York: The Free Press, 1962.

Rogers, Everett M., and Shoemaker, F. Floyd. *Communication of Innovations.* Glencoe, New York: The Free Press, 1971.

Rubin, Louis, ed. *The Future of Education: Perspectives on Tomorrow's Schooling.* Boston: Allyn and Bacon, Inc., 1975.

Runkel, Philip J., and Schmuck, Richard A. *Strategies of Organizational Change Program.* Eugene, Oregon: Center for Educational Policy and Management, University of Oregon, 1974.

Ryan, Charlotte. *The Open Partnership.* New York: McGraw-Hill Book Company, 1976.

Ryan, Kevin, ed. *Teacher Education: The Seventy-fourth Yearbook of the National Society for the Study of Education.* Part II. Chicago: The University of Chicago Press, 1975.

Sarason, Seymour B. *The Culture of the School and the Problem of Change.* Boston: Allyn and Bacon, Inc., 1971.

Saxe, Richard W. *School-Community Interaction.* Berkeley, California: McCutchan Publishing Corporation, 1975.

Schmieder, Allen A., and Yarger, Sam J. *Teaching Centers: Towards the State of the Scene.* Washington, D.C.: American Association of Colleges for Teacher Education, 1974.

Schmuck, Richard A., and Miles, Matthew B., eds. *Organization Development in the Schools.* Palo Alto, California: National Press Books, 1971.

Schmuck, Richard A.; Murray, Donald; Smith, Mary Ann; Schwartz, Mitchell; and Runkel, Margaret. *Consultation for Innovative Schools: OD for Multiunit Structure.* Eugene, Oregon: University of Oregon Press, 1975.

Schmuck, Richard A., and Runkel, Philip J. *Organizational Training for a School Faculty.* Eugene, Oregon: Center for the Advanced Study of Educational Administration, University of Oregon, 1970.

Schmuck, Richard A.; Runkel, P. J.; Arends, Jane; Arends, Richard. *The Second Handbook of Organization Development in Schools.* Palo Alto, California, 1977.

Schmuck, Richard A.; Runkel, Philip J.; Saturen, Steven L.; Martel, Ronald T.; and Derr, C. Brooklyn. *Handbook of Organization Development in Schools.* Palo Alto, California: National Press Books, 1972.

Schmuck, Richard A., and Schmuck, Patricia A. *A Humanistic Psychology of Education: Making the School Everybody's House.* Palo Alto, California: National Press Books, 1974.

Scribner, Jay D., ed. *The Politics of Education: The Seventy-sixth Yearbook of the National Society for the Study of Education.* Part II. Chicago: The University of Chicago Press, 1977.

Sieber, Sam D., and Lazarsfeld, Paul F. *The Organization of Educational Research in the United States.* New York: Bureau of Applied Social Research, Columbia University, 1966.

Sieber, Sam D.; Louis, Karen S.; and Metzgar, Loya. *The Use of Educational Knowledge: Evaluation of the Pilot State Dissemination Program.* New York: Bureau of Applied Social Research, Columbia University, 1972.

Smith, E. Brooks; Olsen, Hans C.; Johnson, Patrick L.; and Barbour, Chandler, eds. *Partnership in Teacher Education.* Washington, D.C.: The American Association of Colleges of Teacher Education, 1966.

Tallmadge, G. Kasten. *The Joint Dissemination Review Panel Ideabook.* Washington, D.C.: U.S. Government Printing Office, 1977.

Thomas, D. Woods; Potter, Harry R.; Miller, William L.; and Aveni, Adrian F. *Institution Building: A Model for Applied Social Change.* Cambridge, Massachusetts: Schenkman Publishing Co., 1972.

U.S. Office of Education. *Better Schools Through Better Partnerships. Final Report and Recommendations of the Council of Chief State School Officers' National Field Task Force on the Improvement and Reform of American Education.* Washington, D.C.: Department of Health, Education, and Welfare, 1974.

U.S. Office of Education. *Educational Programs that Work.* Volume VI, 1979.

Varney, Glenn H. *Organization Development for Managers.* Reading, Mass.: Addison-Wesley Publishing Company, 1977.

Von Haden, Herbert I., and King, Jean Marie. *Educational Innovator's Guide.* Belmont, California: Wadsworth Publishing Co., Inc., 1974.

Watson, Goodwin, ed. *Change in School Systems.* Washington, D.C.: National Training Laboratories, National Education Association, 1967.

Watson, Godwin, ed. *Concepts for Social Change.* Washington, D.C.: National Training Laboratories, National Education Association, 1967.

Zaltman, Gerald; Florio, David; and Sikorski, Linda. *Dynamic Educational Change.* Glencoe, New York: The Free Press, 1977.

# Index

281